Acting on a gut feeling, I slowly swung Bad Girl's two barrels to my right. I just knew the enemy was coming.

The silence lasted almost an hour, then it was broken. The culprit was a paddle. About seventy-five feet away I could barely see a sampan with two men.

I slowly pivoted the M-16/XM-148 toward the enemy, but before I got her fully turned around, the sampan turned and its bow ran up on the beach just ten yards from my bugged-out eyeballs. The men remained in the grounded boat and whispered frantically. Believing that they'd seen me and were about to shoot me, I clicked the M-16 from semi- to full automatic. Snatching the moment out from under the gooks, I squeezed the M-16's trigger, spraying the sampan from end to end with the entire 30-round magazine. . . .

Books published by The Random House Publishing Group are available at quantity discounts on bulk purchases for premium, educational, fund-raising, and special sales use. For details, please call 1-800-733-3000.

DEATH IN THE JUNGLE

Diary of a Navy SEAL

Gary R. Smith
and
Alan Maki

BALLANTINE BOOKS • NEW YORK

This book is dedicated to my mother and dad, my coauthor Alan Maki, my faithful friends Randy and Kathy Bryant and Paul and Helen Martens, and to George A. Maki, who served with the 2nd Division Combat Engineers of the U.S. Army in World War II.

A Presidio Press Book
Published by The Random House Publishing Group
Copyright © 1994 by Gary R. Smith and Alan Maki

Published in the United States by Presidio Press, an imprint of The Random House Publishing Group, a division of Random House, Inc., New York, and distributed in Canada by Random House of Canada Limited, Toronto. Originally published in slightly different form by Paladin Press in 1994.

PRESIDIO PRESS and colophon are trademarks of Random House, Inc.

ISBN 978-0-8041-1341-0

Printed in the United States of America

www.presidiopress.com

First Ballantine Books Edition: January 1996

CONTENTS

FOREWORD

What makes a man like Gary R. Smith spend twenty years of his life in the United States Armed Forces, fifteen of those years assigned to Naval Special Warfare? Certainly not the money. Was it "free" education, retirement benefits, or devotion to one's country? Well, one thing I know for sure is that Gary Smith wasn't looking for a free ride. Any man who is physically and mentally tough enough to endure UDT/SEAL training and survive five Vietnam combat tours in elite units is definitely not taking a free ride and just "putting in his time." Therefore, Gary can honestly say that his hitch in the military was truly a career of which he is proud. This is not the case with all retirees, but you won't find many of those types involved with the Naval Special Warfare program.

Gary's first-person account of his experiences while serving as an enlisted man with SEAL Team 1 in Vietnam is written from the point of view of one who served in the war during 1967 and 1968. He and his co-author, Alan Maki, have tried to reproduce the mind-set Gary brought into the field, in order to share with the reader an honest view of "the way it was" for Gary, his teammates, and all UDT/SEAL personnel who completed BUDS (Basic Underwater Demolition/SEAL) Team Training and served with a UDT or SEAL team in armed conflict against the NVA and Viet Cong in Southeast Asia.

As you will see in this book, during UDT/SEAL training we were instructed in the techniques used by the NVA and Viet Cong. We knew our enemy very well before we deployed to Vietnam. And we called him many offensive names—names like "gook," "dink," "slope," and "slant-eye" were commonly used by many military personnel who served in the war. Unfortunately, the use of ethnic slurs and stereotyping was also an unofficial part of the training—not only with the Teams, but with all armed forces. Certainly this attempted dehumanization of the enemy was cruel, but with the types of missions UDT/SEALs were involved in, many of us might not have survived combat had we thought of our enemy in a better light. To hide this important fact would give the reader a false representation of war in general, because the technique of dehumanizing the enemy has been used throughout history. The authors of this book do not hide this truth, nor do they hide any others.

One of the main reasons Gary decided to share his story with us is because of the large number of phony SEALs who are surfacing, just as people are claiming to have served in U.S. Army Special Forces who did not. Such people are responsible for spreading false information about UDT/SEALs and giving the Teams a bad name. After all the pain that true SEALs suffered just to complete UDT/SEAL training, the blood we shed in combat, and—most important—the men we lost in Vietnam, no one has the right to claim he was in the Teams unless it is a fact. In my experience, those who boast the most about combat experiences in Vietnam were never even there. But you won't find a SEAL bragging about his experiences in the line of duty. Anyone who has been in the Teams can tell very quickly when a "wannabe" is trying to impress people. This book is an attempt to present a factual look at the life of a Navy SEAL, minus the braggadocio and the hype.

The truth, however, is this: with his having survived one combat tour with Underwater Demolition Team 12 and four combat tours with SEAL Team 1, Gary Smith can truly be called one of the heroes of the Vietnam War. The medals on his chest give evidence of that fact. You will not hear that from him, however. Instead, you will hear the story about "the way it was" for a SEAL in Vietnam from someone who knows firsthand. I can honestly say that one reason I, myself, am alive today is because of the experienced combat SEALs like Gary who put me through training; their professionalism in training and combat kept many a young SEAL alive.

I am proud to have the privilege of knowing Gary and of being his friend. His devotion to duty and country distinguishes him from "lifers," career servicemen and women who do nothing more than put in their time. Whether it was pulling a teammate out of waist-deep mud on a SEAL operation deep inside enemy territory in the Mekong Delta or comforting a wounded comrade during a firefight, Gary Smith was a man his teammates could trust and count on.

Darryl Young, SEAL Team 1/UDT-11, 1969–72
Author of *The Element of Surprise:
Navy SEALs in Vietnam*

PROLOGUE

The purpose of this book is to tell a true story about a group of men who loved their country, their command, and, especially, their teammates. Their loyalty to command and teammates was based upon a mutual respect, trust, and dependence upon each other that developed during and after very difficult and dangerous training and combat experiences.

Working as a team required unity, trust, and dependence on each other, and was probably the most important lesson we learned while enduring UDT Training (later changed to BUDS—Basic Underwater Demolition/SEAL). The old axioms, "You're only as strong as the weakest man" and "You're no faster than the slowest man," are absolutes when working as a team. Each man has his strong and weak points. That's why there are no true cynics, pessimists, scorners, or complainers in "the Teams." They simply can't get through training or exist in a confident, optimistic, positive, unified, team-oriented group of men. Don Sutherland in *Kelley's Heroes* said it all: "No negative waves, man." There are no Rambos in the Teams because our strength lies in our unified teamwork. It's attitude more than intelligence that shapes character.

Only after our graduation from UDT Training, and our eventual assignment to SEAL Team 1 and an operational platoon, did we begin to understand what unified teamwork, trust, and dependence upon each other truly meant. Also, in order to function as an effective and efficient platoon under all operational conditions, platoon training was designed to expose any shortcomings or deficiencies, whether they be of equipment, training, leadership, or personnel. We were always conscious of the fact that without proper preparation and unified teamwork, few missions could be accomplished.

An old Chinese axiom, "The more you sweat in peace, the less you bleed in war," was our motto. My good friend Bud Burgess was always quoting this axiom during UDT Training Class 36. Platoon camaraderie, unified teamwork, trust, and confidence are based on mentally and physically difficult and realistic training that is continually being updated and creatively applied. And last, but certainly not least—the men can be no better than their leadership. Another old maxim comes to mind—"Before you can become a good leader you must *first* learn to be a good follower."

On the lighter side, we didn't forget to have fun. When I had worked on the Bridwell Hereford Ranch near Winthorst, Texas, my straw boss, Jack Cheeves, had been very fond of saying, "When you work, you work; when you play, you play." One thing is for sure, we certainly knew how to have fun in the Teams. Sometimes we had to be creative and throw our Commanding Officer, or the platoon chief, or whoever else was handy, in the "dip tank." Sometimes *everyone* got thrown in the tank! Regardless of the motives, we let off a lot of steam, and morale was always high in spite of hard times. When we were training at Camp Kerrey (near Niland) or Camp Billy Machen (near Cuyamaca), we always managed to have a party *after* a long training spell or a hard training mission. Sometimes it was refreshments under a desert ironwood tree, or a rendezvous at the Past Time, Hi-Ho, or the Silver Dollar in

Niland, or Luck O' the Irish on the north shore of the Salton Sea. If we were having a team parachute jump at Rolls Farm (near San Diego) on a Friday morning, we occasionally took along refreshments to the drop zone. After the last jumper had completed his PLF (parachute landing fall), the festivities began. Everyone was laughing and discussing the day's evolutions. The continuous joking and teasing always drew everyone closer together. During the ride back to the command, usually in the back of a two-and-a-half-ton truck, we sang old English and Australian ballads. These memories of "the good ole times," our youthful exuberance, and naivete helped get us through "the hard times."

In summary, I have to say that I consider my fifteen years in SEAL Team 1 and Underwater Demolition Team 12 a perfect example of job satisfaction. Why? Because we always had a true cause, one with a sense of urgency. Not only did I love the excitement and challenges of my job and profession, but I also worked with some of the toughest and most highly motivated men in the world. They were great friends and comrades. They were always there to encourage or comfort a teammate when in need. And finally, it was a privilege and an honor to have served under the officers and with the men of SEAL Team 1 and Underwater Demolition Team 12.

Gary R. Smith, RMCM ret.
May 1, 1992

ACKNOWLEDGMENTS

The authors wish to thank their families for their support; Admiral Elmo Zumwalt for his kind words; LCDR Jerry J. Fletcher; Darryl Young, author of *The Element of Surprise*; Owen Lock, editor, Ivy Books; and Ethan Ellenberg, literary agent. We're especially thankful for Al Betters, Robert Schaedler, Art Streeter, Frank Toms, and Jack Lee for helping me collect lists of Kilo, Alpha, Juliett, Bravo, and Delta Platoon personnel and platoon pictures. A big thanks to Dee Daigle, Frank Toms, and Jack Lee for some of the Delta Platoon pictures and the K-bar knife mission.

Special thanks to all of Gary Smith's UDT/SEAL/ EOD teammates, those still alive and those who have passed over the bar.

AUTHOR'S NOTE

The combat missions described in this book are real. The people are real. Only one name has been changed, to protect a specific person's privacy. The conversations, naturally, are not reproduced verbatim, but are representative of the interplay between my teammates and myself.

Unfortunately, war is real. Death is real. This book covers it all by a Navy SEAL who is lucky enough to have survived five tours of Vietnam. Written with my close friend, Alan Maki, this is my first book. There will be others.

INTRODUCTION

I joined the Navy for a variety of reasons. First and foremost, I was bored with college and my sweetheart had dumped me. Second, I had a burning desire for adventure. I just couldn't bear the thought of living a common, everyday life behind a desk. I had ventured into oil-field work for a couple of years; however, the pay was poor and the hours were long. I had worked on the Bridwell Hereford Ranch Headquarters near Winthorst, Texas, for the '61 and '63 cattle sales. The pay was even worse and the hours were even longer. But my stay in the bunkhouse with four other guys was quite an adventure. Saturday nights were usually spent at the JB Corral, in Wichita Falls, dancing to Hank Thompson and other country-and-western bands. We would return to the ranch in time for chores, which began at 0530 hours. Considering I was young and dumb, and full of things I didn't care to discuss, I was beginning to realize that my life didn't have any direction or purpose. And third, I wanted to be a member of one of the Navy's UDT Teams. With that in mind, and full of youthful idealism, I enlisted on 22 January 1964, at twenty-two years of age.

During boot camp, everyone took a variety of aptitude tests. Sometime afterward, each of us was interviewed by a civilian counselor and asked what basic line of work or training we preferred.

I told him that I wanted to be a UDT diver and that I didn't like anything that had "wires" (electrical) connected to it.

Appearing to ignore me, he looked at my radioman test for copying code (CW or continuous wave). Unfortunately, I had gotten a perfect score. "You'll make a good radioman," he commented without looking at me.

"But I hate anything that has wires to it," I responded.

With a stern look, he stated emphatically, "You'll make a good radioman."

I was crushed! I simply couldn't imagine sitting behind a typewriter and copying code or fiddling with wires for a career.

Prior to boot camp graduation, we had to fill out a "dream sheet" for our first assignment. I doggedly requested UDT Training, Second Class Deep Sea Divers School, and Submariner training.

Upon graduation, I received my orders to Radioman A School at Naval Training Center, San Diego, California. I did well in school, and eventually was able to copy twenty-eight words per minute CW and send twenty words per minute with a standard key; however, I still hated anything that had wires to it.

Again, I was to fill out another dream sheet. Getting wiser, I requested UDT Training, submarine duty, or assignment to any ship in the Pacific fleet. Again I was crushed. I was assigned to the Naval Communications Center of the COMNAVPHIBPAC (Commander Naval Amphibious Pacific) at the Naval Amphibious Base, Coronado, California.

After reporting aboard the 'phib base, I began my short stint as a radioman behind a desk typing messages, monitoring communications nets, maintaining filing records, scrubbing urinals and commodes, and waxing decks. I hadn't been assigned to the comm center over a week before I found out that the UDT Training Command was also located at the amphib base. Then I found out that the guys who were always running in formation and singing songs while waiting for the chow hall to open were UDT trainees, "tadpoles." I immediately submitted a request to be transferred to UDT Training in December 1964. By July '65, I was one of those nuts who were always in a hurry to get somewhere, running in formation, and singing to boot. My life would be forever changed.

The UDT Training area was located at the back end of the base next to the San Diego Bay. The training command office, classrooms, and enlisted barracks were old World War II structures made of plywood. The surrounding grounds were of sand. Every evening we were to rake all trainee boot tracks from it, scrub urinals, et cetera, depending on who was the enlisted duty officer.

There was a two-week pretraining phase for the fortunate trainees who were released early from their previous commands. As it turned out, not all who arrived early would agree that they were fortunate.

Instructor Friendly Frederickson had two weeks to separate the sheep from the goats before Class 36's training was to officially begin. He must have been trained by the Gestapo. His specialty was torturing us in a variety of ways on our half-day mixes of PT, swimming in the surf, and running on the Silver Strand. Frederickson always started off by having us run out into the surf and lie down in it. Then he had us run into the sand dunes, lie down, and roll in the sand, followed by making us put handfuls of sand down our T-shirts and pants. Even our boots got full of sand. One poor fellow had a terrible case of piles after just two days and was shipped out on the third.

All trainee "brown baggers" (married men) were allowed to go home at night. The rest of us maggots were forced to endure continual harassment and occasional physical abuse, especially from Petty Officer Barney "The Ripper" House, after chow and during our daily field-day duties. Then there were the nightly fire watch patrols.

All UDT trainees were issued one and a half rations per meal, and more if requested. During Hell Week we would be issued four meals a day, with the fourth being served at 2400 hours. Considering I loved to eat and that my personal motto was "quantity, not quality," I finally knew what happiness was: "Every day is a holiday and every meal is a feast."

I had finally found "a true cause with a sense of urgency." The best part was the privilege and honor of serving my country and the promise of retirement, if I survived. I had a roof over my head, clothes on my back, food in my belly, and direction in my life. I was delighted and thrilled that I might possibly become a member of a great organization, the Underwater Demolition Team.

Our daily schedule was very basic. We started the day off with one hour of PT or a run of the obstacle course. Afterward, we swam for the rest of the morning, then ran up and down the Silver Strand for the afternoon, or vice versa. All of this physical activity was carefully planned to prepare us for Hell Week.

One morning, after a hard PT, we ran all over the Silver Strand, through the sand dunes, out into the surf, rolled in the sand and raced from one point to another. The "goon squad," which consisted of the slower runners, was continually harassed by Friendly Freddie and Barney Ripper. Even our corpsman, Doc Beaver, a big Indian, had no sympathy. At one point, Doc drove the ambulance past us, dragging one of the goon squad boys behind the ambulance with Freddie and Barney running alongside, cursing and throwing driftwood at him. The next morning, the harassed trainee was shipped out. He must have been a radioman.

For those of us up front, we were forced to inhale Instructor Olivera's cigar smoke as he led us on each day's run. We never did figure out how he could run ten to fifteen miles daily, a burning cigar or a large wad of Beechnut chewing tobacco in his mouth, and outrun every one of us. He was an incredible guy.

After lunch we began a timed two-mile swim in the swimming pool. Progressively, the swim degenerated into a free-for-all at each end of the pool where at least half of the class was bottlenecked. The stronger swimmers were forced to literally swim over the weaker ones. It was not a pretty sight. On occasion, a fistfight would erupt until the combatants were overrun by other swimmers. It was every man for himself!

One day, in the midst of this chaotic situation, I heard Instructor Olivera yell, "Country, get your butt over here."

I quickly swam up to the edge of the pool at the feet of Boatswain Mate Second Class Olivera. "Yes, Olivera?" Olivera was not only a legend, but was also one of the all-time fastest long-distance runners in the Teams. He had been in the Navy for about sixteen years, but in the fifties and early sixties, it was not uncommon for a career sailor to retire as a Second Class Petty Officer (enlisted paygrade E-5). He was also half Arapaho and half Italian. Olivera had a classic hooked nose, balding pate, and dark complexion. He repeatedly made life miserable for those whose attitudes weren't up to snuff; yet, we admired him and greatly respected him. Of course, it was easy to respect someone when he had almost absolute power over one's life. Olivera was able to continually motivate us to push ourselves beyond what we thought to be our absolute physical limits. On rare occasions, Olivera would even move up beside one of us and offer a word of encouragement.

"Country, Instructor Enoch tells me you like chewing tobacco?" Olivera asked while reaching into his well-rounded right cheek and pulling out a well-used wad of Beechnut.

Instinctively, I knew this was one of those times for diversion. "Yes, Olivera. I prefer Days Work," I said, grinning weakly. "It's juicier and more satisfying."

Olivera broke out hee-hawing as only he could. His laughter was a mixture of total control and manipulation, with skepticism and cynicism thrown in for good measure. "Open your mouth and chew on this for a while, and see how satisfying it is." He shoved the large gob of Beechnut into my open mouth. "After you finish the two-mile swim [without fins], report to me at the 'lean and rest' [push-up position]. I want to know how satisfying that Beechnut chewing tobacco was."

"Yes, Olivera! Hoo-yah!" I cried as I returned to a pool filled with about one hundred trainees, all trying to swim a two-mile race and somehow keep from being drowned by the masses of swimmers bottlenecked at the ends of the pool. I had never had the opportunity to swim two miles with a secondhand plug of chewing tobacco in my mouth. Worst of all, the swim was a timed race, and the slower swimmers would later receive special instructions on motivation. Not only was I not interested in motivational training (sand and surf), but I was determined to be in the top twenty-five percent, do or die. And so I achieved, thanks to Olivera's crafty method of motivating me.

Our class was the last one to have the privilege to go through the Colorado River survival week course. We were three-quarters of the way through training at that point. There was a faint light at the end of the tunnel. The scenario we were forced to participate in was based on the premise of our having previously destroyed a military target in North Vietnam. Our problem was that we had to evade all enemy forces lurking at numerous points between Davis and Parker Dams. There was no sanctuary until we reached Parker Dam, and that was to be accomplished no later than 0800 hours on Saturday morning. We were divided into five-man boat crews. Each boat was a seven-man-capable rubber raft called an IBS (inflatable boat, small).

All six boat crews were inserted just below the Davis Dam on Monday evening, south of Lake Mohave. We were to continue traveling south for five nights until we reached Parker Dam at the southern end of Lake Havasu. Each boat crew was to travel independently of the others. All travel was to be done during the night, and we were to hide out during the day. We were not to travel inland from the river more than one hundred yards.

My boat crew consisted of Lt. George Worthington, better known as Lord George Worthingstone; ENS Theodore Roosevelt IV (TR), second in command; then PO2 Bro Moore; followed by PO3 Dick, and yours truly, Seaman Smith. Fortunately for us, the instructors didn't make TR carry that huge club on this trip down the great Colorado River. There must have been times during training that he regretted his Great Granddad's famous policy, "Speak softly and carry a big stick." The route was easy. All we had to do was travel with the current until we reached Devil's Elbow, just south of Needles, California. At that point we expected to encounter the enemy in force. Our intelligence information had been gathered from UDT mates who were graduates of previous classes. Thank goodness for friends! We soon discovered that our instructors not only didn't play by chivalrous rules of war, but also they were our bitter, sadistic, and abusive enemies, whose vocabularies did not include the word *mercy.*

All went well until Tuesday night when we neared the infamous Devil's Elbow. The river became very narrow and the walls of the canyon were absolutely vertical. There was no way to escape except by stealth and concealment. No wonder someone had named the place Devil's Elbow. We did have one tactical advantage though—it was a moonless night.

Lord Worthingstone and TR decided we were to maintain a low profile by not paddling and simply drifting with the current. The "Lord" would occasionally dip his coxswain's paddle into the current to keep us in the center of the stream. You could have heard a pin drop on the rubber boat's main tube. Except for our wicked little hearts thumping at a rhythm of 150 taps a minute, we were quiet as church mice.

Suddenly there was a sound that struck horror in our hearts! Someone had just started an outboard motor. It didn't take much to deduce that it was attached to a boat filled with bloodthirsty instructors intent on making a merry night at our expense. It was about this time that I looked back on the soft life I had had as a radioman behind a typewriter. Being the junior tadpole in the boat and being reminded, on that occasion, that crap runs downhill—I figured that, one way or another, this would be a memorable night.

That outboard motor had barely gotten started when all five of us were stroking, in perfect unison, with all of our strength, and heading downstream, not being too particular where we were going except that it be away from the boat that was gaining on us fast.

We were just beginning to think that we might have a chance to escape when the pursuing boat turned on a powerful spotlight that shined on past us, revealing a heinous reception committee made up of ghoulish individuals awaiting our arrival on a sand bar next to the canyon wall. It was a bewildering situation! I literally didn't know whether to crap or fall back into it. As it turned out, it didn't really make any difference.

Chief McNally's voice came in loud and clear. "Good morning, comrades. We have been anxiously awaiting the arrival of you imperialist dogs."

I was initially confused by his paradoxical greeting—my friend in one breath and my enemy in the next. We were a totally humbled boat crew, seeking forgiveness and receiving only condemnation. Even Lord Worthingstone seemed humbled. As POWs we were allowed to give only our name, rank, date of birth, and serial number. To say any more was treasonous and dishonorable.

McNally gave PO1 Enoch and Friendly Frederickson orders. He said, "Take the dark one and the tall slim one and strip them naked. Bind their feet and hands together and behind their backs. We'll soon see just how tough these warmongering pigs stand up under our compassionate interrogation procedures." He was referring to Bro and me.

Another familiar and deceitful voice spoke up. "I'm so sorry you henchmen of imperialism have blown up our factories, killed our women and children, destroyed our homes and chicken houses, enslaved our retarded brothers and adulterous sisters in the South."

I began to feel real uncomfortable. Truly he was a "slant-eye" with forked tongue. Man, I hope he uses Vaseline, I kept thinking. "Remember, I am your friend regardless of what happens," continued Chief Boatswain Mate Al Huey.

Where had I heard that before? I thought. Good ole Al, the kiddies' pal, had now become "I am your friend," your commie pal.

Lord George, TR, and Dick were made to lie down

with their faces in the sand. McNally interrupted the proceedings by reminding Enoch and Frederickson, "Oh yes, don't forget to place the black bags over their heads and that rattlesnake around their necks. Tie the bag securely around their scrawny necks. I don't want any water to leak inside." He broke into cynical laughter.

The initial procedure was to use a sock filled with sand and to start pounding Bro's kidneys and mine with it.

McNally started the interrogation, "How many other pigs are with you?"

Neither of us answered. The night was very cold so they naturally poured water over our bodies between the beatings and interrogation, claiming we smelled worse than pigs and needed washing. That was probably the only truthful statement they made that night.

"How many more boat crews are there?" McNally continued.

Again, we didn't answer.

"Put that rattler (actually a large gopher snake) inside Moore's bag to keep him company," yelled McNally. Moore began screaming and begging for mercy. "Throw them in the river. They are of no use to us!" McNally said with finality.

I didn't know about Bro, but I was beginning to believe they were really the commies. Especially when they threw me into the river! I began to think about how good that radioman job had been behind that typewriter. The water pressure crushed the black bag tightly over my head. It was a terrible feeling. I couldn't even scream. I hated the thought of having a squirming rattler wrapped around my face.

Just before I blacked out, I was suddenly pulled out of the river and questioned again. It was now my turn to have the rattler crawling inside of the black bag that was tightly secured around my scrawny neck. When we refused to answer their questions, they again threw Bro and me back into the river. My whole body was shaking violently from the cold, the snake, and the realistic training. I made up my mind right then and there that I would never be captured in combat. I would fight to the death. No human being could stand up to that kind of treatment for extended periods of time. It was better to die in honor than to live in disgrace.

To make a long story short, we didn't get captured again during the next three days. The instructors came to within a few feet of catching me again, but I would have died fighting first. It was a lesson well learned. The worst part of my captivity was Enoch stealing the chewing tobacco that I had waterproofed in several condoms. There was no honor among thieves.

In November we spent our last three weeks of training at San Clemente Island, about seventy miles northwest of San Diego. It was entrusted to the Navy and had been used by UDT since the early fifties and probably earlier. It was approximately twenty-three miles in length and one mile wide.

The old UDT Training camp was located at Northwest Harbor and consisted of eight student and four instructor plywood shacks, one long building that served as the mess deck and admin spaces, outside shower, and the ever-present outhouses. Based on the caste system, one was reserved for the mature amphibian frogmen instructors and the other for the immature tadpoles (nonhumans). The berthing shacks' deck dimensions were approximately ten feet by fourteen feet and held four double bunks for eight trainees. Approximately one hundred yards farther inland toward the runway was UDT Training Command's storage/staging barn. All of the buildings were originally built and used during World War II to house the construction workers and their equipment during the building of the nearby runway.

We spent the first two weeks at San Clemente Island free-diving on Japanese and German hulls that had been planted in the Northwest Harbor's cove at depths of twenty to forty feet, depending on the tide, and just outboard of the breakers. Beginning two days after our arrival at the camp, a series of continuous winter storms made our lives miserable for two weeks. It rained over seventeen inches, setting a new record. The surf was very high and the visibility varied from zero to one foot. The water temperature dropped to fifty-seven degrees.

The first eight mornings began at 0400 hours. On those mornings we were briefed on the enemy situation, then grabbed our swim gear and slates, boarded an LCPR (Landing Craft Personnel Ramp) and LCPL MK 4 (Landing Craft Personnel Landing), and headed for China Beach. We were dropped off by using the old swimmer-cast-and-recovery method that had been perfected during World War II. An IBS was secured on portside of the LCPR. Simulating a combat mission and maintaining low profile, the officer in charge signaled one man at a time to slide over the side of the LCPR and into the bouncing IBS. When the enemy beach to be surveyed or reconned was to starboard of the boat, the OIC signaled the first man to enter the water, followed by another every twenty-five yards. The reconnaissance had to be completed before daylight. All swimmers were to swim back out to sea approximately one mile, maintaining one long swimmer line with twenty-five yards separating each swimmer. Eventually, the LCPR returned, traveling at about 15 mph. The pickup man, located in the IBS, held a sling outboard of the raft. As the boat neared the line, each swimmer simply hooked his arm into the sling and was flipped into the boat. By 0700 hours, we were eating breakfast.

After breakfast we mustered on the beach with our wet suit top (that was all we were issued), fins, booties, face mask, life jacket, web belt with knife and MK 13 flare, and, of course, our UDT swim trunks. We were divided into swim pairs and assigned a specific scully. Taking turns diving, our main task was to free-dive down to the scully and tie two 20-pound haversacks of explosives, as instructed, and in such a way that the surge couldn't rip them off. We soon learned that our normal working dive had to be at least one minute in duration.

Upon completion we called to PO1 Dickerson, known as the "Jolly Green Giant," that our scully was ready for inspection. We remained on the surface and anxiously watched him free-dive down and out of sight in the murky water. In less than one minute he appeared on the surface.

"You guys have gotta be kidding me," scolded Dickerson. "One good yank is all it took. Now get your butts back down there and do it right." With that, he swam off to another pair awaiting his inspection. We didn't call him the "Jolly Green Giant" for nothing. It didn't matter how tight we tied the haversacks on, he could somehow rip them off. That meant we would not be allowed to go ashore for another scully assignment and, most importantly, stand beside a large bonfire of driftwood to toast our frozen digits for five minutes.

After lunch we continued our attempts, with occasional success, to load our scully with the two haversacks of explosives until 1800 hours when we were served supper. After supper we prepared for a night mission of one type of reconnaissance or another. We never completed those night missions before 0230 hours. After we took care of our gear, we went to the chow hall for our midnight rations. Hot soup, hot cocoa, lots of peanut butter and cow butter, and bread were always served. Because we were in the cold water for twelve to sixteen hours a day, our bodies started craving peanut butter and cow butter. We were permitted to eat all that we wanted. We literally ate sticks of cow butter like candy bars. Our bodies really needed that fat content for body heat and endurance. Every winter training class reacted the same way.

One afternoon, at the end of the first two weeks, we were taken past Wilson Cove by LCPR and LCPL MK 4 and told to swim back to Northwest Harbor. Unfortunately, the set (tidal current) was moving against us. No doubt our instructors planned it that way. We weren't allowed to freestyle. Only underwater strokes were permitted, which included sidestroke, breaststroke, and backstroke.

Terry Fowler, also a seaman, and I were swim partners. We cut corners by swimming over some of the kelp beds, which were masses of large seaweeds. We literally pulled ourselves, freestyle, through the kelp. With a total time of a little over six hours, we came in fourth out of fifteen pairs.

Terry and I crawled up onto the beach just before dark. We were so numb from the cold that our legs were simply too stiff to do more than crawl. The last swim pair didn't get in for another two hours.

Friendly Frederickson was there to greet us back by saying, "Get off your asses! You pukes. Double time to the shower area, then eat chow. Now!" No encouragement, just a kick in the pants. We continued crawling toward the chow hall until we were able to stand up.

Taking a shower was always a delight. The system was nothing more than pipes secured to posts outside and near our berthing shacks. The water was delivered from a large tank on a hill above the camp by gravity flow. It was always very cold, but very welcome.

The last week before graduation we spent executing demolition raids against enemy positions scattered throughout San Clemente Island and running a timed eight-mile race the last afternoon.

Finally, Class 36 graduated on 3 December 1965. There were a total of thirty survivors. The following men were assigned to UDT-11: Lt. (jg) Charles L. Allen, ENS Richard A. Sleight, ENS John E. Roberts, ENS Theodore Roosevelt, IV, ENS Bruce A. Smathers, Lt. George R. Worthington, BMSN Richmond Cleem, RM3 Robert R. Cramer, BM3 Francis D. Dick, BT1 John E. Fietsch, ETNSN Terry R. Fowler, AQFAN Lewis W. Miller, SFP2 Wash Moore, Jr., ABH3 George W. Raacke, SN Robert A. Schaedler, and MMFN William F. Wright. Last but by far the best were assigned to UDT-12: ENS Robert M. Blum, Lt. Robert E. Condon, Lt. (jg) Joseph G. DeFloria, ENS Thomas J. Hummer, ENS John M. Odusch, BT3 Benjamin O. Azeredo, Jr., EUL3 Bud R. Burgess, RM2 John J. Chalmers, AMHAN Ray E. Markel, ADJ3 David E. McCabe, AK3 Ronald A. Ostrander, BM2 Walter G. Pope, SF1 Donald L. Schwab, and RMSN Gary R. Smith. I was immediately assigned to the 4th Platoon.

Fourth Platoon had just returned from a tour in Vietnam and Subic Bay, Philippines. Not surprisingly the platoon was understrength due to several men getting out of the navy and others on annual leave. In December '65, 4th Platoon's personnel were: Lt. (jg) Hammond, DCC Edwin C. Reynolds, GMG1 George B. McNair, AE2 Walter H. Gustavel, BM3 Stephan F. Cary, RD2 Patrick T. Gruber, MR3 Michael N. Dorfi, AE3 Stephan G. Eastman, BT3 Benjamin O. Azaredo, PHAN Robert D. Totten, MRFN Leroy S. Ray, SN John J. Broda, SFPFN

Alexander, NMN Verduzco, RMSN Gary R. Smith, SN Deeolla, and NMN Van Winkle.

It wasn't long before I was told UDT-12's genealogy. Following World War II, the UDTs became a victim of demobilization by being reduced from thirty to four teams. Two teams were assigned to the Atlantic Fleet, USNAB, Little Creek, Virginia, and two to the Pacific Fleet, USNAB, Coronado, California. On the west coast UDT-3 was the predecessor of UDT-12 and was commissioned on 21 May 1946 under the command of LCDR Walter Cooper and redesignated UDT-12 on 8 February 1954.

SN Van Winkle and PO3 Dorfi were the rugby experts in our platoon. Both were heavily muscled and excellent all-around athletes. They were always cutting up and great for morale. One bright and sunny Southern California day, Van Winkle and Dorfi decided they needed to accept me into the platoon.

Dorfi began the conversation, saying, "I think it's time we initiate Smitty into the platoon, Wink."

Van Winkle gave me a hard look, saying, "Yeah, he even thinks he can outrun us. Let's show him who's the fastest."

"You guys don't know what you're about to get into," I stated as I was backing up. "I'm a whole lot meaner than I look."

It didn't work. I could tell by the gleam in their eyes that it was time for me to head south for the border. The race was on! I struck out for all I was worth by heading down the strand in the soft sand toward the obstacle course. That was my undoing. They eventually caught me, beat the crap out of me, then put their arms around me and said, "Welcome to 4th Platoon, Smitty." It was a good thing they weren't mad at me.

Chief Ed Reynolds was great to work for. Ed had the fastest hands I'd ever seen. When he started giggling, one had best watch out for that uppercut! For some reason he always started giggling just before he threw a series of severe punches and blows to the head and body.

Joe Thrift, who had recently been assigned to 4th Platoon as the LPO, was no slouch, either. He had been a professional boxer until some guy convinced him in the ring that the Navy was the best profession. However, Joe could literally carry on a conversation by using his hands as semaphore flags. He would talk to me using semaphore and I would reply in CW code.

In March '66, all four UDT-12 platoons began the bi-annual Team Olympics, two weeks of operational competition between the platoons. We had a long ocean swim, underwater mine search, beach reconnaissance, parachute accuracy test, long-distance foot race, obstacle course race, timed breath-holding while sitting and while swimming underwater, inland demolition raids, and a variety of administrative, communications, and operational skills tests.

Fourth Platoon won the title. We had the privilege and honor to represent our command during its annual ORI (Operational Readiness Inspection) by the NOSG (Naval Operations Support Group) staff. We spent the next two weeks jumping out of airplanes, diving, demonstrating demolitions, undertaking demolition raids on San Clemente Island, drawing hydrographic charts, et cetera. All went well, with UDT-12 receiving a grade of excellent and a letter to the CO and men for a job well done.

In June '66, six of us were finally sent to Fort Benning, Georgia, to Jump School. Generally, everyone was anxious to go because once we'd graduated, we would receive a second additional fifty-five dollars a month for hazardous duty pay. Because we were divers and worked with demolitions, we were already receiving the first additional fifty-five dollars a month.

The biggest mistake I made at Fort Benning was letting a Marine Force Recon guy give me a Mohawk haircut. It was my idea and his workmanship. All went well concerning my new look during our individual inspection the next morning. No comments were made by the instructors until our daily run after PT. Because PO3 Leslie Funk and I were the fastest runners in the thousand-man class, we were given the privilege of running circles around our platoon while it ran in formation. It was during this time that we passed the Commandant of Jump School, a bird colonel.

Seeing me, he yelled, "You, get over here!" I knew I was in big trouble because of the anger in his voice. I quickly ran to him and dropped to the push-up position, yelling, "Airborne, sir."

Continuing to yell, he spat, "You get out of my school and you get out of here now! And don't you ever come back!"

I was crushed! I immediately jumped up and started running after my platoon, not knowing what else to do. All I could think of was that I would be the first man in UDT to get kicked out of Jump School. Man, you've really done it now! I thought.

The platoon had a big black sergeant running with us. He motioned for me to come over to him. I ran near to him and dropped to the lean and rest, yelling, "Airborne, Sergeant!"

"Go over to OCS (Officers Candidate School) and get a haircut," he instructed. "When you're done, come on back and keep your mouth shut."

I was sure thankful that I had a friend in that sergeant! After I got my haircut and returned to the platoon, I kept my mouth closed for the remainder of the time I was at Fort Benning. I was beginning to understand the wisdom of being slow to speak, slow to anger, quick to listen, and never again to get another Mohawk haircut.

On 22 August 1966, all of UDT-12 departed for Subic Bay, Philippines aboard a Navy C-117, where we relieved UDT-11. We arrived at Naval Air Station (NAS) Cubi Point late on 24 August. Fourth Platoon consisted of the following personnel: ENS John Odusch, Chief Ed Reynolds, Bosn Joe Thrift, "R. E." Saillant, "Moki" Martin, George Nunez, Ben Azeredo, Lou DiCroce, Alex Verduzco, Jim Girardin, Leroy Ray, and Gary Smith.

Shortly after we arrived, 4th Platoon was notified that we would board the USS *Diachenko* (APD 123) the next morning at 0800 hours and head for Vietnam. Until then, we were granted Cinderella liberty (liberty that was canceled at midnight) and told to muster NLT (no later than) 0600 hours at the team area near the enlisted barracks.

The next day I was riding my first "gray ghost." The USS *Diachenko* had originally been a DE (Destroyer Escort) during World War II.

PO1 R. E. Saillant (Fourth Platoon) had been aboard the *Diachenko* during the Korean conflict with UDT-12. He commented, "The only thing that has been changed or added is the air conditioning." The racks were of canvas with aluminum tube rims. They were to be triced up from reveille at 0600 hours till taps at 2200 hours.

Once we reached South Vietnam, we began hydrographic reconnaissance of beaches from the Cambodian border to the Tan Phu Peninsula of Kien Hoa province. Hydrographic reconnaissance was conducted to get an accurate map of the bottom of the ocean along the shore, wherever the possibility of an amphibious landing existed. After the tragedy of Tarawa in World War II, where the landing crafts were grounded on uncharted reefs and where many Marines were shot to pieces and drowned in deep tidal pools, the Navy perfected the procedures of creating hydrographic charts by two methods:

1) combat reconnaissance with UDT swimmers; the UDT reconnaissance of an enemy-held beach was usually completed the night before the amphibious landing with the combat demolition of the obstacles at predawn; and 2) administrative reconnaissance; usually done after the amphibious landing had taken place, or at any time, to gather hydrographic information of any designated beach or area. It was done during the day under secure conditions and was more accurate.

Generally, we were able to perform administrative recons because the U.S. Army Special Forces and their indigenous troops secured the beaches for us. Seldom did we come under fire. Some days we swam for twelve hours or more. Because I was also a cartographer, I had to work on the development of the hydrographic charts after swimming all day. Occasionally, Chief Reynolds would have mercy on me and let me be beach security for a day or so.

On 1 September, we got to go to Singapore for five days' liberty. I really enjoyed visiting the famous Raffles Hotel, where "Bring 'em Back Alive" Frank Buck used to stay in the thirties and forties.

After our short stay in Singapore, we headed south for the equator. When we reached the magic point, all hands who weren't Shellbacks were called "Pollywogs" and were hand-delivered a "Subpoena and Summons Extraordinary" from "The Royal High Court of the Raging Main." It read:

WHEREAS, the good ship USS *Diachenko* (APD 123), bound for Subic Bay, Philippines, is about to enter our domain, and the aforesaid ship carries a large and slimy cargo of land-lubbers, beach-combers, cargo-rats, sea-lawyers, lounge-lizards, parlor dunnigans, plow-deserters, park-bench warmers, chicken-chasers, hay-tossers, sand-crabs, four-flushers, crossword-puzzle bugs and all other living creatures of the land, and last but not least, he-vamps, liberty-hounds and drugstore cowboys falsely masquerading as seamen and man-o'-warsmen of which you are a member, having never appeared before us; and

WHEREAS, the Royal High Court of the Raging Main has been convened by us on board of the good ship USS *Diachenko* (APD 123) on the seventh day of September, 1966 at Longitude 105 degrees and Latitude 0 degrees 0 minutes 0 seconds, and an inspection of our Royal High Roster shows that it is high time the sad and wandering nautical soul of that much abused body of yours appeared before the High Tribunal of Neptune; and

BE IT KNOWN, That we hereby summon and command you, Gary Smith, RM3, now a plow-deserter, U.S.N., to appear before the Royal High Court and Our August Presence on the aforesaid date at such time as may best suit our pleasure, and to accept most heartily and with a good grace the pains and penalties of the awful tortures that will be inflicted upon you for daring to enter our aqueous and equinoctial regions without due and submissive ceremony to be examined as to fitness to become one of our Trusty Shellbacks, and a worthy Son of the Sea and answer to the following charges:

CHARGE I. In that Gary Smith, RM3, now a hay-tosser, U.S.N., has hitherto willfully and maliciously failed to show reverence and allegiance to our Royal Person, and is therein and thereby a vile land-lubber and pollywog.

CHARGE II. In that you brush your teeth with onion sauce causing a Trusty Shellback to become ill by your bad breath.

CHARGE III. In that you take a shower with Right Guard only and have no decency among the Sons of the Sea. Disobey this summons under pain of our swift and terrible displeasure. Our vigilance is ever wakeful, our vengeance is just and sure!!!

Given under our hand and seal

Attest, for the King:

DAVY JONES, Scribe.

<u>NEPTUNUS REX</u>

Shortly after the Summons, the humiliation and torture that went with crossing the equator began. The Corpsman and the ship's head cook got together and concocted a terrible mess of goo that smelled and looked worse than a bucket filled with rotted toads and maggots. The long trail of humiliation and gagging began as we were forced to crawl on our hands and knees and to kiss the belly of the Royal Baby, who just happened to be the head cook, who stood about five foot six and weighed 225 pounds.

I didn't mind the thought of having to gingerly kiss his revolting stomach; it was the mass of rotted toads and maggots smeared on it that made me gag. Yessir, the Royal Baby was a fine-looking specimen, sitting there in his boxer shorts, crown on his head, and crap on his gut.

I didn't crawl any closer than I had to. I stretched out my neck and tried for a light kiss—I wasn't interested in getting that mess smeared all over my face. The smell was absolutely revolting! Suddenly the Royal Baby grabbed my head and forced my face into the pit of hell, rubbing my face around and around in it.

"Shit!" was my immediate response, followed by gagging and trying to get away from that retarded pig. Wait till I get my hands on Doc, I thought. I'm gonna put this evil mess in all of his shoes, fill his toothpaste tube with it, and smear it all over his pillow. Damn his worthless hide! I might even take their "aqueous and equinoctial regions" and, with a total lack of "submissive ceremony," shove it up their armpits.

My next travail was to crawl through a passageway where good ole Trusty Shellbacks were standing on both sides waiting with three foot sections of canvas fire hose. This ought to be fun, I thought; all I've got on is my UDT swim trunks! Shit!

I lowered my head and charged like a sex-crazed water buffalo, growling and snorting until the blows of the fire hose started taking effect. By the time I got through the gauntlet, I felt more like a neutered warthog.

Continuing to crawl, I was forced to enter into the back end of a thirty-foot beast, made of sheets. It was filled with vile-smelling, decomposed, leftover food, and other unknown ingredients. No doubt Doc and Cookie had something to do with that, too.

I hadn't gotten more than six feet inside the sheets when I began to feel that I was in the stomach of a large and nasty saltwater crocodile. He began to twist, roll and toss me to and fro. At one point I was totally buried in a mass of slimy ground beef, chicken liver and gizzards, flour, hydrogen peroxide, baking soda, squashed tomatoes, boiled okra, food coloring, et cetera. My nose and ears were filled with the foul mess! It was impossible to breathe. If I only had had my SCUBA gear!

I finally managed to reach the opposite end of the beast, and crawled out its mouth to the fantail (open main deck in the after part of the ship) where I was then considered a Trusty Shellback. A fellow Trusty Shellback started washing me down with a fire hose. By the end of the day, everyone had had enough of Neptunus Rex and his stinking equator.

The USS *Diachenko* and 4th Platoon were then directed to the DMZ to participate in the DECKHOUSE

IV amphibious operation, which would take place about three miles south of the DMZ. Myself and PO2 Azeredo were dropped off one mile from the coast by motorized IBS the night before the Marines assaulted the beach at dawn. Our mission was to swim to the beach and take surf observations. That entailed visually measuring the heights of the waves for the high and low series, the distance from the beach to the first breakers, the time between each wave, condition of the beach, et cetera, information that was very important for the assault boat coxswains, the Seabee Beachmaster Unit, not to mention the Marines and support units involved in the task force.

It was a moonless night with ideal conditions for clandestine swimmers. All went well until we began swimming back to our rendezvous with the IBS. A large dark shadow gradually drifted toward us. As it got closer we recognized it as a Vietnamese junk. When it came within fifty feet of us, we saw that our only options were to wave our K-bar knives at them, dive underwater, or remain very quiet and still. We chose the latter, and the junk drifted by without spotting us.

We continued toward our rendezvous point, where we turned on a strobe light that was covered with an infrared lens. Within a half hour, the motorized IBS crew spotted us with their metascope infrared receiver and picked us up.

The next morning, the Marines, Beach Master Unit, and Seabees hit the beach. Initially, the Marines encountered little resistance on the beach. However, it was a different story as they moved inland while paralleling the Cua Viet River. Eventually, they established a small base at Dong Ha where they could be resupplied by Navy LCU (Landing Craft Utility) boats and aircraft.

In January '67, while 4th Platoon was based out of the Navy's Camp Tien Sha just outside Da Nang, Jim

Girardin and I were assigned to go to Don Ha with our diving gear to change a damaged screw on an LCM-8 (Landing Craft Mechanized). We traveled up the Cua Viet by LCU. Surprisingly, we were never fired upon by the NVA.

Once we accomplished our task at Don Ha, we were taken back out to the mouth of the Qua Viet River where we rendezvoused with the Navy Beachmaster LARKs. Jim and I spent several days diving on a broken land-intake fuel line that supplied fuel for the Marine and Navy operations to and from Dong Ha. The intake fuel line was buoyed approximately one mile to sea from the mouth of the Cua Viet River. Apparently the refueling tankers regularly got underway without disconnecting their fuel line from the buoyed land line intake! The weather was stormy, the seas were rough, the underwater surge tossed us to and fro and against the bottom. The visibility was usually less than a foot. With the Beachmasters' help, we finally got the fuel line intake repaired.

In February of '67, 4th Platoon was tasked to administratively recon several beaches south of Chu Lai shortly after the Marines had landed nearby during the DECKHOUSE IV amphibious operation. Again the weather was stormy and the seas were very rough. The surf was plunging and about ten feet in height. The inshore winds didn't help the surf situation, either. Occasionally, the Marines received sniper fire and several men were killed or wounded. Other than our folks on the beach running the recon, the swimmers were in little danger of getting shot. Our worst enemy was the tidal current and rip tides.

The 4th Platoon's swimmer line was to run perpendicular to the beach and out to sea for five hundred yards. There was a swimmer stationed at each of the twenty-five-yard markers on the line. The beach party would control the movement of the swimmer line by using two flagpoles to ensure swimmer alignment and to signal the swimmers, once they were lined up, when to take a sounding with their lead-line. In good weather, calm seas, and low surf, the admin recon was a lot of fun. However, when conditions were like those at Chu Lai, it was very dangerous. We had a terrible time getting ourselves and the swimmer line just to the two-hundred-yard mark. Actually, we never got through the surf zone because it extended much farther than five hundred yards. The waves were spaced so closely together that there was no chance to take a sounding and record the reading on our slates, much less keep a straight swimmer line.

When we ran into a very powerful rip tide, some of us were forced to abandon the swimmer line and go out to sea with the current until we could swim away and down the coast several hundred yards. Only then could we return to the beach to regroup. We fought the elements for about four hours until several men got entangled in the swimmer line and had to inflate their life jackets to keep from being drowned in the surf. Reluctantly, we had to admit that we couldn't complete the recon. However, we were thankful that no one was hurt badly or drowned.

In late February '67, we returned to Subic Bay for a few days before returning to Coronado and the beautiful Silver Strand. In the meantime, we concentrated on getting our parachute, demolition, and diving requalifications up to date.

One Saturday we were jumping with the NAS Cubi Point Skydivers sport parachute club. I was given permission to jump a new "Para Commander" for my fifth freefall and my sixteenth jump overall. We were jumping from an UH-2B helicopter into the Subic Bay trap and skeet range. The jumpmaster, MM2 Moki Martin, and I went up to six thousand feet together. Martin and I had started out freefalling together at the small airport near Lakeside, California, during the summer of '66. We hadn't made a freefall since then. Both of us were a bit nervous but determined to joke and grin at each other in spite of the butterflies in our stomachs. I was to go first because I was jumping the Para Commander. When I was motioned to exit by the jumpmaster, I immediately leaped out with my back arched, arms and feet spread out wide in the "frog" position. I stabled out and enjoyed the scenery, occasionally glancing at my altimeter.

As I neared three thousand feet, I visually checked my rip cord's position with my right hand. When I did, my body dipped to the right and I spun rapidly clockwise. To stable out, I simply put my right arm back even with my left.

When my altimeter's needle reached three thousand feet, I reached in with my right hand and pulled the rip cord, being careful to not lose it, which would have cost me a case of beer.

I waited and waited, and the parachute failed to open! My reserve was located in front of my stomach exactly like the military reserve was when jumping the T-10 at Jump School and the T-10 with the Tojo modification in UDT and SEAL Teams. I doubled over, gripping the reserve with my left and the rip cord with my right hand. My body flipped upside down with my butt pointing at the ground. I pulled the reserve, and the next second I was sitting in the reserve saddle. It opened incredibly fast, followed by the Para Commander, which gradually inflated. Then I had two canopies over my head. I was slowly swinging around and around until I landed in the high grass between the skeet range and the hillside.

Martin's and the jumpmaster's jumps went well. We grabbed three more chutes and went back up for another thrill. While we were gaining altitude in the helo, the wind came up suddenly without our knowing it. We weren't using smoke grenades for wind indicators on the DZ (drop zone) because it wasn't an official military jump, and being young and dumb and a little on the cocky side, we figured we could handle just about anything.

Again the jumpmaster put me out first. I was jumping a steerable, twenty-eight-foot military surplus canopy with the double-L modification. I pulled at twenty-five hundred feet with my chute opening just fine, but when I looked down at the ground, I noticed that the jumpmaster's spot was off by a couple hundred yards.

I immediately faced into the wind and looked between my Cocharan boots to check my drift speed. I was drifting across the road from the skeet range, passing over the spare sixteen-inch gun barrels for the battleship USS *Missouri*, and rapidly moving toward the Kalaklan, commonly called Shit River because of the open sewage it carried away from the town of Olongapo.

As I neared the river, it appeared I would miss the high power lines by about a foot, but I would definitely hit an open metal shed about midsection. I was considering pulling my capewell releases to plunge to the ground, but before I could make a decision my feet hit a high power line.

It was a shocking experience and reinforced my hatred for wires. There was a loud pop and sparks flew everywhere when my feet hit the line. I was also paralyzed from the waist down. My parachute canopy hung over the high power lines, suspending me about twenty-five feet from the ground. I hung there, stunned.

Gradually, I realized what had happened. The base had to cut off the electrical current and get a large cherry picker to reach me. Jim Girardin rode the cherry picker forks up in the air and released me from the parachute.

I was taken to the hospital, where the doctor examined me. The current had entered my feet, traveled up to my waist, and exited through my butt. The bottoms of my feet and the back part of my buns were blistered. If the current had continued up and through my heart, I would have been instantly killed.

I remembered an old Irish proverb that said, "A man that's born to hang will never drown." Now I knew what that meant. Within two hours, I was back to normal with no aftereffects other than the blisters.

The Navy doctor asked me to what unit I was assigned. I told him UDT-12. He looked at me with a grin and said, "Get out of here. You guys are too much."

We were only too glad to leave. We headed directly for the Navy Enlisted Men's Sampaquita Club for a few San Miguel beers. In a short time Moki Martin, Jim Girardin, the guys, and I were boasting and reminiscing of the day's excitement and experiences. We didn't have much time to do a lot of thinking; we were too busy having fun!

We departed Subic Bay, Philippines on 3 March by a Navy C-117, and arrived at NAS North Island, Coronado, California, on 8 March '67. Within two weeks, about half of us were assigned to SEAL Team 1.

Our first week with SEAL Team 1 was spent getting moved into the SEAL barracks, getting our personal records turned in to admin, medical records turned in to medical, drawing our operating gear from supply, getting assigned to Foxtrot Platoon, being issued personal weapons, et cetera.

The next week, we (Foxtrot Platoon) began the six-week course of SBI (SEAL Basic Instruction) that involved weapons familiarization and training, small unit tactics, prisoner handling, map and compass, SOPs

(Standard Operating Procedures) that included hand signals and individual responsibilities, rappelling, emergency extraction by McGuire rig, operational insertion and extraction by helicopter, boat, and parachute, emergency first aid, uses of ordnance, et cetera.

Our weapons training took place in the Chocolate Mountains on the Navy Bombing Range at Siphon ten of Coachella Irrigation Canal and the Beal Well area. We fired the 57mm and 75mm recoilless rifles, 60mm and 81mm mortars, M-60 and Stoner machine guns, M-79 grenade launchers, M-16/XM-148 combination rifle and grenade launchers, .30-caliber BAR (Browning Automatic Rifle), Thompson and M3A1 ("grease") submachine guns, Swedish-K submachine guns, Browning .30- and .50-caliber machine guns, and silencers.

Most of our squad and platoon training missions took place on the Alamo River, which drains into the Salton Sea, and other marshy terrain that was very similar to the Rung Sat Special Zone (RSSZ) in the South Vietnamese delta that was just a few miles southwest of Saigon.

One particular night we were given a mission that took us across a muddy flat of the Salton Sea. The mud was bottomless in places and impassable by walking. We soon learned that we had to lie down in the mess and pull ourselves along with our hands and knees. It was exhausting.

It took us all night to get across that muddy flat. We were covered with mud from head to toe. Our weapons were caked and filled with the salty muck, but we learned many lessons that night. We had gotten only a taste of what we would be experiencing in the Rung Sat Special Zone (RSSZ).

When we returned to Siphon ten, we bathed and cleaned our weapons in the Coachella Canal.

We remained at Siphon ten for a couple of weeks, concentrating heavily on weapons training. We spread sleeping bags under the desert ironwood trees and grabbed a few hours of rest when we could.

The last week, Foxtrot Platoon was given an ORI (Operational Readiness Inspection). The Cadre (SEAL Team 1 instructors) had us running all over the prickly Chocolate Mountains and the mucky Salton Sea, blowing up enemy targets with explosives, capturing specific individuals, rehearsing area and point ambushes and reconnaissance, and in general, doing RP&B (Rape, Pillage, and Burn). We were beginning to work smoothly as a platoon, and also as a squad, when we split up. Each man was beginning to feel comfortable and confident with his responsibilities and how he fit into the platoon. And every man knew exactly what the other men's responsibilities were.

It was at this point that our instructors began teaching us the art of flexibility applied to contingency planning (when the enemy had gained the element of surprise over us). The key was to take the unexpected and turn it into victory. Continuous training in immediate action drills prepared us to respond instinctively and aggressively and for the best chance of survival. For example, if we were to patrol into an enemy ambush, our immediate response would be to charge directly into the midst of the ambush, thereby changing a defensive action into an offensive action, that is, direct assault against the enemy. If we could pull it off, we were winners; if not, then the enemy would surely hold us in great awe and respect for our courage. Even in death, it was good to be a winner.

We gradually became more confident as a fighting unit because we knew we could count on the Navy Seawolves, Navy Boat Support Unit personnel, and others to respond to our cries for help or reinforcement. In other words, we would use our strength against the enemy's weakness, neutralize the enemy's strength, and conceal our vulnerability. The enemy had a larger force, but we had superior firepower, and/or maneuverability. Because we were a small, offensive unit, we always had to try to seize and hold the initiative. Without going into all of the elements of war, our strengths were due to our good leadership, up-to-date training, state-of-the-art equipment, and teamwork. Take away any one of the four, we would be in trouble.

The last three weeks in July '67 were spent at the Army's Jungle Warfare School at Fort Gulick in the Canal Zone in Panama. It was an excellent school, staffed by U.S. Army Special Forces personnel.

There, Foxtrot Platoon was used primarily as point element for company- or battalion-size operations. During one evolution, we were to E&E (escape and evade) the enemy from point *A* to point *B*. Naturally, the "enemy" consisted of Special Forces staff members. We were given all day to complete the course. All of Foxtrot ran the distance and none were captured. However, one sergeant was hot on my trail, and got close enough to get a hand on my right shoulder, when I dove into a creek. I swam to the other side and kept on moving. I hadn't forgotten the lessons learned at Devil's Elbow on the Colorado River during UDT Training.

We learned how to make comfortable shelters (called bohios) from a mosquito net, poncho, and inflatable mattress. We learned how to cook coatimundi, boa constrictor, iguana, sea foods, et cetera, and how tasty their flesh was.

The highlight of the trip occurred when a sergeant said I could have a small boa constrictor for a pet. All I had to do was reach into a cage where a fifteen-foot mama boa lay with several hundred babies, each twelve inches in length, wiggling all together in one bundle. I couldn't back out, as SEAL Team 1's image was at stake. I reached down into the mass of squirming evil and came up with none other than Bolivar. He and I became fast friends. I simply put him into my pocket and smuggled him back to Coronado.

When we returned to the Silver Strand, we had just one week to get our gear packed to leave for Vietnam.

On 7 August, Foxtrot and Alpha Platoons departed for Vietnam on board a Navy C-117. Foxtrot Platoon members were as follows: Lt. Stanley S. Meston (OIC), Lt. (jg) Francis E. Schrader (AOIC), PR1 Richard A. Pearson, MM2 Harlan W. Funkhouser, BT2 Michael E. McCollum, HM2 William L. Brown, RM2 Gary R. Smith, SM3 Leslie H. Funk (Katsma), ADJ3 Mitchell L. Bucklew, ADJ3 John F. Flynn, BT3 Ivan C. L. Moses, AMH3 Ray E. Markel, and SA Vernon L. Dicey. Alpha Platoon members were as follows: Lt. (jg) Joseph DeFloria, Lt. (jg) Nelson, PHC James M. Cignarella, PT1 Gerald M. "Ace" Bowen, Phillip L. "Moki" Martin, QM2 Talmadge W. Bohannon, SK2 Gouveia, HM2 Mahner, BM3 Al "Apache" Williams, RM3 Byrum, ICFN Guidry, and SK2 Ronald A. Ostrander. Even Bolivar, my snake, enjoyed the trip. I took him out of my field jacket pocket and let him crawl around in my lap and on Funkhouser's neck while he was asleep.

All went well until we reached Barbers Point Naval Air Station on Oahu. One of the crewmen had snitched to U.S. Customs that there was a snake on board. We were not allowed to depart the plane until we had been questioned and searched by Customs. Naturally, I denied having a snake with me because I knew my teammates wouldn't give me away.

Finally, the Customs men gave up the search and departed. Apparently, Hawaii didn't have snakes. And they didn't want any.

Mr. Meston, my platoon officer, came over to me afterward and asked, "Where is that damn snake?"

I could tell he wasn't in a mood for humor. Without hesitating, I replied, "Right here in my coat pocket, sir."

Obviously irritated, he ordered, "Never do this again! You almost got us all into trouble. Do you understand?"

"Yes, sir," I replied as I stood at attention. I decided that I had better leave Bolivar in my coat pocket the whole trip coming back, unless, of course, I put him in Funky's coat pocket. Now that's what I'd call a good, covert scheme, I thought. After Lieutenant Meston walked away, I looked over to Funkhouser, grinned, and said, "How would you like for me to buy you a beer?"

"Lead the way, matey," was his cheerful reply.

I bought him the beer, which was one of our last in the States. Two days later, we arrived at Tan Son Nhut Airport in Saigon. Nha Be Naval Support Activity was to be our home for the next six months, and the VC were to be our targets for assassination.

My platoon, Foxtrot, relieved Kilo Platoon. The Kilo Platoon members were: Lt. E. D. Gill (OIC), Lt. (jg) D. Mann (AOIC), SM1 Wilson, DC1 Mack, EM1 Christensen, GMG2 Swepston, MM2 David Lee Sitter, BUI Payne, TM3 Haldeman, RM3 Neal, IC3 Boston, PH3 Kelmell, SN Cary, and HM2 Lappohn. Alpha Platoon relieved Juliett Platoon. The Juliett Platoon members were: Lt. (jg) Grabowsky (OIC), ENS Seiple (AOIC), HMC "Doc" Jones, BT1 John Fietsch, BM1 Donald L. "Goody" Goodman, EM2 William T. Doyle, SFP2 Wash Moore, ABH2 George Raacke, ETN3 Robert Schaedler, BM3 Richmond Cleem, SN Frank Toms, RM3 Robert Cramer, IC2 Michael J. Scrafford, MM3 Art Streeter, and FA Coy Ray Humphrey.

Echo Platoon had previously arrived at Nha Be in June and wouldn't be relieved until December by Bravo Platoon. Echo Platoon members were as follows: Lt. R. G. Brereton, Lt. (jg) R. F. Redding, QM1 D. D. Daley, BM2 J. S. Cirardin, SM1 Tommy L. Hatchett,

MR2 C. D. "Tobacco Lou" Lewis, HM1 H. C. Marshall, GMG1 H. F. Matthews, PR2 Gary W. Shadduck, EMC W. A. Tobin, and BM1 R. Tullas.

It was really good to see the guys again. We were soon told the details of what had happened last April 7th, when members of Juliett and Kilo Platoons were aboard the *Mighty Moe* (a modified Mike-Six boat) deep in the Rung Sat Special Zone. Frank Toms stated that they were ambushed by a well-armed VC/NVA unit with automatic weapons and shoulder-fired B-40 rocket rounds. Of the sixteen SEAL platoon members aboard (not counting MST casualties), thirteen were wounded and three killed. Kilo Platoon lost Mr. Mann, Neal, and Boston. Sadly, Mr. Mann had been married only a year at the time of his death. Boston had married a couple of weeks prior to Kilo Platoon's deployment to Nam in early April '67. It was to have been Boston's last trip to Vietnam before his discharge from the navy. It's easier to be brave when you don't have a wife and kids to worry about, I thought.

CHAPTER ONE
Mission One

"Valor is a gift. Those having it never know for sure whether they have it till the test comes. And those having it in one test never know for sure if they will have it when the next test comes."

Carl Sandburg, December 14, 1954

DATE: 18, 19 August 1967
TIME: 180400H to 190830H
COORDINATES: YSO74634, 077644, 083643, 086639, 086633
UNITS INVOLVED: Foxtrot, 1st Squad, MST-3 (Mobile Support Team)
TASK: Reconnaissance patrol and overnight ambush
METHOD OF INSERTION: LCPL MK-4
METHOD OF EXTRACTION: LCPL MK-4
TERRAIN: Defoliated swampland, mangrove swamp
TIDE: 0905H Low, 1309H High, 2023H Low
MOON: Full
WEATHER: Cloudy with rain
SEAL TEAM PERSONNEL:
Lt. Meston, Patrol Leader/Rifleman, M-16
Lt. Gill, Ass't Patrol Leader/Rifleman, M-16
RM2 Smith, Point/Rifleman, Shotgun
MM2 Funkhouser, Automatic Weapons, M-60

BT2 McCollum, Grenadier, M-79
HM2 Brown, Radioman/Rifleman, M-16
ADJ3 Bucklew, Rifleman, M-16
AZIMUTHS: 000 degrees-500m, 045
   degrees-175m, 035 degrees-350m, 090
   degrees-500m, 135 degrees-500m, 180
   degrees-800m
ESCAPE: 180 degrees
PHASE LINES: Tijuana, San Diego, Los Angeles
CODE WORDS: Challenge and Reply—Two
   numbers total 10

This was it—Foxtrot Platoon, our first mission. We had a good bunch of guys in the squad, but we were all green. We were untested. Still, we were ready. This is what we'd been training for, and now the time had come.

I was keyed up and excited. If I was scared, I didn't notice it. My excitement overwhelmed all other emotions. As I glanced around at the others, none of them looked scared either. Of course, their faces were covered with green-and-black camouflage paint, but even that couldn't hide their eyes. And their eyes looked clear and confident.

Personally, the fact that a SEAL had never been captured made everything black-and-white for me. No SEAL had ever been captured, and I wouldn't be the first. I would never surrender. I would fight to the last breath. I would never leave my platoon; rather, I'd stay, and if death came, it would come to us all or to all who attempted to kill us. Do or die: That gave me courage. Knowing I wouldn't allow capture, and consequent torture, took away my fear of the unknown. I'd make it back alive from this mission, or I'd flat-out die trying.

Since this was our first time out, Lieutenant Gill had agreed to come along to make sure we didn't do anything stupid, like getting killed. He was experienced and was finishing up his tour of duty. He'd advise our OIC (officer in charge), Lieutenant Meston. Mr. Meston looked a bit like he needed some help. He wasn't scared, but seemed unsettled. I'll keep an eye on him, I thought; the jury's still out on what kind of platoon leader he'll turn out to be.

Seven of us went out in the dark. That seemed like a lucky number to me. Seven. Maybe that was a sign this tour would go well, or at least this first mission. I hoped so. But where we were going wasn't a place swarming with luck. It was the Rung Sat Special Zone, swarming with Communist forces. The Rung Sat was a thirty-by-thirty-five kilometer area of mangrove swamp located on the northeastern edge of the Mekong Delta and contained some of the most toilsome terrain in Vietnam. It was a haven for the VC and NVA, who used the area as a resting place after operations. The Vietnamese called the area "The Forest of Assassins," due to its history as a hideout for pirates, outlaws, and contrabandists. And now we SEALs were invading the territory, ambushing the enemy in his own backyard.

It was just past 0200 hours when we boarded the LCPL MK-4 that would take us to our insertion point off the Quan Quang Xuyen, which was a tributary of the Soirap River. The LCPL was a thirty-six-foot-long, V-bottom, steel-hull landing craft, which sat low in the water because of the armor plating on the outboard sides, therefore affording us protection and a low silhouette. The boat was powered by a 300-horsepower turbine exhaust diesel engine. There was a four-man crew, including two gunners, whose job was to drop us at the correct insertion point, and not two miles off course. Once we jumped off the boat and into the jungle, we'd march to our own drummer.

As we sped along down the middle of the river, the

early morning air was cool and invigorating. An occasional spit of rain slapped me in the face. Once, I spit back. Eat it, Vietnam.

I stood behind the coxswain and the two lieutenants, who were using radar to pick up any enemy boat traffic and to monitor terrain features. All the others were seated aft on the steel deck with their weapons pointed toward the black jungle. I held Sweet Lips, my Ithaca model 37 pump shotgun. The point man generally got his weapon of choice; on this mission, I was point, and Sweet Lips was my choice. I'd sawed off the last few inches of her barrel, making her one evil little lady. I'd loaded her with six rounds of 00 buckshot. No one had looked down her hole, yet, with his last gasp and his heart throbbing in his mouth, but, I thought, today might be the day.

The moon was full and I saw its smiling face every few minutes when it promenaded from behind the dark clouds. I didn't like its big face, though, right at that moment. It was not my friend when it lighted up my platoon for enemy eyes to see. I pointed Sweet Lips in the air as a silent warning for Mister Moon to disappear. Funny, but in a few moments, he did.

One of the men took advantage of the blackness and got up and urinated over the side into the river. He must really have to go, I thought. Sure enough, he was at it a long, long time, which told me he was excited. Either that, or he hadn't relieved himself since the eighth grade.

Lieutenant Meston told me to pass the word that insertion would be in fifteen minutes. That meant it was time to get mentally prepared and to run one last check on equipment. I wore an H-harness and web belt with two ammunition pouches attached on my left side and two more on my right. Each pouch contained fifteen rounds of 00 buck, giving me sixty-six rounds including the half dozen already loaded. A K-bar knife was taped, handle down, on the left shoulder strap of my H-harness. Taped on the knife sheath was an MK-13 day/night flare. Two M-26 fragmentation grenades hung from my web belt. A full two-quart collapsible canteen was attached to the H-harness high on my back. A quart canteen was hooked on the web belt over my right buttock, and another over my left. In the center of my back, a small, nylon backpack containing C rations and a first aid kit was attached.

Finding everything in order, I looked through the dark at the men behind me. Funkhouser patted the belted ammo for his M-60 machine gun. He looked at me and grinned, indicating that he, too, was ready.

Finally, the coxswain cut back on the throttles and Lieutenant Meston signaled for us to lock and load. The LCPL, with its engine now just above idle, glided closer to the ominous shoreline. I climbed onto the bow and crouched down at the starboard side of the boat. Lieutenants Meston and Gill and Doc Brown gathered behind me. Funkhouser, Bucklew, and McCollum assembled on the port side of the bow.

I looked down at the reflection of the moon in the water. Small waves rippled as the bow sliced through. Just ahead, the water lapped at the beach. A peacefulness hung in the air. I was mesmerized by the beauty of the moment. This can't be war, I thought. My thoughts drifted with the current.

A second later, I snapped back to reality. This is war, dummy, I censured myself. Life and death. I had to get my head on straight and do my job. These guys were depending on me. Wake up. The enemy had the element of surprise during insertion, and here I was, daydreaming.

I watched the bank as the bow nudged into some ghostly black snags. I jumped onto the muddy shore. As the others followed, I heard a splash. Someone had jumped short of the bank, but I didn't look back. My eyes and concentration had to focus on the ground ahead. Still, I wanted to snicker at the mental picture of a comrade falling in. Of course, I couldn't snicker; strict noise discipline had to be maintained. Sounds, especially talk, carried incredibly far in the jungle, as I had learned in Panama only a few weeks earlier. I wondered now about the sound of the boat motor: Had it been heard by any bad boys? I squeezed my bad girl a little tighter.

I dropped to one knee in the mud, my gun at the ready. My ears strained for sounds of enemy movement. Lieutenants Meston and Gill were a few feet behind me. At first, the only thing I detected was the drifting away of our support boat. A couple minutes later, there was silence. I only heard the ringing in my ears. Then I heard someone speak, which startled me until I realized the voice was only in my mind. It said, "Be careful, Smitty."

Another ten minutes passed. I saw and heard nothing. Lieutenant Meston signaled me to lead on. I moved slowly and painstakingly, which was the only possible way to walk in muck and mud. With each step, I felt like some little dirt devil was trying to suck my hundred-and-seventy-five-pound frame down into his private pit.

I knew from Meston's PLO (patrol leader's order) that the first three hundred meters was defoliated swampland, which, translated, meant "our butts are exposed." We wanted to get to cover as quickly as possible, but we'd been trained too well to screw up by senseless haste, so I proceeded cautiously on point. The lieutenants were right behind me, with the radioman, Brown, behind them. The others followed single file, but I couldn't see them in the dark.

After almost an hour, the open ground was behind us. We entered a mangrove swamp, which consisted of nipa palm and other tropical maritime trees and shrubs in dense masses. One hundred meters into the bush, I found a creek flowing into the Rach Long Vuong, which was the minor tributary we were to follow in a big U-shape back to the Quan Quang Xuyen and the extraction point the next morning. It was at this finger of water that Meston wanted to hide out for a couple hours, looking and listening for enemy activity. He signaled me to scout the creek, both north and south of the platoon, while the rest waited.

The sky was lightening as I patrolled, and the bushes gradually changed color from night-black to green. I patrolled the bank up and down the creek, looking for human tracks in the mud. My eyes scanned the foliage across the water. There were no signs of life, except for the mosquitos.

Working my way back to the platoon, I gave Meston the "all clear." He motioned me to crawl into some brush along the creek, assuming the right flank. I picked my way through the bushes and vines and found the driest spot I could, where my rump would sink in the mud only a couple inches. Each man in the platoon followed suit, finding a hiding place off to my left, ending up spread out in a perimeter overlooking the creek.

I'd been warned that armor-piercing mosquitos loved the dawn, and they loved SEALs. Sure enough, hundreds of the nasty things lost little time in locating my position. But I'd worked hard at covering every square inch of meat from my neck down with military-issue camouflage greens and cotton long johns. And my head held a thick layer of mosquito repellent, courtesy of the United States Navy.

On my legs, dozens of the hairy-legged gooks tried to penetrate my clothing. I didn't feel anything, so I guessed my protection was adequate. Another whole division buzzed my head. I watched them for several seconds, wishing I could identify the big shot of the bunch. I'd have liked to put him out of commission, but I couldn't pick him out. All of them were huge.

Just before the sun glinted over the horizon, the mosquitos mounted a final offensive, attacking me from all quarters. There was no way to swat a thousand ace flyers, so I didn't swat any. I just allowed the repellent and clothing to do the job.

After a while, I looked through the hordes of mosquitos at the foliage around me, and I discovered the red ants. They, too, appeared to have heard the dinner bell. It amazed me that such little creatures showed no fear of such a large beast as myself. I looked forward to killing some of them.

A couple hours went by, and things had changed. The mosquitos had retired to who-knows-where, somewhere to escape the heat of the day. Eleven enemy dead—red ants—lay at my feet. Eight had died without warning; the other three, well, suffice it to say that their deaths had been drawn out and painful because each one had put a round of teeth in me before his capture. I went down in their books as a WIA; they went down dead.

I looked over at ADJ3 Bucklew, who was visible to my left about ten meters away. He was hard to see through all the vegetation and cammo paint, but I knew exactly where to look. Besides that, I could smell him. I stared at him for a full minute, fully aware that I was gazing at the nephew of the famous Captain Bucklew of World War II.

Eventually, Bucklew's head slowly turned toward me. He looked for a few seconds, then his white teeth flashed behind a big, silly grin. I smiled back, then stuck out my tongue at him.

The temperature rose toward a hundred degrees. Inside my long johns, I felt like a baked potato wrapped in tinfoil. Still, I was grateful, for without the long johns, the mosquitos would've drained me dry. As it stood, I believed I'd lost only a pint of high octane.

Bucklew abruptly waved at me and signaled that it was time to move. I crawled out of the mud and waited for the lieutenant. Two minutes later, I was back on point and guiding the platoon north. Our planned mission was to follow the creek to the Rach Long Vuong and a checkpoint we'd designated Tijuana, then circle east with the river to checkpoint San Diego. From there, we were to recon six hundred meters southeast before setting up an all-night ambush site on the riverbank at Los Angeles.

Suddenly the rains came. Hard. I didn't mind, though, because the mosquitos were awash. My body and my clothing needed a good rinse, anyway. I couldn't stand myself an hour earlier, but I had put it out of my mind then. I wished I had some shampoo and soap.

In the downpour, my vision was limited. I glanced behind me at Meston, who was right on my tail. I turned away and continued guiding the procession.

As point, I was supposed to look for the enemy himself, his footprints, and the little gifts he leaves for nice guys like me, namely, booby traps—all shapes and sizes.

One of the friendliest booby traps was the "toe-popper," a small pressure-activated mine that usually only blew off the foot of the unfortunate who stepped on it. Punji stakes, barbed sticks planted in a camouflaged hole, also were partial to American feet. The ones with a nastier streak were those dipped in dung, designed to infect through intimate contact.

The booby traps that were totally antagonistic and anti-American were those made to destroy whole bodies: antipersonnel mines similar to our M18A1 claymore mine, specially adapted grenades, and many other types of mechanically and electrically initiated booby traps. These were set off by stepping on them or just barely moving one of them, tripping a wire, or by the concealed enemy himself. Oh, the joys of the point man.

Upon reaching Tijuana, Mr. Meston motioned for me to leave the water's edge and to take a shortcut over some higher ground toward San Diego. I checked the compass on my watchband, took a reading, then steered the platoon due east through the jungle. There was less muck throughout the shortcut, but I knew the vacation would be brief. High tide was coming soon.

Before reaching San Diego, we stopped to eat our C rats and drink water from our canteens. The two lieutenants and I set up a security watch while the others ate, then we got our turn at some nourishment. The C rats tasted pretty good to me after all the hours of reconnaissance, and the water tasted like life itself, even though it was tepid.

After a half-hour rest, I guided the platoon down to the Rach Long Vuong. At San Diego the mud was soft and we were in water that was knee-deep. The time was 1300 hours and high tide was in. That meant conditions wouldn't get any worse, unless a crocodile erupted out of the mire. If so, strict noise discipline was off. Sweet Lips would see to that.

I turned with the river toward the southeast, heading toward Los Angeles, our ambush site. We were only six hundred meters away, which was not very far unless one was walking in mud, water, rain, and a "free-fire" zone where people shot everything they have at anything that moved. Not that I was complaining. It beat being on the fiftieth floor of a skyscraper in an earthquake registering nine on the Richter scale.

I wondered about Los Angeles, the primary ambush site of this mission. I wondered whether we'd cause the earth to shake there with all of the firepower we were lugging, our platoon of angels. Not that any of us were very angelic, though right then I wished I had wings. Come to think of it, I did. I'd already earned my Navy/Marine Corps parachute wings. Maybe there was some angel in me, after all.

Just then, I stumbled over something and halfway fell into the water. Quickly regaining my balance, I felt with my feet for the submerged object. I touched something solid, and, holding Sweet Lips in my right hand, I reached carefully underwater with my left. My fingers found a hold on the thing, and I slowly raised it out of the mud and water. As water rushed out of the nose and eye sockets, I saw I was holding a human skull.

Lieutenants Meston and Gill joined me for a few seconds in admiring the prize. They offered thirty more seconds of patience while I ran a short line through the eye sockets and fastened the souvenir to my web belt. Then I was back in the saddle.

After another thirty minutes, the rain lightened up, and an hour later it stopped. Lieutenant Meston pointed a finger down the river and then held up one finger at me, indicating we were inside the city limits of L.A., and downtown was just a hundred meters away.

The water I was walking in became a couple inches lower. I wished it were suitable for drinking, as I was thirsty again. It was brackish, however, so I'd drink from my canteen after I pulled up a chair in the ambush site, that is, if I wanted to hang Sweet Lips in a bush and sit in water up to my armpits. Twenty minutes later, I thought I'd found the living room.

Soon Lieutenants Meston and Gill confirmed that it was time to set up our ambush. First, I had to scout up and down through the bush growing along the channel.

As I did so, the remainder of the platoon waited back in the brush.

After a thorough check of the area, I rejoined the others. Meston signaled me to select a spot for the right flank. I slipped in between two bushes.

Within a few minutes, our perimeter was set up along the flooded bank of the Rach Long Vuong. I carefully rested Sweet Lips in a small tree just above the water, which was almost two feet deep, then I sat down in the warm stuff. My buttocks sank a few inches in the mud, which put the water just beneath my chin. No problem. I'd endured much worse in UDT training at the Naval Amphibious Base in Coronado, California. There I had been introduced to Hell Week and the infamous mud flats in the Silver Strand. The mud flats was an old sewage area, where the watery muck was two to four feet deep. On two consecutive days, my instructors had harassed Class 36 at the flats while timing boat crew competitions in the mud. For the better part of each day, I had stood in mud, swum in mud, crawled in mud, got stuck in mud, and almost had become mud. In fact, the instructors had tossed my paper-bagged lunch out to me when I had stood in mud at chest level; hence, half of what I had eaten had been mud.

Then there was the time at Stead Air Force Base Survival School when I had spent forty-eight hours in a simulated POW camp. After many hours of mental torture, I literally had been pushed, squeezed, and compacted into a wooden box barely big enough for a rabbit. So tight was the fit that it had taken two men to pressure the door of the box shut. When I had heard the *click* of the lock, I had almost lost it. There I was, in a compressed fetal position, so crushed that my lungs couldn't expand—I couldn't breathe. I had mentally scolded and ordered myself to calm down, then started inhaling and exhaling tiny, rapid breaths of air. This had kept me alive until four hours later when the door was opened and I was pried back into civilization. With incidents like these in my past, sitting in two feet of water for a few hours was as easy as ogling the curves of Raquel Welch.

Two hours later, I felt something nibbling on my left wrist. I hastily brushed the creature away, but another swam through my arms. Then another. I was surrounded by several tiny fish. I chased them away with my hands, then they were back in a matter of seconds. I decided not to resist, and they continued to play and nibble.

The fish stuck around for a long while, and suddenly they were gone. Maybe the smell of Bucklew down the line had done the trick. Or perhaps it was the fact that I had just urinated through my clothing. At any rate, my little friends departed. I was left to my mission, which was to ambush the enemy.

Since I was on the right flank of our point ambush, my responsibility was to watch for any sampans approaching from the right, which in this case was south. In the event of a sighting, I was to tug three times on the parachute suspension line that I'd strung between me and Bucklew, who was several meters to my left with the line tied to his right wrist. Bucklew was to then pull on another line linking him to Lieutenant Meston, who would likewise pass the message. We were to hold our fire until the enemy skiff reached the middle of the kill zone, which was right in front of our middle man. Once the center of the kill zone was penetrated, the platoon commander would initiate the ambush. That was when all seven of us would open fire, and when some gooks would wish they were dreaming. It was my job to put them to sleep.

More hours slid by and the sun went down. The fish hadn't returned. Just a few mosquitos annoyed me. No

VC had yet made an appearance, but we were not really expecting them until late in the night.

I gazed at Bucklew one last time before it was too dark to see him.

I tugged once on the suspension line, which asked, "Are you okay?" I thought he was looking at me, then he smiled, and I knew he was. I smiled back.

Darkness settled on us shortly thereafter and Bucklew disappeared. I stared at the moonlit water in front of me and reflected a while about why I was there. I blamed it on *Life* magazine (or was it *The Saturday Evening Post*?), which had printed a cover picture of a soldier looking up to the heavens and a hand reaching down to him. I had been in grade school in Abilene, Texas, at the time, and I had tacked that picture up in my bedroom. It had made me think: Am I predestined to be a career military man? From that time forward, I had been obsessed with playing war.

The man who had lived next door to my family had served in World War II, and he had fueled my obsession by giving me some German and Jap gear, including a gas mask, web gear, and dummy grenades. When I was fifteen, my family had moved to Wichita Falls, where I became a frequent visitor of a country club. I had dressed in military utility greens and boots, wielding my pellet rifle, and I had carried out secret operations all over the club's golf course, which had been "enemy controlled territory." Occasionally I had shot a grey squirrel for my taxidermy projects; however, the country club's security personnel had thought dimly of my actions. Whenever they had spotted me with my rifle, they had assaulted my position in their golf carts.

Escape had not always been easy, especially when I had had my goofy Brittany Spaniel with me. Sometimes I had done what Hawkeye in *The Last of the Mohicans* did—I had crawled (dragging my dog) to the creek, slid into its dirty water, and maintained a low profile in the weeds that grew in and around it. Never mind the water moccasins—the water had become my friend. Fortunately, I had never been caught. After three years of numerous close calls, I had retired to the campus of Midwestern University, where I had figured out ways of hiding from my professors without being missed.

Now, here I was, twenty-five years old and still playing hide-and-seek. Up until that day, it always had been just a game; never again would it be just a game. Never again.

It became difficult to see in the dark, especially when the moon vanished behind the clouds. I had to rely on my ears. I listened hard. To hear things at any distance, I had to block out the hum of mosquitos circling my head. It was their supper time, but my tenderloins and hindquarters were underwater.

The buzzing became hypnotic when I allowed myself to relax too much. It reminded me of the purring of a rotating fan that I had liked to sleep to when I was a kid. I had to watch it to avoid dozing off. The mission had begun almost twenty hours before, and my head and eyes felt it.

I decided to close my eyes and trust my ears. My hearing was acute, and besides, I was a light sleeper. I was sure I'd be alert with any unusual noise.

Some time later, I woke up. At least I thought I had been asleep. Really, it was hard to say. I sensed that I had slipped over the edge between waking and sleeping, but I was not sure. Nothing seemed to have changed. It was still dark and the mosquitos were with me. I saw very little, and there were no distant sounds. The only difference I noted was the smell.

I smelled the jungle then, really for the first time. It was the odor of decomposing nipa palm. The smell of wet and rot. An Oriental smell like I'd not smelled before. It had probably been there all along, but I'd missed it. I hadn't concentrated on it. But then it filled my nostrils and registered in my brain. The smell of Vietnam.

I looked in Bucklew's direction, but I saw only black. Tugging once on the suspension line, I received no response. That meant he was asleep, or dead. I pulled again. The second time, he pulled back, once. I'm okay—you're okay. Then we were alone with ourselves, again.

The night passed. Nothing happened. No sampans, no VC. Not even a croc, thank God.

The sun was sneaking up to peek at us, so we had to get on the move. Our extraction point was eight hundred meters and a couple hours south. At Lieutenant Meston's signal, I climbed to my feet. Water rushed out of my clothing as I pulled Sweet Lips from the branches. She felt funny in my hands and I wasn't sure why. Slipping her under my right arm, I rubbed my hands together. My skin felt like the exterior of a shriveled prune.

Bucklew motioned for me to roll up the suspension line. I did and shoved it in a pants pocket. A minute later, the platoon was ready to go.

Back on point, I was wet and cold in the cool morning air as I guided the platoon south toward the Quan Quang Xuyen. The sun was still struggling to climb over the horizon, but its quest had lit up the land. Ahead of me, some nipa palm trees looked black against the brightening sky.

Looking back down, I watched the water and protruding brush before and to the sides of me. Many nasty things could await me—booby traps, crocs, and snakes to name three. And then there were the NVA, gooks.

Fortunately, we made it all the way to the extraction point with nothing more to show than a souvenir skull and five million mosquito-inflicted puncture wounds for

the seven of us. Four and a half million of them be-
longed to BT2 McCollum, our grenadier, who hadn't
worn his long johns. His facial expressions as we
awaited the LCPL were a sight to behold, and his incessant scratching of his thighs told the whole story. He'd
been had, royally.

Twenty minutes later, though, we were all on board
the Navy boat and were headed back to the barracks at
Nha Be Naval Base. I glanced from one SEAL to another, all seated and chattering; strict noise discipline
was off. Each guy was wet and dirty, caked with mud.
Filthy as they were, they were downright ugly, but it
was a good-looking ugly to me. They were the bravest
and toughest men in the world. They were my teammates, my buddies, my brothers. I would fight to the
death for any one of them.

Personally, I was feeling really good, almost euphoric. I couldn't wait to grab a shower, clean my gear,
oil Sweet Lips, eat some vittles, and hit the rack. The
thought of it all made me smile.

Mission One was a complete success. Seven men out,
seven came back, all alive and well. Only McCollum
would argue the point. Scratch, scratch.

CHAPTER TWO

Mission Five

"That is at bottom the only courage demanded of us: to have courage for the most strange, the most singular and the most inexplicable that we may encounter."

Rainer Maria Rilke, *Letters to a Young Poet*

DATE: 3, 4 September 1967
TIME: 030315H to 041030H
COORDINATES: YS143736
UNITS INVOLVED: Foxtrot, 1st Squad, MST-3
TASK: Line reconnaissance and river ambush
METHOD OF INSERTION: LCM-6 *(Mighty Moe)*
METHOD OF EXTRACTION: LCM-6
TERRAIN: Mangrove swamp
MOON: None
WEATHER: Cloudy
SEAL TEAM PERSONNEL:
Lt. Meston, Patrol Leader/Rifleman, M-16
RM2 Smith, Ass't Patrol Leader/Point, shotgun
MM2 Funkhouser, Automatic Weapons, M-60
BT2 McCollum, Grenadier, M-79
ADJ3 Bucklew, Radioman/Rifleman, CAR-15
ENS Khan (LDNN SEAL), Rifleman, M-16
AZIMUTHS: 000 degrees
ESCAPE: 000 degrees

CODE WORDS: Challenge and Reply—Two
   numbers total 10

There I was, back on point with Sweet Lips. I was
moving through the mud of a mangrove swamp on my
fifth mission. In the previous two weeks I'd been point
man on three other missions; all had been uneventful. I
wasn't complaining. I was glad we'd had the good for-
tune to get a few placid missions under our belts; we
had needed to get our feet wet, which we'd done in every sense of the phrase.

Mr. Meston liked me on point. He'd noticed my
country-boy instincts and knew my Texas upbringing,
so he'd put his faith in me. I'd reciprocated that trust.
Since the first couple of missions, Mr. Meston had settled down and impressed me with his decision making.
He was a well-balanced man, cautious yet creative, and
not afraid to hear new ideas. My kind of leader.

I glanced back at Meston. He was five meters behind
me, just visible in the first light of day. Behind him,
invisible to me, was Bucklew with the radio, then
followed Funkhouser, Khan, who was a Vietnamese
SEAL, and McCollum. All of them were likeable guys,
especially McCollum.

McCollum was a jovial fellow and had turned out to
be the life of the party whenever there was a party,
which was every available night. At Nha Be Naval
Base, the Seabees had erected a prefabricated twenty-
by-forty-foot shelter with a semicircular arching roof of
corrugated metal. It was a Quonset hut over a concrete
floor. Inside was a plywood bar, a large refrigerator for
storing beer, a few tables with chairs, and a beat-up piano stolen from Saigon. It was there where many
SEALs hung out, and where McCollum sat at the piano
and sang endless off-color English and Australian ballads. Our platoon had nicknamed him "Muck," which

was simpler to say than McCollum, and is British for "engaging in aimless activity," which was what hanging around the Quonset hut entailed.

Also part of Muck's repertoire were the love songs from the *Navy Song Book,* which he saved for the nights when he'd especially miss his wife back home in the States. His last song two nights earlier, sung with great feeling, had been "Sweethearts and Wives." The words were well known to me:

"Now comrades fill your glasses,
And cease each merry jest;
Let ev'ry one among you think of her whom he loves best.
From Maine to California, in lands far off or near,
God bless the girls who love us, the girls our hearts hold dear!
Sweethearts and wives, wherever we may roam,
Back fly our thoughts to you and home.
Sweethearts and wives, fond hearts and true,
With tear-dimmed eyes, we drink to you.
Make it a bumper, comrades, and each one standing here
Can whisper soft above his glass, the name he holds most dear.
While as we drink in silence, across the ocean foam,
Our loving greetings fly tonight, we drink to those at home!
Sweethearts and wives, wherever we may roam,
Back fly our thoughts to you and home.
Sweethearts and wives, fond hearts and true,
With tear-dimmed eyes, we drink to you."

Suddenly my brain screamed, "Stop!" and my right leg froze in midair. My heart slammed in my throat as I realized there was a trip wire across my shin. The next few seconds took forever; part of me wanted to draw back, the rest of me refused to move. I stayed put, and nothing happened. It became apparent that I'd stopped my forward momentum in the nick of time.

As Mr. Meston approached, I waved at him to back off. He did, and I looked hard to see where the trip wire lead. I spotted a tin can, camouflaged and tied to the trunk of a small tree in front of me and to my left. The can was tied parallel to the ground with the open end facing me. Inside the can was an object which I couldn't make out, but I knew what it was. It was a VC grenade. The trip wire was attached to the grenade, which had had the safety pin removed. Fortunately for me, the grenade was still inside the can where the spoon was held in place. Had I finished my step, the grenade would've been pulled out of the can, releasing the spoon and detonating the grenade. It's fair to say I would've earned a Purple Heart, but I'd have been a bit too stiff to shake hands at the award ceremony.

Sure of myself, I stepped back and allowed the trip wire to slacken. I got free of it, then took a few seconds to choke my heart back down my esophagus.

I carefully approached the booby trap and took my K-bar knife and cut the monofilament trip wire. I didn't slide out the grenade. I simply left the grenade in its nest and rejoined the platoon.

Mr. Meston slapped me on the back, then motioned for me to take point and lead the way. Gee, thanks for the compassion, Lieutenant. Couldn't I have had another five seconds, first, to recover from my nervous breakdown? Nevertheless, I guided the platoon eastward to the place where our intelligence indicated a VC hootch was located. Our job was to check the hootch, looking for enemy activity.

We located the hootch two hours later. From our position, forty meters from the hootch, it looked vacant.

Mr. Meston decided to play it by the book, spreading us out into a skirmish line facing the hootch. He then signaled me to skirt the area around the hootch, maintaining visual contact with the platoon.

I carefully walked the minor trail leading to the hootch, looking for more booby traps. Staying close to the brush, I circled the hootch from west to east, finding only old human tracks in the mud. I signaled Mr. Meston, and he slowly advanced toward the front of the hootch.

As Meston reached the open door, I joined him. He motioned for me to go inside. Sweet Lips was the first to stick her nose in, with me coaxing her from behind. I saw immediately that there was no one in the hootch, and in the few seconds it took for my vision to adjust, my eyes told my brain the place had been cleaned out. The only things left were a broken clay stove in one corner of the dirt floor and a makeshift bed constructed of lashed limbs in another.

Meston entered the hootch and participated in the perusal, then we exited and rejoined the platoon.

As we continued our reconnaissance, I couldn't help but analyze each member of the platoon strung out behind me. Khan, the Vietnamese SEAL, was impressive. He was a short, slender man with penetrating, predator-type eyes. He was steady and exhibited no fear at all. He had a deep scar on his left cheek as a reminder of a knife fight with a gook, who had a deeper scar across his decaying chest.

Funkhouser was just as impressive as Khan. He was a husky six-footer who was so familiar with the M-60 machine gun that I believed the barrel had been his pacifier in his cradle days. He was as cool as a cobra in the field, warming up only when we partied.

Mr. Meston was a clean-cut man of medium build, standing five feet, ten inches tall. He had been making good decisions, including his choices of beautiful, exotic women.

McCollum was better behind the piano than he was in the field; to tell the truth, we were all better at the bar than at recon. "Muck," though, was a bit uncomfortable with his assignment to rear security. Bringing up the rear on a pitch-black night in an enemy-infested jungle was enough to make most men jittery. Still, I'd rather have "Muck" with his M-79 grenade launcher protecting our posteriors than most.

Bucklew was the most handsome one of the platoon, with the possible exception of myself. He was a muscular, six-foot, hundred and eighty pounder. He was a great runner and swimmer, but his athleticism wasn't helping him in the swamplands. That was because his mind was giving him problems, negating his physical advantages. Mr. Meston had given him a try on point a couple missions back, but the stress had eaten him up. Bucklew by then seemed too nervous to me. I was hoping he would hold up when we engaged the enemy, which was an eventual surety.

I pondered my analysis of my buddies for a minute. It seemed to me as though I'd been a little hard on some of them, until I remembered I was judging their performance under extremely dangerous conditions and not simply how they'd fare on a frog hunt back in Texas. In a jungle with gooks and snakes and crocs all around, nobody was perfect, believe me. But these imperfect SEALs, of which I was one, were not quitters. Regardless of their individual quirks and shortcomings, collectively they composed a group of fighting men that no sane enemy would want to face. Of that I was sure. I knew these men. They'd been trained to the max. Someone would have to pay for all that training, and his name would be gook.

I continued on point, moving in ankle-deep mud,

until 1200 hours when Mr. Meston decided to take a break. In fairly thick cover, the six of us set up a perimeter in a circle, with each man facing outboard. I sat down in the mud and leaned my head back against a nipa palm and closed my eyes for half a minute. It felt good to rest my eyes and daydream of the little house in the country I planned to buy near my parents' home in Scotland, Texas. Right then I really wanted the house because it was built on a hill where I'd seldom ever have to walk in mud.

Knowing I must stay alert, I opened my eyes and looked for trouble. He was only present in his mosquito disguise. Feeling safe, I stood Sweet Lips against the palm tree and took a can of C rations from my backpack, along with a P-38 can opener and a spoon. I opened the can of ham and lima beans and stared at the stuff, smothered in solidified grease. I set the can down to my right in the mud, hoping the ninety-degree heat would liquefy the grease so I could pour some of it out.

In the meantime, I drank from my canteen. The water was warm, as usual, but refreshing. It was wet; that's all that mattered.

While my meal slowly corroded, I decided to relieve myself at the nearest bush. I pulled down my pants and long johns, realizing that shining a full moon at hungry mosquitos needed to be a short-lived experience. Two minutes was as short as I could make it, and I think I incurred only one slight wound. The responsible mosquito, though, was dead.

After covering up my exposed parts, I sat down next to my food and my shotgun. I reflected for a couple of minutes on our mission, which involved reconnaissance and then sitting overnight on an ambush site on the Rach Nuoc Hoi waterway. This particular river was only forty meters wide and was still six hundred meters north of our position. We had to cross two minor tribu-

taries before we got there. Also, one hundred meters before the stream, there was a hootch to inspect.

I looked at Mr. Meston, who was a few meters to my
right, and he flashed the thumbs-up at me. I nodded,
then he went back to digging into his C rats can. He
looked like he was enjoying the stuff.

I looked at my can and saw the grease was still hard.
Disgusted, I picked it up and thrust in my spoon, scoop-
ing out a blob. This brought back the pleasant child-
hood memory of a picnic when I had sat beneath a tree
and shoveled pork and beans out of a can and into my
mouth. Right then, I wished I had the pork and beans;
the grease in my C rats was sticking to the roof of my
mouth, guaranteeing me an unpleasant memory.

Fifteen minutes later, Meston gave the signal to get
ready to move. After forcing down a last bite, I stuck
the can upside-down in the mud, then stood up and
stepped on it. It sank and vanished. On recon, we never
left behind anything but our tracks.

Ignoring the gurgling noises in my gut, I briefly inspected my gear, picked up my weapon, and fell into
line. I took point, as always, and, after reading my compass and checking with Mr. Meston, I began guiding the
platoon on a northeasterly course which would take us
to the first creek crossing.

As I advanced through the bush and the mud toward
the creek, I was walking in an inch of water, which soon
rose to two inches. I knew the water would get a little
deeper, as high tide was still an hour away. The creek,
however, was then only sixty meters in front of me.

My eyes darted from the water before me to a bush
on my left, a tree on my right, the water ahead, and
back toward my feet. Three meters directly in front of
me there was something in the bushes growing out of
the water. Something strange, a peculiar-looking log. I

stepped closer, then the log rose higher in the water and became a seven-foot crocodile.

My heart exploded. The croc eyeballed me from six feet as I turned Sweet Lips toward its jaws. Instantly, the creature whirled and seemingly flew into the distant creek. Never had I witnessed anything move so swiftly, its legs a mere blur in the muck. My heart was getting its best workout in years.

I looked at Mr. Meston behind me, and I jokingly examined my pants to see if I'd wet them. At least I wanted Mr. Meston to believe I was joking. Then I proceeded toward the creek, Sweet Lips still shaking in my hands.

Once I reached the creek, Mr. Meston gave the hand signal for "danger point." With that, Funkhouser deployed himself on our left flank with his M-60 machine gun, and McCollum, with the grenade launcher, positioned himself on our right flank. Mr. Meston, Bucklew, and Mr. Khan moved up behind me as I prepared to drop into the deep water of the creek.

Knowing that most of the creeks and tributaries in the Rung Sat Special Zone were over-the-head deep, all of us took a minute to blow up our UDT life jackets already in place beneath the H-harnesses we were wearing. On Mr. Meston's signal, I took a moment to look for smiling crocodiles, then I waded into the creek, which was twenty feet wide. The water met me at the neck on the first step, so I didn't even try for a second; instead, I swam across.

Upon my reaching the foliage on the far side, I crawled out onto the watery, muddy bank and poured the water out of Sweet Lips. Then I did a short recon before waving the other SEALs over.

McCollum came first, and then Funkhouser. Once out of the creek, they set up on right and left flank positions, as usual. The others followed single file.

After the brief swim, everyone deflated his life jacket and quickly inspected his gear. Mr. Meston pointed a finger at a stand of nipa palm trees, then whipped his finger around in tight, little circles in front of his face. That was the signal for "rally point," which meant if we somehow got separated, we were to meet here. The only thing that could split us up was one whale of an enemy assault. I hoped I never would see the day I'd have to scramble back to a rally point.

From the stand of nipa palm, we were less than a hundred meters south of the second creek crossing. I guided the platoon there in twenty minutes. This creek, like the first, was not very wide, but it was deep.

I inflated my life jacket, then swam across. A short recon turned up nothing nasty, so I gave Meston the "all clear." Funkhouser slid into the creek, and halfway across, he disappeared underwater. A moment later, his M-60 made an appearance, followed by Funky's head. As he grasped some tree branches on my side of the creek, Funkhouser shook his head like a Labrador retriever, sending water droplets everywhere. He looked at me and grinned, then dumped the water out of the machine gun's barrel.

I turned away and looked to the northwest where a hootch was supposedly located. I couldn't see it, but I knew it was not far. Maybe a hundred meters.

As the rest of the platoon crossed the creek, I continued watching the bushes. Funkhouser's splashing had been a little noisy. VC may have heard us.

At Mr. Meston's signal, I started for the hootch in ankle-deep water. Fifty meters later, I saw the hootch ahead and to my left, about forty meters away. It was sitting on a muddy plateau several inches above the water. I guided the platoon ten meters closer, then Mr. Meston motioned for us to form a skirmish line. McCollum and Funkhouser took the flank positions, their weapons pointed toward the hootch. Mr. Meston signaled for me to go in alone.

Everything worked the same as before. I skirted the hootch, noting its decayed condition: the palm fronds were disintegrating on the walls, and the roof was caving in. Around the hootch, there were only muddy deer tracks. Meston met me at the front, then I went in with my Sweet Lips.

Inside the only signs that people once had lived there were a remnant of mosquito net hanging near the entrance and some charcoal residue in one corner of the hard-packed mud floor.

Mr. Meston came in and made a studious walk around the floor, shrugged, and left. I followed right behind him. There was only one thing left to do on the mission, and the doing of it was just eighty meters to the northwest. That was where we'd find the main channel of the Rach Nuoc Hoi, close to where it met the Song Ba Gioi. That was also where we hoped to raise a brouhaha for which formal invitations would be unnecessary.

I took the point and started for the river ambush site. The tide was receding and I was walking in thick, slick mud. Also, the closer I got to the river, the heavier the brush I had to penetrate. I was in a real jungle, all right. Our regular army stayed away from hellholes like that. Only SEALs were crazy enough to explore and duke it out in the muck and mire of the Rung Sat Special Zone.

After almost an hour of fighting the bushes, and vines, and mud, I saw the river through the foliage just ahead. I signaled to Mr. Meston that we were there, and he waved for me to recon the riverbank and our ambush site. In this dense brush, he was asking a lot. Of course, I agreed with his decision and didn't hesitate to follow his order.

I began my laborious exploration at 1640 hours and

didn't make it back to Mr. Meston until 1700. I nodded my head that all was well, and he pointed me to left flank. I crept through the thick undergrowth until I found myself on the riverbank. A couple of bushes separated me from the stream.

I sat down in the muck in a place where I could see the river between the bushes and where I could get off some shots at anything that moved in the water. Sweet Lips would have no problem doing some damage because the river was less than forty meters wide. Should the VC float by on a sampan bringing supplies to their troops, they'd be awfully close to the kiss of death.

As Funkhouser settled into position several meters to my right, I untied my boots and took them off. I pulled a pair of coral booties from my pack and slipped them on, then placed a pair of swim fins on top of the mud to my right. Mr. Meston had me prepared to go into the river to retrieve the sampan and supplies should we wipe out some gooks. Again, I was assigned to the risky business. That was what I got for comparing myself to Hawkeye. Now some of the guys were even calling me that.

I took the roll of parachute suspension line out of my pants pocket and crawled with it toward Funkhouser. He met me halfway. I gave him the end of the line, which he wrapped around the middle finger of his left hand, then playfully saluted me with it. I whispered for him to go to places further south, then scooted back to my position. Funky and I were now linked and ready for nightfall, which was yet three hours away.

I stared at the current for a while. It was very fast, and I wondered how quickly a sampan would move in it. Just as fast as the current, I informed myself. That meant I'd have to discharge the six rounds in Sweet Lips as fast and accurately as my arms could work.

Sluggish action on my part would result in only one or two shots before the sampan was out of reach; therefore, I had to stay awake and alert.

As I watched the water, a sea snake floated past me. It was black with white rings, and I knew it was venomous. This one looked four feet long; in a few seconds it was gone. I prayed that no shark would come that night.

The day gradually, but very slowly, passed. The heat and humidity sucked pints of water through my skin's pores in an unrelenting effort to weaken me. Man, it was hot. The VC didn't appear foolish enough to have left their hootches for a boat ride in that furnace. At least I hadn't seen any.

Time went by and nothing grabbed my attention until the mosquitos began swarming over the water. A cloud of them was active right in front of me. Night was near, and with it, the bloodsuckers. How I wished I could unload on them with Sweet Lips, just for the satisfaction of it. Perhaps another time.

At dusk, the thought of vipers, crocs, sharks, and gooks stepped front and center from the back of my mind, where I'd been able to store it for a good, long two minutes. The thought contained a lineup of adversaries, all able and more than willing to remove fifty years from my life span. The men in my platoon had invented a name for these death dealers from the deep: "man-eating man-a-cheetahs." Any creature that swam and had a deadly bite qualified.

I remembered that Billy Machen, the first SEAL to die in Vietnam, had been killed near there last year. He had been a good point man, too. But I liked point. I wanted it. If I died there, so be it.

I remembered reading in a magazine about a man and his epitaph. On his tombstone was inscribed:

> "Here lies Leslie Moore,
> Shot by a .44;
> No less, no more."

I liked that inscription, and I'd been thinking about a similar one for me:

> "Here lies Hawkeye Smitty,
> His death was not very pretty;
> Oh, what a pity."

Whether I got torn apart by a couple dozen bullets or a couple rows of razor-sharp teeth, there wouldn't be anything pretty about it.

As the last light faded into darkness, so did my thoughts of dying. Now I had to concentrate on killing. I was totally concealed, as were my buddies, and I was ready. All the odds were in our favor. We had the element of surprise, and we had the firepower to blow the *Queen Mary* out of the water. A tiny sampan had absolutely no prayer, unless it could drift past unseen and unheard, and if that was ever possible, that night might have been the night. It was as black as Aunt Jemima's posterior. But I had great ears. I could hear farts clear at the other end of the line. Must have been the beans in the C rats talking.

McCollum ejected an occasional noise for half an hour, then apparently got his intestines under control. It was quiet for all of three hours. Then something in the water to my left wheezed, then sucked in a lot of air. After the gulp, it made a little splashing sound. It was a crocodile. He had come up for air, then went underwater again.

I didn't think about the croc for long. The suspension line tied to my right wrist jerked three times. Three times meant "the enemy is here!" I raised Sweet Lips between the two bushes and squinted hard at the river. Before I saw anything, the thundering crack of M-16 fire erupted on my right. A moment later, the black figures of two men in a sampan were just ten feet in front of me. One of them gasped the Vietnamese equivalent of "My God!"

I squeezed the shotgun's trigger as Funkhouser let loose with the M-60 machine gun. I pumped in rounds and pulled the trigger again and again. Tracer bullets streaked across the river from Funkhouser's machine gun. Continuous M-16 fire, along with Bucklew's CAR-15, pounded my eardrums. Three grenades from McCollum's M-79 exploded out front and to my left. I sent three more loads into the dark.

The wall of sound was deafening as I reloaded Sweet Lips, then I fired three more rounds as part of the foray. Another grenade blasted the night in the midst of the heavy gunfire, and I wondered when Mr. Meston would stop the firing. One thing was perfectly clear to me: whoever and whatever was in front of us could no longer exist.

After another fifteen long seconds of ear-shattering and brain-jarring noise, I yelled at the top of my lungs for the men to cease fire. After all, enough was enough. There was no need to use up two tons of ammunition on one little sampan. Since it was time for a cease-fire and Mr. Meston hadn't called for one, and I couldn't see him to check on his condition, then it was my job as assistant squad leader to stop the firing and save a couple bullets for the trip out of there.

The shooting stopped for a few seconds, then one of the M-16 riflemen opened up on full automatic. I shouted again for a cease-fire. I didn't have to whisper since noise discipline had been blown all the way down the river.

The gun stopped firing, and Mr. Meston called out,

"Don't worry, Smitty, it's me." A few seconds later, a concussion grenade blew up in the river. "Just me again," Mr. Meston said. "I wanna get any swimmers." I saw spots before my eyes; all else was black. Silence returned with a wallop and cranked up the volume on the high-pitched ringing in my ears. My hands were shaking and my nervous system was in some kind of shock.

Through the ringing, I made out Mr. Meston on the radio calling in the boys on the Boston Whaler. Then he called to me and said to forget about trying to retrieve anything from the fast-moving water. That was good news to me. I would have just as soon vamoosed.

I heard more talking. This time it was Vietnamese, and it was coming from across the river. Maybe an enemy unit was moving in. I asked Funky if he heard the voices, and he said he did.

Half a minute later, Mr. Meston was again talking on the radio. I heard him say something about holding the Boston Whaler, and then something about Navy Seawolves. Putting it all together from there was easy: he was calling in the helo gunships.

After Mr. Meston ended his radio communication, he passed word for the man on each flank to put a blue-colored lens on his battery-powered strobe light. I found the strobe in my pack and prepared it as ordered, knowing the helo pilots needed the light to identify our position.

We reestablished noise discipline for the next ten minutes. During that time, I didn't hear us, and I didn't hear the VC. It was dead still. Then I heard the Seawolves coming.

Knowing what was about to happen, I didn't lose a second in prostrating myself in the watery mud of the riverbank. From there I flashed my blue strobe light at the black sky.

I heard Mr. Meston say, "You identify. Over."

The reply via the radio was, "Blue light. Over."

Mr. Meston said, "Roger that." Five seconds later, silence got blown apart. A Seawolf swooped in on our location from downstream and opened up. M-60 machine guns strafed the opposite bank, just forty meters from my nose. I saw the tracer bullets streaking through the dark.

As the Seawolf flew away, a second helo came in, firing 2.75-inch rockets at the shore. The rockets exploded along the bank as another M-60 barked dozens of bullets. At that point I was sure that whoever was speaking Vietnamese over there earlier was speaking expletives now.

No sooner was the Seawolf gone than the first gunship, following a racetrack pattern, circled and started its second pass down the river. Again, the machine guns wreaked havoc. More rockets demolished the jungle. The second helo dove in for more, then the first, circling and hitting again and again, like two sharks in a feeding frenzy.

Finally satiated, and after communicating with Mr. Meston, they flew away. I sat up and listened as they faded into the night, spellbound by the precision of their attack.

Seconds later, my ears reverberated in the quiet. There was a pressure against my eardrums that I not only felt, but I could also hear. The sound of rushing blood. The thud of my heartbeat. The thunder of existence in a sphere where others no longer existed. I was alive. I could hear it.

I also heard Mr. Meston using the radio to call our extraction team with the Boston Whaler. The Whaler was an eighteen-foot, W-bottom, fiberglass boat that had a nine-man capacity, including a crew of two. I expected she would be zipping in with her

105-horsepower Chrysler outboard engine and power prop humming.

While waiting for the boat, I readied myself for another assault. Sweet Lips was fully loaded and pointed at the dark river. After all of the earlier firepower, I doubted I'd be looking eyeball to eyeball with a gook in the next twenty minutes, but I wouldn't be caught making mud castles, just in case.

I noticed my hands were no longer shaking, and I wondered when they had stopped. I thought they had only shaken for a few minutes after our attack. Just a normal reaction to sudden excitement. I remember them having shaken after I killed a big whitetail buck a few years earlier. I had spent a whole day hunting for him, and in an unexpected moment, there he was. I had quickly raised my rifle and fired once, and as I had looked on the ground for signs of blood, my hands had shaken. Same as that night.

My ears quit ringing in a little while, and minutes later I heard a boat coming fast downstream. Using prearranged long and short radio clicks, Mr. Meston directed the coxswain toward our location.

As the boat drew closer, Mr. Meston signaled with his red-lens flashlight. The coxswain cut way back on the throttle and softly nudged the bow of the boat into the vegetation on the riverbank. I could see the silhouette of the coxswain and the gunner, who were the only crew aboard.

Mr. Khan and Funkhouser climbed over the bow and into the boat, followed by myself and McCollum. Mr. Meston and Bucklew, with the radio, came last. Usually, the patrol leader and the radioman were the last to extract simply because they had the radio for communications, and the patrol leader had to set the example. The boat then backed away from the foliage while all of us trained our weapons on both banks of the river.

Once we turned upstream, the coxswain poured it on and we sped the two hundred and fifty meters to the Song Ba Gioi. There we swung westward and went full throttle, which was thirty-five knots with a full load. I was wet all over, and the wind seemed colder on the big river. But it was no biggie. In ten minutes we'd climb aboard *Mighty Moe*, the big LCM-6 which would escort us back to Nha Be and a beer party I was still alive to enjoy.

I raised Sweet Lips defiantly toward the night sky and, with all eyes on me, whispered "Hoo-yah!" which was the cry of UDT/SEALs. The others responded with quiet *hoo-yahs*, maintaining a semblance of noise discipline. Still, the release felt good. Our morale was high. Another mission was over, this time with two estimated KIAs. Thank God, I wasn't one of them. It was not my epitaph being inscribed that day.

CHAPTER THREE

It was a long boat ride back to Nha Be on *Mighty Moe*, and as we reached the naval base, the sun was already lifting over the horizon. I'd been awake for thirty hours but couldn't sleep had I wanted to, and I wanted to. But the whole squad was flying high. We'd had our first action of the tour, and it was time to let everyone on the base know it.

As we disembarked, there were many howls and *hoo-yahs*. One of the Seawolf pilots stood near his gunship on the helo pad and gave us a quick wave. I raised Sweet Lips high over my head in salute to that courageous man. Funkhouser sauntered beside me and wrapped an arm around my neck for a friendly squeeze. I looked right into his face and yelled, "Hoo-yah!"

Funky slid away, saying, "Smitty, your breath smells like a three-day-old dead dink!" I puckered my lips and sent my buddy a kiss. He just grinned.

We entered the barracks and headed immediately upstairs to the twenty-by-twenty-foot briefing/intelligence room for debriefing. Our squad entered the room with the mobile support team right behind us, followed by the Seawolf crews and Lieutenant Salisbury. Altogether there were twenty men in the room, all of whom had had a part in the mission, with the exception of Mr. Salisbury, the detachment OIC.

The door to the room closed and Mr. Meston began

the debriefing. He spent several minutes reviewing the mission, then specially thanked the mobile support and Seawolf crews for their assistance.

Finally, Mr. Meston asked for suggestions. After a few statements of lessons learned and recommendations, I had one: "Next time out, McCollum needs to avoid beans." With that comment, Mr. Salisbury congratulated us, then excused us to clean up.

Cleanup started with the basics. Everything was muddy, and the mud had to go. Wearing my muddy cammies and all my gear, holding Sweet Lips in my hands, I stepped into the rough shower the Seabees had made for us. I turned on the overhead spray and salty water, pumped from the Long Tau River, washed over me. The water was unheated, but it was not very cold.

After rinsing Sweet Lips, I set her outside the shower room. I began stripping off my gear and clothes while standing beneath the running water, cleaning things as I went. The water at my feet was brown as it swirled around the extra-large drain. Several minutes later, though, my clothes and gear were thoroughly flushed, and I was as clean and shiny as a real seal.

Once out of the shower, I slipped into my blue-and-gold T-shirt, UDT swim trunks, and coral booties. The wet clothes and gear I hung on pegs in a dressing room adjacent to the showers, intending to take the clothes to Nga's, a laundry in Nha Be, the next day. The cleaning of Sweet Lips, however, had barely started.

I took the shotgun to a small wooden table with a jerry-built tin roof over it, located next to our barracks. A big metal tub filled with diesel fuel sat on the ground beside the table. There I disassembled the weapon and washed it in the diesel, using several sizes of firm-bristle brushes to scrub each part. A meticulous cleansing got off all of the salt and carbon residue.

After the diesel bath, I wiped the parts dry with a

towel, then used special lubricants on every inch of the weapon before putting it back together. When I was done, Sweet Lips looked and smelled like a new girl.

I returned Sweet Lips to the armory, where she would be stored until I needed her again. Then I entered the ground floor of our twenty-two-by-seventy-five-foot barracks, which housed three SEAL platoons, minus the officers, totaling thirty-six men. Eighteen cots were lined up, three feet apart, on each side of the center aisle running from one end of the building to the other. My platoon had done some trading with the Seabees for several four-by-eight-foot plywood sheets and some two-by-fours with which to build partition walls between every second and third cot. This gave us some semblance of privacy with two-man cubicles to share. My cubicle was eight by eight feet, and my mate was Funkhouser. Each cot had a mosquito net draped over its four tall corner posts, the ends of which could be tucked under the cot's mattress to keep out mosquitos. At the foot of each cot was an individual locker for storing personal items.

I went to my cubicle, where I put on a fresh pair of camouflage pants, a cammo shirt, and dry pairs of socks and boots. I reached underneath my cot and pulled out a two-by-two-foot wooden cage that held Bolivar, my twenty-inch pet boa constrictor.

I opened the mesh wire top of the cage and took Bolivar in my hands for a minute of petting. The snake seemed appreciative of the show of affection, after which I put him back and slid the cage under the bed. Then I went to the chow hall to eat.

There were no C rats in the mess hall; instead, it was time for some real food, or at least as real as the cooks could get it in an out-of-the-way place like Nha Be.

Bucklew and Khan were seated at a table and were digging into ham and eggs, toast, and coffee. I grabbed a tray at the serving counter and filled a plate with the same menu, opting also for some Tabasco sauce.

"Mr. Meston and McCollum took a chopper to go look for the sampan we shot up," Bucklew informed me as I sat down at his table. "It's low tide, so they may find something in the mud."

"Prob'ly two dead VC," snarled Khan, staring right through me with those penetrating eyes of his. He looked mean. I was glad he was my friend and not my enemy.

Bucklew swallowed a bite of food and said, "Hawk-eye, you sure were lucky yesterday."

I grinned. "You mean with that booby trap?"

"Yeah," replied Bucklew, nodding his head, "not to mention that croc. Volunteering for point must involve some kinda death wish."

I gazed hard at Bucklew. "I don't wanna die. That's why I'm on point. I trust myself more than anybody else." I looked at Khan, who was looking at me. "If I ever get shot up, Khan, make sure the Communist pig who shoots me gets paid back in full."

Khan slowly nodded once, then went back to eating. I poured some Tabasco sauce on my eggs as Funkhouser approached with Mojica, a Mexican-American member of the Boat Support Unit.

"That's the way to smother those eggs!" agreed Mojica, pulling a chair away from the table and sitting down.

"There's plenty more where this came from," I informed him.

"Don't stuff yourself," said Funkhouser as he, too, sat down. "Save room for the beer. The party starts at 1200 hours, and we're buyin' for everybody on base in honor of our first successful mission."

It was the custom, after every successful encounter with the enemy, for the returning platoon to invite ev-

eryone to the Quonset hut for free beer. At 1200 hours,
I tossed a five-dollar bill on the bar counter, which paid
for fifty beers at ten cents apiece. Funkhouser, Bucklew,
and Khan did likewise. Within minutes, there were forty
guys in the building, including SEALs, boat support
people, and helo crews. They were all in a festive
mood.

Hoo-yah! was the cry of the afternoon. Backslapping
and neck-hugging were a frequent exercise, which accelerated when Meston and McCollum entered with two
recovered Communist weapons in their hands.

"Look what we got!" boasted Mr. Meston as he held
up an AK-47 and McCollum showed off an Enfield
rifle. "We found the sampan, full of holes, along with
these rifles, three rifle grenades, a paddle, and a cook-
ing pan."

"What about the dinks?" Funkhouser shouted.

"Probably washed downstream," answered Lieutenant Meston, setting the AK-47 on a table.

"Shark meat!" someone yelled, and all of us shouted
hoo-yah! and raised our glasses high.

McCollum wasted no time dropping a five-spot on
the counter and grabbing a beer before heading for the
piano. He drank half the beer in one swig, set it on top
of the piano, then sat down on the piano bench. After
playing a short introduction, he began to sing:

"Hail! Hail! The gang's all here!
What the hell do we care? What the hell do we care?
Hail! Hail! The gang's all here!
What the hell do we care now?"

As he went through the words again, everyone joined
in. Bucklew hoisted his glass over his head, splashing
beer on himself and on my back, as I happened to be
the fortunate one standing in front of him. But I was

only momentarily irritated. Five beers and a dozen songs later, I was not worried much about anything. And five beers after that, I was the one doing the splashing.

One of the SEALs from Echo Platoon made a big show out of downing two beers in ten seconds, then challenged Foxtrot Platoon to beat his feat.

"No problem," I retorted. "Just give me a minute." I spent the next few minutes searching the dark and dusty places of the building until I found what I needed to win the bet: a cockroach.

With all eyes upon me, I pinched the cockroach between the thumb and index finger of my right hand, while with my left I lined up two beers on the bar counter in front of me. After a final look into the fuzzy, bug-eyed face of the two-inch insect, I tossed it into my mouth and chewed it in half. Then I swallowed the two beers as fast as I could.

"Nineteen seconds!" someone from Echo Platoon bellowed. "You lose, Smitty!"

I coughed and said, "The cockroach is crawlin' back up my throat."

One SEAL from Echo Platoon ran out of the Quonset hut, hands cupped over his mouth.

McCollum watched the man go, then hollered, "It looks to me like Smitty won!" My platoon buddies shouted several *hoo-yahs* in agreement.

The party continued nonstop for nine hours, with many of the 230 men on base making an appearance. The Seabees who worked the day shift were the last to show, but by the time they did, I was too inebriated to care.

At 2100 hours, after countless beers and shuffleboard games, I called it quits and wended my way to the barracks and my bed. I remembered tucking in the mosquito netting and my head hitting the pillow, but that was all I remembered.

The next morning, despite headaches and hangovers, our entire platoon of fourteen men was awake at 0600 hours for breakfast, and at 0730 were assembled for calisthenics. All of us were wearing UDT swim trunks and lightweight tennis shoes. A few men wore T-shirts, but the rest were bare-chested, including me.

Lieutenant Meston told me to lead the PT, which I did. After half an hour of vigorous exercises, everyone was perspiring heavily, which was good. I'd found PT to be the best way of sweating out all the beer I'd consumed at a party.

When I finished guiding the platoon through the numerous routines, Meston ordered a six-mile run. That put a smile on my face, as I loved to run. At six feet, two inches, and a hundred and seventy-five pounds, lean and mean, with a good pair of lungs, I was blessed with a runner's body and the ability to fly. Bucklew, who was another running enthusiast, and I grabbed the front and led the others out the gate of the ten-acre naval base and onto a narrow, hard-packed gravel road. The road extended all the way to Saigon, which was seven miles northwest.

Immediately upon leaving the base, we began passing by the four dozen hootches which were built on stilts on both sides of the road. I noticed Nga's hootch and was reminded that I had to take in my dirty clothes for cleaning and pressing.

It took less than a minute for Bucklew and me to run through the village of Nha Be, and as we left it behind, Katsma from Foxtrot 2d Squad caught up to us. He was a five-foot-nine, barrel-chested strong man, built like Atlas, and he was no slouch of a runner, either. We were running at a sub-six-minute-per-mile pace as "Kats" joined us.

"You call this fast?" Kats taunted us.

"Fast enough to keep you lookin' at our cute little butts," I said, glancing over my left shoulder at this determined runner.

"They're cute, all right," Kats chuckled, then loudly sucked in some air.

Bucklew picked up the pace a notch. "We'll show you fast on the way back when there's a mile to go."

Kats stayed right behind us. "I'll be here waiting."

"Yeah," I said between breaths, "watchin' our lovely buns." I smiled. Katsma intended to run directly behind me, drafting off me for five and a half miles. Then, as usual, he'd try to pass and beat us to the naval base's front gate.

I checked my watch after a mile. We were cruising at a 5:38 pace. Not extremely fast, but quick enough to put two hundred yards between the three of us and the next two SEALs. The pace was also fast enough to make talking tough. Still, Kats persisted.

"Remember last year, Smitty, when you won the SEAL Team Olympic run on the Silver Strand?" he asked, grabbing air every few words.

"I'll never forget it," I answered, "especially since I beat you." I looked at Bucklew, who was alongside my right shoulder and the perfect picture of a runner. He took a brief look at me, and I winked at him.

Kats gave a short laugh. "Ha! It was a twelve-and-a-half-mile run, and I tore my thigh muscle after eight miles." He paused for a couple deep drags of oxygen. "You call that a victory?"

I made him wait several seconds for an answer, then I boasted loudly, "Yeah!"

"Bull," he grumbled, and the conversation ended. There was to be no more talking as the pace quickened again.

Bucklew moved half a stride ahead of me for a few

seconds until I kicked it up a bit to draw even. I looked off to my left at the mud flats and rice paddies, enjoying the exhilaration and sense of freedom that running brought. It felt good to be alive and strong.

My good feelings didn't last long. We'd run the second mile in 5:26, and Bucklew was cranking the pace higher. Kats was running right up my back.

Crap, I thought, these guys were crazy. Then I ran faster. My body was working hard now, and my brain told me I was in for a real workout. At that pace, I couldn't enjoy the scenery; instead, I had to concentrate on my form, my breathing, and on relaxing my body. Sweat poured into my eyes as I focused on the road ahead. My breathing was loud, and I could hear Bucklew and Kats, as well. Suck in, blow out. Slap, slap, slap, slap, slap, slap. Man, it was getting fast.

I saw the old Buddhist pagoda ahead on the left, which sat at the three-mile mark and our turnaround point. As we reached it, I glanced at my watch; we'd run the third mile in 5:18.

"Piece of cake," I lied as I broke to my right and made a tight-circle turnabout on the road. Bucklew and Kats revolved with me until we were all running south, retracing our steps.

The pace stayed fast. Bucklew and I kept abreast of each other, while Kats continued benefiting from my cutting a path through the heavy, humid air for him. Not until we covered a quarter of a mile did we approach one of the other SEALs still running north. ADJ3 Flynn, an automatic weapons man with Foxtrot 2nd Squad, recognized the battle we were having and shouted encouragement at us.

"What the hell are you idiots tryin' to prove?" he yelled. None of us answered as we flew by him. "Beat 'em, Kats!" he shouted after his squad buddy.

Bucklew raised high his right hand with the middle finger extended as we distanced ourselves from Flynn.

We continued pushing the pace, passing the other men going the opposite direction, one by one, until we saw the last two, Funkhouser and Lieutenant (jg) Schrader, bringing up the rear. They reminded me of two sick Texas longhorns loping down the road.

"Run, Funky!" I gasped as I blew by the two joggers.

"Too much beer and whiskey last night!" bellowed Funkhouser. I smiled to myself, knowing that Funky would be last even if he hadn't touched a drop of the party drinks.

As water, booze, coffee, and every other liquid I'd drunk lately gushed out of my pores, I wiped the sweat off my watch face and noted that we'd run the fourth mile in 5:15. Only two miles to go, I encouraged myself. Then I forced a quick burst of speed and pulled away from Bucklew and Kats, just to keep them psyched out and guessing. They struggled to catch me, even as I struggled to keep the new pace. All of us seemed relieved when I slowed back down, and we resumed our earlier positions.

With the surprise blast that I had tossed in, we ended up racing the fifth mile in a fast 5:08. My heart was busy letting me know it was there; I heard it beating against my temples. I ran my left hand over my face and wiped it off. My body fluids were definitely at high tide.

Kats, still right behind me, farted rapidly three times.

"Need some more gas?" he blurted in a barely audible voice. I could tell he was dying, like I was dying. But death under those circumstances didn't deserve the least consideration. The only thing that mattered was pride and manhood and pouring your stinking guts out to the bitter end. And the end was less than five minutes away.

Bucklew was puffing fast and hard to my right. I heard someone else puffing, and I realized it was me. I couldn't hear Kats, but I couldn't afford to lose my concentration with a look back. I just assumed he was there, even though his feet striking the road couldn't be heard. We were moving so fast that any sounds to my rear couldn't catch my ears.

Suddenly Bucklew let out a short *hoo-yah!* and sped up. I couldn't believe it, but I went with him. Still, he was a step in front of me. Beads of sweat sailed off his flailing left arm and struck me on the chest. Then, to my amazement, Kats moved up on my left. They were both making their big move with three-quarters of a mile to go.

In the five seconds I was in limbo, deciding what to do, Bucklew and Kats ended up running side by side, four meters in front of me. I dug deep into my bag of intestinal fortitude and closed the gap to two. Placing myself behind Kats, I used the draft to my advantage, hoping I could hang on.

A minute later, the village of Nha Be was in sight, a quarter of a mile away. Through the sweat, I focused my eyes on the nearest hootch, believing if I made it to the hootch I'd somehow be rewarded with a last surge of energy for the four-hundred-meter-sprint to the base gate.

Bucklew and Kats weren't wavering a bit in front of me. They were neck-and-neck and showed no signs of weakening. Here I was, though, feeling like I was running in an oven. It was getting hotter every second. Even my feet seemed to be on fire. My head screamed for me to stop, but my body was somehow stuck on automatic pilot. I was a robot, a machine revved to the max. I could barely think. I just was.

As we reached the hootch, my mind suddenly caught up with my body. I snapped out of my bewildered state and thought clearly again. I knew I was okay because I noticed that Bucklew's butt wasn't as cute as Kats had said. And it was a butt I intended to beat.

One hundred meters into the village, I experienced the flood of adrenaline I needed. With every ounce of power left in me, I surged to Kats's left side. He glanced at me with a look of desperation, then focused his gaze on the gate, 250 meters ahead. Bucklew was at Kats's right; we were dead even.

Nga, the laundry mamma-san, was slowly walking across the road just fifty meters away. As she noticed us bearing down on her, her body stiffened in alarm.

Bucklew panted, "Look out!"

Nga scurried for the edge of the road on my side. I took a chance and didn't break stride, hoping she'd get out of the way. As I rushed by her, my left arm brushed her back. Kats took advantage of the distraction and went full throttle. This was it. He threw everything he had into a final sprint. Bucklew and I were a split second behind in going with him, but instantly we gave it our all. Two hundred meters, full out. Nothing got held back. Absolutely nothing. Three bodies with engines burning, all in overdrive.

I strained for all I was worth, but Kats stayed half a step ahead; Bucklew, however, dropped a shade behind me. Then, with one hundred meters to go, Bucklew fell a step back.

Okay, I told myself, it was me and Kats. Go!

I ran into what felt like a time warp. I sped up while everything around me seemed to slow down. All that mattered was just Kats and me, me and Kats. Straining, grunting, striving, driving, grasping, heaving. Gunning for the gate.

With forty meters left, I drew even. At ten meters, Kats gained a mutinous inch or two that I couldn't see, but I felt it. At the finish, I could feel it still. So did

Kats. He flew through the gate with his right fist in the air. He had won, barely.

As I slowed to a walk, I looked at my watch, which I had stopped when I had passed through the gate; it read 31:42 for the six-mile run. I bent over at the waist and almost heaved my guts, but I didn't. I stared at my feet for a few seconds, watching a multitude of sweat drops fall from my face onto my shoes.

Standing up again, I was dizzy, but I began jogging to help my body to cool down gradually. Kats and Bucklew were doing the same twenty meters ahead of me. As I followed them, I made a quick calculation and realized we'd run the last mile in an incredible 4:57. Flynn was right, I told myself, we were idiots. It was too hot to run that fast.

"Hey, idiot!" Kats shouted at me. "I gotcha!"

With perspiration still streaming into my eyes, I looked at Kats and shook my head. "If I hadn't bumped into Nga, I would've won by ten yards!" I fibbed.

Kats spun around and started to backpedal. "Bumped?" he said with a laugh. "Is that all you did to her? I thought you had a full-blown affair!"

I couldn't help myself. I laughed. "Even if you discard the bump," I argued, "there's still the cockroach issue."

"What do you mean?" Kats asked as I caught up to him, and he turned around to jog with me. His breathing was still fast and heavy, like mine.

I grinned at my friend. "If it hadn't been for that cockroach," I said, "the winner here today would've been a horse of a different color."

Kats gave me a playful shove, then laid back his head and whinnied. "Excuses, excuses," he muttered, "but I won the race. Bucklew is my witness."

I looked at Bucklew, who was jogging to our right. "What about it, Buck?"

Bucklew smiled at me. "Kats and I already struck up a deal while you were back there tossing your cookies."

"And?" I wondered.

"He promised me a couple beers if I tell the others who won."

"And?" I persisted.

Bucklew chuckled. "You lost."

I moved over and slapped at his head, but he blocked my assault.

"You lousy Communist!" I said.

As the other runners began showing up, Kats, Bucklew, and I jogged to the gate and waited to cheer for my roommate and Schrader, who I knew would be the last two. "What kinda pace do they run?" Kats asked me.

"Eight minutes a mile at best," I reported.

Kats looked at his watch. "Well, it's been forty-nine minutes already, so where are they?"

Bucklew grunted. "Probably at the pagoda prayin' for a gook to shoot 'em so they won't have to run back!"

Lieutenant Meston, who ran the course in forty-one minutes, walked toward us.

"Who's left?" he asked.

"Funky and Schrader," I answered. "Any minute now."

Bucklew pointed down the road. "There they are entering the village."

I watched the two men jogging side by side. Even at a distance, they still looked like sick cows.

When they were two hundred meters from the gate, we all started hollering.

"Come on, Funky!" I yelled. "Shake the lead out!"

"Run, girls!" shouted Pearson, the point man for 2nd Squad. He began clapping and howling like a coyote.

We were quickly joined by the other SEALs, all of whom wanted to get in on the action.

"I'll bet five bucks on Schrader," I heard Flynn offer from behind me.

I turned and looked at him. "You're on, Flynn."

As Funkhouser and Schrader picked up their pace, I joined in the cheering. Then the two men really started running. It was obvious that neither wanted to be last.

"The loser buys a round of beer!" McCollum cried out.

"Hoo-yah!" someone shouted.

Funkhouser and Schrader drew much closer. Their faces were beet-red from their effort. They were wet with sweat, neck-and-neck, and I thought of how Kats and I must've looked driving for the gate.

Then, fifteen meters from the gate, Funkhouser stumbled and started to fall. With arms flailing and body contorting and twisting, he somehow regained his balance. No, I thought, that was not how Kats or I had looked.

Funkhouser lost most of his speed in the near collision with the road, and he lost all of the race. I lost five bucks.

CHAPTER FOUR

Mission Six

"The impulse to mar and to destroy is as ancient and almost as nearly universal as the impulse to create. The one is an easier way than the other of demonstrating power."

Joseph Wood Krutch, *The Best of Two Worlds*

DATE: 12, 13, 14 September 1967
TIME: 120600H to 140130H
COORDINATES: YS073779
UNITS INVOLVED: Foxtrot 1, Alpha 1, MST-3, Navy Seawolves
TASK: Recon patrol and 4-hr. river ambush
METHOD OF INSERTION: Navy Seawolves
METHOD OF EXTRACTION: LCPL
TERRAIN: Mangrove, nipa palm, thick undergrowth
MOON: 3/4
WEATHER: Clear with occasional clouds
SEAL TEAM PERSONNEL:
Lt. Meston, Patrol Leader/Rifleman, M-16
Lt. DeFloria, Ass't PL/Rifleman, M-16
QM2 Bohannon, Automatic Weapons, M-60
RM2 Smith, Point/Rifleman, Shotgun
MM2 Funkhouser, AW, M-60
BT2 McCollum, Grenadier, M-79
HM2 Mahner, Corpsman/Rifleman, M-16

BM2 Williams, Radioman/Rifleman, M-16
ADJ3 Bucklew, Radioman/Rifleman, M-16
Ty, Ass't Point/Rifleman, M-2 carbine
AZIMUTHS: 260 degrees-550m, 180
    degrees-100m, 260 degrees-300m
ESCAPE: 225 degrees
CODE WORDS: Challenge and Reply—Two
    numbers total 10

The T-10 area of the Rung Sat Zone, located a few kilometers south of Saigon, was a dangerous place for good guys. It was an area where one hundred percent contact with the enemy occurred. There were big NVA units in the T-10, and we were going in. Ten men from Foxtrot and Alpha Platoons. It was like sending a mouse after a lion, but the lion was drowsy and unsuspecting while the mouse was sneaky and packing a bazooka.

At first light on September 12, 1967, five of us from first squad boarded a Seawolf slick. Five others from Alpha Platoon climbed aboard another Seawolf slick, and together the helos flew us toward our insertion point for my sixth mission as a SEAL in Vietnam.

It was a twenty-minute flight, just above the treetops at a hundred miles per hour to our drop-off, and as we went, I ran the mission through my mind. The plan was to insert in defoliated swampland, about 250 meters north of Rach Vuna Gam, a tributary of the Quan Nhon Trach, then patrol eight hundred meters southwest to our forty-eight-hour ambush site on the stream. The two squads would split twelve-hour shifts on the riverbank with the resting squad maintaining rear security several meters back in the bush.

I looked at the men seated on the deck next to me, and it was obvious they were ready for war. Funkhouser caressed his M-60 machine gun. He was loaded down with five hundred rounds of 7.62mm linked ammunition belted around his upper torso.

McCollum carried the M-79 grenade launcher with seventy rounds of 40mm HE and ten specialized 40mm canister rounds loaded with 00 buck. Attached to his web belt and ammo pouches were two M-26 fragmentation grenades, two M-3A2 concussion grenades, and two hand-fired pop parachute flares.

Besides carrying the PRC-25 radio, Bucklew was packing an M-16 with 350 rounds of ammo. He was also heavy with grenades: two frags, one concussion, one red and one green smoke grenade, and two red and two white pop para flares.

Mr. Meston boasted an M-16 with three hundred rounds, a frag and concussion grenade, one red and one green smoke grenade, two pop para flares, and a Starlight Scope. Adding to our destructive capabilities, Mr. Meston also carried one thermite incendiary grenade and one white phosphorus ("Willy Peter") grenade.

I, of course, squeezed Sweet Lips in my hands and toted sixty-six rounds of 00 and an extra fifteen rounds of flechettes.

Each flechette round contained several miniature aluminum arrows packed into its 12-gauge shell. Attached to my ammo pouches were three fragmentation grenades, two concussion grenades, a green smoke grenade, and one M-18 antipersonnel claymore mine. I also carried in my backpack a prisoner-handling kit with gag, blindfold, and line.

In addition, each man packed a strobe light, a pencil flare kit, K-bar knife, an MK-13 day/night flare, bright orange aircraft panel, and a lensatic compass, along with C rats, water, and a first aid kit. On top of all that, the designated swimmer had the fins, coral booties, and stream-crossing line. Guess who?

The five men on the other slick were just as well prepared and ready for bear, and anybody in his right mind would not have wanted to mess with the ten of us. Nor anybody in his left mind, for that matter.

Bucklew handed me a roll of olive-drab ordnance tape for sealing the bottom of my pants. I wrapped the tape snugly around the tops of my jungle boots, making sure not to leave any opening where leeches and small crabs would be sure to crawl. It was bad enough having malaria-infected mosquitos creeping into my ear canals and nostrils without having bloodsuckers and pincers up my crotch.

After fifteen minutes of flying, the pilot made a fake insertion, and then another a few miles later, to confuse the Viet Cong. Mr. Meston hollered that the next insertion was real and we should prepare to insert.

I slid over to the starboard door and hung my feet out above the strut. Bucklew eased beside me. Funkhouser and McCollum dangled out the portside door as the helo flared and started to descend. Looking down, I wondered where the pilot was going to attempt to drop us. There was nothing but thick, stinking, double-canopy jungle below us.

As we sank lower, I looked out at the propeller rotating above the fast-closing treetops. A few more feet and the blade would be carving out chopsticks. Still, the pilot risked another yard.

The helo ended up hovering a good fifteen feet above the brush and muck when the pilot told Meston, "Go!" My God, I thought, that was a long way down, especially when we were all so heavy with equipment.

Mr. Meston yelled, "Go!" Without hesitation, I jumped. Two seconds later, after sending a shockwave of pain through my knees, I was sitting on my butt in the mud.

Bucklew jumped next, ending up on his rear end

right beside me. Mud splattered onto my left arm and cheek, but I didn't mind; it went with the territory.

When McCollum landed behind me, he managed to stay on his feet, but Funkhouser followed with a total collapse. He ended up spread-eagled and face down, four inches deep in the mud. I climbed to my feet as Mr. Meston leapt from the helicopter and finished on his knees at Funkhouser's side, and together we hoisted Funky out of the wallow he'd created. Funky spit mud through his teeth as I wiped a glob from his left eye.

"Geronimo," he said without emotion, spitting some more.

I felt like laughing, but one look at the menacing jungle around us stifled the urge. Nothing but thick vegetation—mangrove roots, nipa palm trees, bushes, elephant grass, and Mekong muck. Somehow we had to patrol eight hundred meters through that tangled maze of tropical wait-a-minute to our ambush site.

As the helicopters flew away, I advanced a few meters into a thicket crisscrossed so heavily with branches and vines it resembled a network of huge spider webs. Working my way forward, I felt like the most uncoordinated person on the planet as I pulled one foot out of six inches of mud, lifted it high over a cluster of branches while I shoved others away from my face, then found a place to step down without snapping twigs, as my other foot jerked out of the mud behind me. Every step was a struggle, and the mosquitos made it even tougher.

As I continued my plodding, making more noise than I liked, the nine men trailing me sounded like sundry three-legged crocodiles doing the cha-cha. It was so noisy that any NVA unit within three hundred meters easily would have mistaken us for Dumbo the elephant and his mother. The good news was there probably weren't any NVA units within three hundred meters, or three thousand meters. After all, who would R&R in this wretched hellhole of a place? Only SEALs, for whom R&R stood for "raid 'em and rattle 'em." Right then, however, all the racket was rattling me.

Mr. Meston, breaking too many branches, followed directly behind me, keeping an eye on his watch compass and our direction. Bucklew, carrying the radio behind Mr. Meston, was keeping the pace count, meaning he was counting every step as we went. In thick jungle, where one could see only a few feet through the foliage, compass use and pace count were essential to not getting lost. The T-10 area was not a place in which red, white, and blue lovers could afford to lose their way.

After an hour, the pace count was three hundred. It had taken sixty minutes to travel approximately two hundred meters. I looked back at Mr. Meston and he signaled for me to stop. Everyone halted and we listened awhile.

I heard something in the brush to my left. As I slowly turned my body toward the sound, Sweet Lips pivoted with me at hip-level. I spotted a movement low to the ground, and when it moved again I identified a brown hare. It was a little fellow, perhaps ten inches long. He didn't appear to notice me, and after a few carefree hops, he was gone.

Mr. Meston waited a couple minutes more, then motioned to me to move.

Two hours later, we'd covered a total of six hundred meters from the point of insertion. We were still two hundred meters from our ambush site, and my attitude was poor. The platoon as a whole was making far too much noise, which increased our danger, and I could hardly stand it anymore. There wasn't a hint of a breeze, and in the dead quiet outside our perimeter, every snapping stick must have resounded like a rifle shot. The air temperature was at least ninety, and perspiration seeped out of every sweat gland in my body. I rubbed countless sweat beads off my forehead with my hand and with them came some of the camouflage paint I'd applied several hours before. I was too late with the wipe as sweat ran into my eyes, forcing them shut with a burning sensation. I squeezed my eyelids, wrinkling up my face, then popped open my eyes just in time to see a twig snap in two against my right shoulder. More of our noise discipline down the toilet. But I didn't halfway care anymore. Let the gooks hear us and come after us. Then we could get the confrontation and the mission over with.

Come on, Smitty, I scolded myself. Get it together, man. Stay focused. You're the point man and the guys are trusting you with their lives. Shake off the heat and the problems. Concentrate on your job. Stay alert.

A few seconds later, I was back in the saddle. I knew what I must do and I'd do it as well as was possible under the most trying conditions. But I went only another twenty meters before Mr. Meston signaled me to stop. I watched him as he stepped over a vine and approached me through the brush. He stopped four feet away and looked intently into my eyes. His stare was one of concern, and I knew he was wondering if I was okay. Somehow he had sensed my mental struggle.

I nodded my head and winked at him, which was all the reassurance he needed. With that, he looked back and signaled Bucklew to pass the word for the men to set up a perimeter and to repose right where they were. It was obvious there was no need to form a circle of any kind as we were not moving down an established trail. The terrain dictated much of the tactics, and in that thick mess we simply had to maintain visual contact and strict noise discipline while we rested.

I sat down on some root offshoots of a bush, which kept my backside out of the mud. The heels of my jungle boots sank a few inches into the slime, however. It was almost impossible not to have some kind of bodily contact with the mud.

Mr. Meston settled down a couple yards away and took a drink of water from one of his canteens. The image of it presented a message to my dehydrated brain that I should do the same. Removing a quart canteen from my web belt, I took a sip, swished it around in my mouth, then swallowed. The water tasted great, even though it was warm. The second swig was long and better yet. I thought I might live through that god-awful day, after all.

I slipped the canteen back into its canvas pouch and took my cammo paint kit out of my pants pocket. The sweat had streaked the cammo on my face, I knew without looking.

After applying the green and black cammo to my cheeks, nose, and forehead, I slid the kit back into my pocket. As I did, something bit the back of my neck. Without too quick of a motion, I reached up with my right hand and found the culprit with my fingers: a red ant. I used the nails on my thumb and index fingers to cut off its malevolent head.

No sooner had I performed the execution and flicked the corpse away than another ant bit my left wrist. This one I brushed onto a ridge of mud near my left boot. My instantly devised plan was to step on it and push it deep into the muck, but I couldn't get my boot out of the hole it had made.

As the ant raced away, I caught it with the shotgun's stock and rammed it underground. Sweet Lips delivered the kiss of death again, albeit in a rather unusual style.

Wondering where the ants were coming from, I looked around at the bush behind my back. Sure enough, there were red ants on every limb and leaf. I also counted six ants on me, crawling on my sleeves and pant legs.

I got Mr. Meston's attention, made a creepy-crawly motion with my fingers, and pointed at the bush. Mr. Meston nodded at me to go ahead and move. I eased up into a squatting position and gradually pried my feet free of their coffins. Even pulling slowly, I couldn't eliminate all of the sucking sounds.

After a seminoisy minute, I was sitting on a large root facing the ant bush, which was then seven feet away. From there I could watch the nasty critters and pick them off, one at a time, as they came for me. I hated the ants and I hated their bites; of course, I couldn't criticize their tactics, which were essentially the same as ours: sneak up on your prey, bite them real hard, and get away.

Only three ants got close enough in the next ten minutes for me to deal with. The first two I killed immediately. The last one I used in practicing my Vietnamese and prisoner interrogation techniques.

With the ant pinched between my thumb and index finger, I whispered at it, "*Ong co thay Viet-cong khong* (Have you seen any Viet Cong)?" When the creature didn't answer, I tore off one of its rear legs.

"*Nhung bay no o dau* (Where are the booby traps)?" No response, so off came the other hind leg.

"*Ho co chon nguoi-My nao o day khong* (Are there any Americans buried here)?" The ant would not cooperate. I ripped out the remaining four legs, then set the ant on the muddy ground.

"*Dung yen,*" I commanded, which meant "Don't move." This time the ant obeyed, out of necessity, of course, so I decided to be merciful and let it live.

Mr. Meston signaled me that it was time to go. I rose to my feet and began the chore of picking my way through the jungle. My mind was sharp and focused the way it had to be.

After fifty meters of slow going, I saw the Rach Vuna Gam on my left. It was a stream, only thirty meters wide, on the banks of which we would position our ambush site. I remembered Mr. Meston saying during our mission briefing that he wanted to set up where the stream bends to the south, and since the stream was going east-west right there, I knew we must patrol farther.

I moved very cautiously a couple meters inland in thick brush as I followed the stream. Every twenty or thirty meters I stopped and listened. Once I heard some birds flush about forty meters ahead, so we waited several minutes, attempting to discover what caused them to spook. Receiving no clues, Mr. Meston finally motioned for me to proceed.

I didn't have to go far. After fifteen meters, the stream began winding to the south. I followed the curve a short distance until Mr. Meston signaled me. He wanted me to recon the riverbank by myself, until I located the best ambush site somewhere in the immediate vicinity.

I spent ten minutes scouting the dense shoreline, determining that one spot was as good as any other. After all, thick was thick, and muck was muck. I relayed this information to Mr. Meston, who decided to settle in right where he stood.

As predetermined, Mr. DeFloria, Bohannon, Williams, Mahner, and Ty set up a perimeter on the bank overlooking the stream, while Mr. Meston, Bucklew, Funkhouser, McCollum, and I sat down ten meters back in the bush to relax and act as rear security. I looked at my watch and saw that it was 1015 hours. That told me three things: first, it had taken four hours to patrol the eight hundred yucky meters from insertion to ambush site; second, I had more than eight hours to kick back and doze there in the bush before we relieved Mr. DeFloria's squad on the riverbank; third, it would only get hotter during the next several hours.

After a drink of water, I laid Sweet Lips across my lap, wrapped my arms around my propped-up knees, and hung my head to sleep. Just when I drifted off, a rustling sound tap-danced on my ears. I thought I was dreaming until I heard the noise again, louder the second time. I opened my eyes and snapped my brain to attention. I focused on the sound, moving toward me from the west.

Glancing at Funkhouser on my right, I saw he was asleep. Looking to my left, I saw Bucklew with his M-16 already pointed toward the bushes. I raised Sweet Lips, safety off, at the oncoming threat. A few seconds later, a flicker of movement low in the brush caught my eye. I aimed down the barrel of the shotgun, my finger caressing the curvature of the trigger. I was ready to atomize the enemy.

Suddenly a bird of some kind darted through the brush into an open spot where I could get a good look at it. Then another joined it. I realized I was gazing at two domestic chickens.

Bucklew lowered his rifle, looked at me and raised his eyebrows. I dropped Sweet Lips onto my lap and shook my head. First a rabbit, now chickens. I'd imagine I were back home in Texas if I took to daydreaming just a bit.

I watched the chickens for a few minutes until they disappeared from sight. Listening to them wander away, I realized there must be a VC base camp nearby for domestic fowl to be about. That meant the odds were great that we'd engage the enemy sooner or later on this mission.

It was harder to doze off knowing VC were close at hand, but eventually I did. When I awoke, it was 1340 hours and hot as hell. The air was humid and thick, causing me to sweat like a roasting water buffalo.

I looked at Bucklew. His head was hanging limp,

with his chin against his chest. A couple mosquitos were busy getting a fill-up on his right cheek.

Mr. Meston and McCollum were to Buck's left. I picked out pieces of their clothing in the brush, but they were too well camouflaged for me to know whether they were awake.

Funkhouser was sitting in the mud a few yards to my right, staring off into the jungle.

I decided it was time to eat. I took a can of C rats out of my backpack and opened it with the P-38 can opener. I looked at the spaghetti and meatballs and it looked ready to pounce at me. As was often the case, there was a lot of hardened grease forming an undesirable topping.

I stood the can in the mud where the sun could melt the grease, and I could dump it on an ant or two. Just another field-tested method of insect torture.

While I waited for the grease to liquefy, my thoughts turned to my favorite author, Robert Ruark. In his book, *Horn of the Hunter*, which I had read five times, Mr. Ruark told of lion hunts, leopard hunts, elephant hunts, rhino hunts, cape buffalo hunts, and every bloody kind of hunt one could conduct in bloody Africa. I'd hunted dangerous African big game animals only vicariously through Mr. Ruark's books, so I wasn't sure of the validity of what I thought. But what I thought was this: the most dangerous big game animal is man.

An animal had only one way to kill, which was its body ripping up yours. A man, however, had reason and technology, which lent him several options: he could kill you with his hands or blow you in half with guns or grenades when he was near, or he could kill you with booby traps or mortar rounds when he was miles away. Also, while an animal instinctively tore out your life and finished you as swiftly as possible, a man could elect to stretch your death out over hours or days.

Yes, I thought, man was the animal to fear the most.

I wished Mr. Ruark had been alive to discuss hunting and life and death and jungle survival tips, but he was not. Mr. Ruark, and I did mean the Mister, had died two years earlier in London at the age of forty-nine. I wished he were there with me in Vietnam and we were hunting deer, tigers, elephants, and crocs. Everything except man.

Then back to reality. I was hunting man. Damn.

Thirty minutes later, I poured the grease out of the C rats can over a red ant as planned, then ate every bite of the spaghetti and meatballs as I watched the ant wade through the fat. I finished as the ant finally struggled out of the mess.

I also stepped on the C rats can and pushed it into the mud until it was gone. That was when I felt it. The wind had suddenly picked up. I looked above the brush and saw the sky was dark to the west. A foreboding stripe of lightning telegraphed the severity of the advancing storm. But it only made me smile. Come on, Vietnam! Rain like mad and wash away the one-hundred-degree heat!

I watched for several minutes as the thunderclouds marched my way, and I was reminded of the west Texas storms of my youth. I remembered the many times when everything had become totally quiet, the vacuum before the storm. I'd stand in my yard and stare apprehensively at the sky, waiting for the sixty- or seventy-mile-an-hour winds. Soon a great, ominous red cloud would appear in the distance, as the advancing element of Texas dirt had blown toward me. The first time I had seen this, I couldn't have been more frightened if it had been an ax murderer bearing down on me. The second time, though, I had stood my ground, my heart pounding.

When the winds had finally lashed into my little body, the transient dirt had bit my eyes and reddened my teeth. Minutes later, with black clouds climbing all over me, rain had made its assault, then hail, bouncing off the ground all around me like ricocheting bullets.

One time when the hail seemingly had stopped, I had actually heard a hailstone falling out of the sky. I had looked up, and not seeing anything or knowing which way to run, I had stayed put and covered my head with my arms. A moment later, a chunk of hail the size of a hardball had slammed into the ground just five yards from me.

The thunderclouds were now directly above and unloading on me. I looked up and relished the wet on my face. For two hours, I was drenched with heavy rain, then the rain and the clouds were gone. Left behind was a wonderful, fresh, clean smell. The Rung Sat had been put through the rinse cycle and felt like a new place. I was refreshed. I was happy. I fell asleep.

When I awoke, it was hot again. I checked the time and saw it was 1755 hours. In thirty-five minutes it would be our turn on the riverbank. I had just enough time to eat something and cammo up again. I was sure the paint had streaked from all the rain I had permitted to wash over my face.

As planned, at 1830 hours Mr. Meston, Bucklew, Funkhouser, McCollum, and I relieved Mr. DeFloria's squad on ambush. McCollum took the left flank and I positioned myself five meters to his right. As usual, we strung a line between us for communication purposes. In a couple hours it would be too dark to see each other; actually, I could barely see Muck then because of his camouflaged clothing and the brush between us.

Even though the air temperature was in the mid-nineties, I felt pretty good. I was sitting in the shade of a big bush, and looking at the smooth-flowing stream just a yard from my feet brought cool impressions to my mind.

After an hour, a large gray heron flew up and landed

in a few inches of water about five feet to my left. I could have poked it with the barrel of my shotgun if I had tried, but the bird was oblivious to my presence. It stood perfectly still, looking across the water.

I was thrilled by this bird, and I studied it closely. Its long tapering bill and long neck combined to form a gentle hook, like the crook in a shepherd's staff. The plumage appeared very soft, and I wished I could touch it. The legs were long and spindly, ideally created for wading in several inches of water where the heron did its fishing.

The great bird finally took a step toward me, then another, with its eyes cast toward the water. A third step brought its head up. Instantly the wings opened and thrusted powerfully downward, beating the water with the feathery tips. The heron burst out of the stream and into the air, a trail of water cascading off its wings and feet. Some of the droplets splattered on my legs and hands.

As the heron flew away down the river, I whispered a "thank you" after it. Thank you, beautiful bird, for reminding me how much I loved living. How precious it was to interact with the good Lord's masterpieces. Even that swampland had its appeal and splendid moments. I had to savor those moments, as hideous times were sure to follow. Later that night, bullets, rockets, and blood could shroud the beautiful shore.

During the last hour of daylight, only the usual occurred: the sun sank below the horizon, a pair of crocodiles wheezed somewhere downstream, and the mosquitos mounted an offensive any military general would applaud. Darkness installed itself, and the moon's reflection glittered on the water.

The night made me drowsy. I reached into my pants pocket for one of the Dexamil capsules Doc Mahner had given me and the others when we had relieved him on ambush. The pill was a stimulant, which I'd used on two previous missions. My experience had been that half an hour after ingesting one, I would suddenly "get high" and get happy, almost to giggling. My central nervous system would feel like it was plugged into 120 hummingbirds. I would believe I could write six books in the following hour.

Of course, what went up must come down. And coming down from a Dexamil high was rough. My senses were dull, tiredness overwhelmed me, and it was doubly difficult to stay alert. If I fell asleep, it was a deep sleep from which I hardly could awake. With that in mind, I slipped the capsule back into my pocket, deciding to tackle the night without the drug.

At 2400 hours I was wide awake and glad I hadn't taken the Dexamil. McCollum had taken the pill, I was sure, because he was jabbering something about pink elephants across the river. I tugged the line between us, trying to snap him back to reality. The line, which was tied to my left wrist, jerked back so hard I almost dropped Sweet Lips.

"There's elephants over there," I heard Muck say.

I leaned in McCollum's direction and whispered, "Shut up!" The line tied to my right wrist jerked once, so I pulled it once to reassure Bucklew that everything was okay.

McCollum babbled a couple more times in the next half hour, then I heard nothing further from him. I figured he was probably coming down from his high and was falling asleep.

The stream was rising rapidly due to the incoming tide. By 0100 hours, I was sitting in water up to my waist. I could stand up, but after a day of extreme heat and humidity, the coolness of the water felt good to me.

I had to urinate, so I went through my pants. A circle of warmth lingered for several seconds and the contrast in temperature was pleasant. Another splendid moment to cherish.

At 0115 my ears picked up a thumping sound about two hundred meters downstream, just around the bend in the river. A few seconds later I heard voices. I tugged thrice on both lines, the one attached to McCollum and the other to Bucklew. Neither man responded. I tried again and nothing happened. Obviously, they were sleeping soundly. My easy guess was that both were suffering from the aftereffects of Dexamil.

With Sweet Lips off safe and pointing at the dark water, I listened intently for more human voices. My eyes watched for a silhouette of men in a sampan. Many minutes passed by . . .

An hour later, I heard several coughing sounds across the stream and in the jungle. Again I tugged on the lines, and again I discovered I was alone in my vigilance.

I didn't hear or see anything unusual the rest of the night on ambush. It was clear that what I had heard earlier were Viet Cong, but they were not nearby anymore. I thought they had beached their sampans around the bend and then had gone inland. Perhaps they had walked to a base camp located somewhere on the opposite side of the stream.

At dawn, the line on my left wrist jerked once. I looked toward McCollum in the aurora of first light, but it was still too dark to pick him out in the bushes. I jerked the line hard to let him know I was all right. The hard pull also relayed a bit of disgust. After all, it was one thing to see elephants that weren't really there. It was another thing to hang strict noise discipline and jeopardize the entire mission with gibberish. I intended to ask Muck to avoid Dexamil in the future.

At 0630 hours, Mr. DeFloria's squad relieved us on the ambush site. I sneaked back to the previous day's resting spot.

Mr. Meston moved over to me and whispered, "Anything last night?"

"Heard a paddle two hundred meters downstream," I whispered, "then voices across the river just after 0200 hours."

Mr. Meston got real close. "Did you signal?"

"Dexamil sucks," I grumbled. "Muck saw pink elephants. He and Buck slept like babies."

With this information, Mr. Meston decided to recon the riverbank with Bucklew and me. He informed Lieutenant DeFloria, then we went northeast toward the area where I had heard the sampan.

I was on point, and after two hours and four hundred meters of nothing but thick jungle, we returned to the rest of the squad. I sat down in a dry spot, happy to have had the exercise.

Throughout the remainder of the day, little was different from the previous day. It was hot and I sweated like I was sitting in a sauna. I was thankful when thunderheads rolled in at 1400 hours, and rain came shortly thereafter. For two and a half hours I enjoyed the shower.

At 1645 hours, Williams signaled from the riverbank that he saw one VC about four hundred meters upstream on our side of the river. This reawakened the wariness in every man, even though the VC disappeared in the bush after less than a minute. We knew that we were in the lion's den. The good news was the lion didn't know we were there. We hoped.

At 1730 hours, a half dozen bosun birds flushed from their roost in a tree about 150 meters downriver. I wondered what had alarmed them, knowing it may have been Victor Charlie. If so, he was getting close.

When it was time to relieve Mr. DeFloria's squad on ambush at 1830 hours, I was keyed up. I had a strong premonition that night would be the night. Somebody was going to lose his future.

First Squad set up the same as the previous night. McCollum had left flank and Funkhouser right. Mr. Meston, Bucklew, and I were in between, in that order from right to left.

All was still until just after dark at 2100 hours. That was when I heard a banging like the sound of a paddle against a sampan. It was coming from the same area as before, about two hundred meters to the northeast around the bend of the river. I tugged twice on the suspension line both ways, and Muck and Buck tugged back twice each. They, too, had heard the noise.

Seconds passed. I stared into the darkness in front of me. The moon was hidden behind clouds and the jungle was blacker than the previous night. It was even possible for a sampan to float by without our knowing it. I strained my ears, listening for a muffled voice, the thump of a pole against a sampan, or a tiny splash of water.

Three hours crept by. The water level crept up. At midnight I was up to my waist in brackish water. That was the time for the VC to travel, I thought. They used the cover of darkness and peak high tides for the movement of supplies and personnel. Sometimes highly classified documents were handcarried by a commo-liaison for maximum security.

At 0100 hours, I wondered about McCollum and Bucklew. On the previous night at this time, they had been hibernating. I tugged once on both lines to check on them. McCollum pulled back, but not Bucklew. I tugged again and received no reaction. Buck must have ignored my advice to cease and desist the taking of Dexamil. With him out of it, there was no way to relay a message down the line to Mr. Meston and Funkhouser.

Fifteen minutes later, I heard talking and bumping noises two hundred meters downstream. The sounds were louder and more numerous, making me think there were three or four sampans and at least a half dozen Viet Cong.

McCollum pulled three times on the line. I quickly jerked three times on Buck's line and prepared to fire my shotgun over the stream. My eyes frisked the dark for the enemy. Nothing showed up.

Splashing sounds, then the sound of boats being dragged onto the shore filled my ears. The VC were going inland, ditto the previous night.

I climbed to my feet, rising slowly so the water running off me made little noise. I waded along the bank to McCollum's side.

"Psst. Two hundred meters downstream around the bend," I whispered to him. "They're on the shore. Load up with HE and lob all you can right in on them."

Muck got ready and I jerked the line to Bucklew three more times. Still no response.

"Fire!" I whispered at Muck. "That'll wake everybody up!" He wasted no time in firing the first 40mm round down the river. I opened up with Sweet Lips directly across the water. If any gooks were there, I planned to make them keep their heads down.

Instantly, Mr. Meston and Funkhouser fired their weapons. I saw the red tracer rounds from Funky's M-60 machine gun zipping over the water. A couple seconds later, Bucklew was firing his M-16. McCollum was shooting round after round of high explosives downstream, where they were blowing up ashore.

Firing my shotgun, I kept the trigger pulled and pumped the gun as fast as I could, emptying it in a couple of seconds. As I reloaded, Mr. DeFloria's squad moved quickly into position on the ambush site, interspersing themselves with 1st Squad. Each of them began firing his weapon into the jungle across the stream, and specifically where Muck's 40mm HE rounds were exploding. That made ten of us flinging everything we had into the night.

The eruption of sound almost defied description. Two machine guns, five M-16s, one M-2 carbine, one shot-gun, and a grenade launcher firing like crazy. The blasting noises conglomerated into one continuous, deafening roar. To top it off, all three claymore mines were blown. Then Mr. Meston tossed a concussion grenade into the river to kill any swimmers.

I squeezed off six more rounds of 00 buckshot, then I heaved a fragmentation grenade toward the opposite shore. The grenade fell short and exploded in the water. Tearing another from my ammo pouch, I jerked the pin and threw the thing with all my might. This time there was an explosion in the brush across the river.

I watched as McCollum fired three more rounds from his M-79. When they blew up downriver, Bohannon turned his M-60 machine gun toward the explosions and let go with about seventy rounds of 7.62mm bullets. I pulled the pin on my third frag grenade and tossed it into the river. It blew, then Mr. Meston shouted, "Cease fire!" At least that's what I thought he shouted. My battle-blown eardrums were vibrating so violently with all the racket that a screaming jet engine at ten feet wouldn't have done any more damage.

In a few seconds, I saw no more tracer rounds or explosions. The terrific firepower had stopped, but the roar continued to bang off the walls of my brain.

Mingled with the ringing in my ears was a cry of pain. Then another. The sounds were from downstream. I thought I heard a moaning, too.

As I listened harder, Mr. Meston sounded like a bomb going off when he called on the radio for the two LCPL boats to extract us. Using predesignated code words, he said, "Stingray Eleven, this is X-ray Two. Be advised, enemy contact. Request extraction as soon as possible. Over." He next requested the Seawolves to fly in and strafe the opposite riverbank. Then he communicated with Caisson 69, which was the U.S. Army artillery battery on an island called "French Fort," requesting an artillery H-and-I (Harassment and Interdiction) strike soon after our extraction.

Giving the radio handset back to Bucklew, Mr. Meston passed the word to mark our flanks with strobe lights, which McCollum and Funkhouser handled.

A couple minutes later, Mr. Meston told me to mark the Viet Cong's position with a hand-held parachute flare. I took one off my web gear, aimed it skyward over the bullet-torn jungle and slammed the bottom against the palm of my left hand. The flare rocketed out of its case and soared into the sky over the VC's position. Reaching its peak height, the parachute deployed and the illuminating charge ignited. The flare burned so brightly that it turned our dark little world into brilliant daylight. The light was mesmerizing as it hung a while, then gradually floated downward, reflecting off the water. It shone brightly for almost a minute, and, as it slowly died, I sent up another. McCollum waited forty-five seconds, then shot up a 40mm parachute flare.

Then I heard the helos. They flew single file over our heads and opened up, strafing the opposite shore with M-60 machine guns and 2.75-inch rockets. I watched as the rockets exploded and bullets sheared branches off trees.

The gunships circled in their usual racetrack pattern. As they swooped in for a second attack, I heard a partially-muted yelling across the river. I listened for more, but the Seawolves erupted in a wave of gun and rocket fire to drown out every other sound. More rockets blew the life out of the jungle; more trees and bushes were shredded.

As the helos flew away, I watched the flares peter

out. Eerie shadows were cast on the water and jungle in the fading light. Seconds later, it was lights out.

While my eyes worked to adjust themselves to the sudden darkness, I couldn't see a thing. My night vision was totally shot. I held my hand in front of my face. Where I should see my hand there were red, white, and blue spots. I smiled at the thought: I was patriotic even in my blindness.

I tuned my ears toward the opposite shore and listened intently for a few minutes, but I heard only a humming in my ears.

Minutes later, I heard the boats coming for us. Mr. Meston used the radio to guide them right to us.

First squad swiftly boarded one boat, Mr. DeFloria's squad the other.

Moving upstream, the coxswain of our LCPL flashed a spotlight along the shoreline, looking for sampans hidden in the vegetation. He spotted pieces of a sampan floating on the water.

Filled with blood lust, the gunners on the boats began destroying the jungle with their .50-caliber machine guns. I saw branches and leaves dropping in the light of the spotlight. An entire tree was cut in half and fell into the stream.

I fired Sweet Lips twice at the shore. Funkhouser joined in with his M-60. McCollum sent two rounds of HE into the foray. Mr. Meston and Bucklew added semiautomatic rifle fire. My eardrums took another licking, but so did the VC.

As we stopped firing and the boats accelerated up the river, a great feeling of relief washed over me. We had survived the T-10 area, leaving a vivid reminder of our visit carved in tree trunks and, we hoped, human bodies.

We heard incoming artillery rounds as we disappeared into the night. The "men with green faces" had scored again.

CHAPTER FIVE

I awoke at 0630 hours on September 29, my birthday. Twenty-six years old, nine missions under my belt, and still in one piece. I did, however, have a couple long gashes on my legs, incurred while prowling through a nightmarish mangrove swamp.

Sitting up on my bed, I checked the cuts. One was four inches long, right of my left knee, just above the Wiley Coyote tattoo on my calf. Another two-inch incision sliced through the neck of the Road Runner tattoo on my right calf. Both tattoos had been artfully done by old Doc Webb in May of 1964, while I had enjoyed my first liberty in San Diego after boot camp. Doc, known all over the world, had had a parlor not far off Broadway. Right then, I was not too happy that the Road Runner had been decapitated. I'd always hated the thought that any part of me that has a head would someday lose it. Someday for the Road Runner had been three days earlier.

I slipped on my UDT swim trunks, then raised the mosquito netting, and stepped out of bed onto the concrete floor. Dropping the net, I slid into my coral booties.

Funkhouser was lying on his back on the other bed, snoring softly. I decided to take Bolivar, my twenty-inch boa constrictor, out of his cage and set him on the topside of Funky's mosquito net, three feet above Funky's face.

As the snake slithered around, I dropped down on my haunches and blew through the netting into Funkhouser's ear. He squirmed a little, but after thirty seconds, he was still asleep.

A better idea popped into my mind. "Viper," I whispered. Funky stirred. His eyes began moving beneath his eyelids.

"Viper!" I tried again. This time, Funky's eyes popped open and focused straight up at the snake. For a seemingly endless few seconds, nothing happened. Just as I was ready to laugh and call off the prank, Funkhouser rolled his body toward me with tremendous speed and force. He crashed into the netting and flopped out of the bed and into my lap, pulling the net and Bolivar down with him. I, too, ended up sprawled out on the floor.

"Don't hurt the snake!" I shouted as Funkhouser scrambled to his feet, stark naked. "It's Bolivar!"

I looked up at Funky's face; it was wearing a wild-eyed, helter-skelter expression. Bolivar was at my feet, and while Funky was still trying to get a grasp on things, I grabbed the snake and put it back into its cage.

"I oughta kill you!" Funkhouser hissed at me.

I laughed. "Come on, Funky, be nice to me. It's my birthday."

"Birthday, hell," Funkhouser mumbled, picking up his mosquito net. "It's your funeral if you ever do that again. I guarantee it. And the snake's, too."

I chuckled as I walked away and out of the barracks. That had been so much fun, I thought I'd do it again. But not soon. First I'd let Funky get over it. And next time I'd use a real viper. After all, if Funky was going to kill a snake, I didn't want it to be Bolivar.

I walked into the chow hall and spotted Katsma and

Bucklew sitting together. After heaping scrambled eggs and bacon on a plate and stacking four pieces of toast on top at the food counter, I poured coffee into a cup and walked the hungry man's meal to my buddies' table.

"Chow, Hawkeye," greeted Katsma, looking up at me.

I set my cup and plate on the table and pulled out a chair.

"I'd invite you to sit your ass down," continued Kats, "but it looks like you don't need an invitation."

I smiled and sat down.

Bucklew reached for one of my twelve pieces of bacon, but I stabbed my fork at his hand. He jerked away just in time.

"Come on, Smitty!" he complained. "You can't eat all that! We've got PT in less than an hour!"

I shoved two pieces of bacon into my mouth at once. "No biggie," I said while I chewed. "I'm not interested in a foot race against you two today. I've got other things on my mind."

"Like what?" asked Katsma, plopping his fork down on his now-empty plate.

"Like going to Saigon and buying a radio," I informed him, then I put a forkload of eggs in my mouth.

"Oh, yeah?" said Kats. "Who's goin' with you?"

I chewed some more, then swallowed before answering, "You are."

"Me?"

"All of us are going," I told him. "Foxtrot Platoon."

The mess hall door opened and Funkhouser, wearing UDT swim trunks and a blue-and-gold T-shirt, entered. He immediately yelled, "It's Gary Smith's birthday today! Drinks are on him this afternoon!" He looked around, then saw me.

"There he is! The bastard himself!"

I gave Funky the finger. He gave me the same. Both of us were smiling, however, so I didn't have to worry about losing my eggs due to a fist slamming into my stomach. I'd had the "fist-in-the-gut-upchuck experience" back in high school, where my girlfriend of a week hadn't been charmed by the splatter on her dress. I had lost my hamburger and fries and her puppy love, even though I had won the fight.

Funkhouser served himself at the food counter and approached our table with a tray full of breakfast.

"After what you did to me, I shouldn't be sittin' with you, Smitty," Funky grumbled, setting his tray on the table across from me. "But since it's your birthday, I'll make an exception."

As he sat in a chair, I retorted, "Since it's my birthday, do me a favor and sit someplace else." He looked hard at me, not at all amused, so I smiled real wide. I still wanted to keep my eggs in my breadbasket.

"Smitty, tell me more about this trip to Saigon," Katsma said.

Before I answered, QM2 Bohannon hurried to our table and called my name.

"Your snake is on the loose!"

"Where?" I asked, dropping my fork and preparing to rise.

"South side of the barracks," Bohannon replied.

I pushed my chair away from the table and gave Funkhouser an accusatory look. He choked down the food in his mouth.

"Don't look at me!" he spit. "I didn't let him go!"

I started for the door.

"Why didn't you grab the snake, Bo?" I barked while not looking back.

"I hate snakes!" Bo called after me.

I jogged to the south side of the barracks, keeping my eyes peeled for Bolivar's slithering in the sparse grass.

Finding only pesky mosquitos, I searched the west side around the gun-cleaning table and diesel tub. Nothing there.

After inspecting the head and shower stalls, I covered the ground around the Seabees barracks, then the helo pad and Quonset hut. Then I started all over again.

Funkhouser, Bucklew, and Katsma spread out and helped me the second time around, but when we met fifteen minutes later at my cubicle in our barracks, none of us was holding a boa constrictor named Bolivar.

The snake's cage was halfway beneath my bed with the mesh-wire top flopped open. I kicked at it in disgust.

"Man, I didn't let him go," Funkhouser said again.

Katsma patted me on the back. "Don't worry, Hawk," he said soothingly, "we'll find him. He'll be all right."

"PT time!" someone yelled from outside the barracks.

Kats again slapped my back. "Let's go. Your snake will prob'ly join us for sit-ups."

All fourteen men of Foxtrot Platoon, along with a couple of other officers, gathered near the front gate at 0730 hours for PT. Katsma was told to lead us through the various exercises, and he did a good job out front. Contrary to my usual exuberance during PT, I just went through the motions; my mind was on Bolivar, and I was upset with myself for my apparent carelessness in properly securing the cage door.

After almost thirty minutes of sweating through the workout, Mr. Meston announced the Saigon trip would begin at 1000 hours, then called for us to jog twice around the perimeter of the ten-acre base. I was happy for the run, as someone might spot my snake.

With everyone breaking into a scamper, I loudly broadcast my predicament and asked my teammates to watch for my pet.

"Holler if you see him!" I directed.

"I'll scream with delight, like the house maid did last week when she saw my private stock!" McCollum blew from behind me.

"Knowin' you, you were as limp as a snake!" Funkhouser teased him.

"You've never seen me coiled up and ready to strike!" McCollum retaliated. "That's a sight to behold! The eighth wonder of the world!"

Katsma and I jogged a little faster, joining the others at the front of the pack.

"The ninth and tenth wonders are in my family, too!" Muck yelled after us.

"What are they?" Kats yelled back.

"My wife's bazookas! They're awesome! I call one Victor and the other Charlie, and I do love the way they torture me!"

Laughing, we ran away from the slower runners. McCollum was still getting guffaws behind us, but his words were now unintelligible.

Katsma soon made a move to take the lead over everyone, and even though breakfast was still heavy in my stomach, I couldn't help but go with him. The lead was what I was used to. It was where runners like Kats and me just naturally ended up. Not that we were so great—we simply loved to run, to stride out, to make tracks.

That morning, the rush of wind and the feeling of strength was stimulating. I almost forgot about Bolivar's being lost as Kats and I intermittently challenged one another with short bursts of speed as we circled the base. When we completed the run, however, Bolivar was all I thought about.

Sweating profusely, Kats and I made a beeline for the showers. As we approached them, Kats pointed toward the Seabees barracks.

"There's a snake!" he exclaimed.

I looked and saw the snake, but it was easy for me to tell that it wasn't mine. This snake was more than two feet long and had different colored stripes.

"That's a viper," I informed Katsma, who concurred. We watched as the venomous snake slid through the new door leading into the barracks.

"Should we go warn the Seabees?" Kats wondered aloud. We looked at each other. Smiles broke across our faces.

"Naw!" we sang in unison.

"Viper bites are rarely fatal," I stated as we headed for the showers.

After a short shower, I walked back to my barracks wearing only my UDT swim trunks. Just outside the open door, I threw my wet towel on top of a scurrying, three-inch shrew and gathered it up. Bolivar would have breakfast awaiting him, should he come home.

I entered my cubicle and deposited the shrew in Bolivar's cage, making sure to fasten the latch. I slid the cage under my bed, then dug a pair of Levi's jeans and a sports shirt out of my footlocker. I'd wear those clothes to Saigon.

I checked my Rolex. It was only 0835 hours, so I decided to read. I draped the fresh clothes over the locker, then crawled under the mosquito netting with Louis L'Amour's *The First Fast Draw* that I had received from my mother a few days earlier.

I should go look for Bolivar, I told myself. Yes, in a half hour, I would. Give him some time to surface. First, I thought I'd get lost myself in the story.

I was lost only twenty minutes when I was snapped back to reality by someone shouting curses from outside the barracks. I listened more intently and I realized it was Flynn yelling something about a snake.

Funkhouser rushed into the cubicle. "Flynn's got Bolivar cornered in the john!"

I dropped my book on the bed and flew out from beneath the mosquito net. A few seconds' sprint brought me into the lavatory, where I found Flynn in his undershorts and wearing sandals, swearing and holding his right index finger in his left hand.

"Your damn snake bit me!" he informed me, showing me the wound. His finger had been punctured slightly.

"Where is he?" I asked, unconcerned about Flynn's little bite.

"Look in that first stall," Flynn directed, then he moaned. I entered the stall and spied Bolivar's tail behind the toilet. Looking around the other side, I saw my pet's head, placed my hand behind it, and then grabbed. I pulled Bolivar out of his hiding place.

Holding the snake with both hands, I started out of the latrine.

"Thanks for finding him, Flynn."

"Next time I'll kill that little gook!" my teammate called after me.

I chuckled. "You'll have to stand in line!"

Several other SEALs, having heard the commotion, met me outside the john.

"Flynn got bit on his finger," I announced, continuing toward the barracks.

Katsma walked beside me. "That's what we get for not telling the Seabees about that viper. What goes around, comes around."

I grinned. "At least it was Flynn who got the come-around, and not us. *Hoo-yah!*"

I put Bolivar in his cage with his new companion, whom I'd dubbed "Squeaky."

I crawled back into my bed and read another thirty pages, then dressed for the Saigon trip.

At 0955 hours, thirteen SEALs from Foxtrot Platoon,

along with Lieutenant Salisbury and Mojica, our boat support buddy, assembled near the front gate and watched as Leading Petty Officer Pearson drove up in a late model Chevy pickup truck. A previous SEAL platoon had stolen the truck from the U.S. Army on a street in Saigon, where it had been parked, looking very olive drab, a few months earlier. Now it was very black, with the false license number 93-4127 painted on the doors.

There being nothing quite as audacious as thieves returning to the scene of their crime, the fifteen of us joined Pearson in the truck. Lieutenants Meston and Salisbury climbed into the cab with Pearson, and the rest of us climbed into the open box in the back. A few of the guys carried sidearms, which they weren't supposed to do in Saigon, but they kept the weapons "hidden," actually bulging, inside their shirts and belts. Smith and Wesson 9mms and .38 Specials were the weapons of concealment.

McCollum and Flynn jumped in the back of the truck after handing up a case of beer apiece.

"These are in celebration of Smitty's birthday!" McCollum declared, flashing me a smile. I chuckled to myself, knowing the beer would have come along regardless. Any excuse for beer was a good excuse. As a matter of fact, on a previous trip to Saigon we had commemorated Mickey and Minnie Mouse's anniversary, and God only knew if we had had the correct date or even if the two rodents had ever formally been married. But the beer had tasted particularly good that day.

With all on board, Pearson drove us through the base gate. Down the hard-packed gravel road past the hootches of Nha Be we went. A couple of Vietnamese children, naked at the side of the road, waved at us. I waved back.

A distinguished old man with a white goatee just stared as we went by. He was short and frail, and his clothes literally hung on him. He looked despondent. Like most elderly Vietnamese men, I was sure he cared not for war but wanted only to live peaceably with his family.

As we left the old man and the village of Nha Be behind us, Pearson sped up. Since the road to Saigon was immediately west of the northern end of the Rung Sat Special Zone, and was, in fact, separated from the RSSZ initially only by the Long Tau River, the trip was potentially dangerous. The VC sometimes mined the road, using both pressure and command-detonated mines. The most effective mines were usually command-detonated. The VC, while hiding in the jungle, chose their target and detonated the mine, using the current from flashlight batteries, when the target moved into the kill zone. After blowing a vehicle off the road, they killed any survivors. Also, VC snipers occasionally sat in wait of a good target. Obviously, a rig carrying a bunch of beer-guzzling men from a U.S. naval base made an exceptionally enticing target.

As Pearson drove faster, we opted for our number one defense against the thought of a possible ambush, which was the cold beer. It took but a few more seconds before everyone in the box had a beer can in his hand.

"To Smitty!" Funkhouser called out, hoisting his can over his head. The others saluted me in the same fashion, then McCollum started singing "Happy Birthday." All joined in, then gulped their beers when the last word was sung.

Halfway through the second round, I heard the blast of a rifle from the east side of the road. I looked into a rice paddy, but I didn't see the shooter.

Another shot rang out, then a third.

"Sniper!" Mojica warned us.

Doc Mahner, standing just behind the cab, slapped the roof of the cab with his hand to get Pearson's immediate attention from behind the wheel.

"Sniper!" he shouted. "Go faster!"

I heard the sonic pop of a fourth bullet fly by my head before I heard the report of the rifle. Out of reflex, I ducked. Of course, the bullet was already buried in a palm tree on the other side of the road by the time I had reacted.

Pearson was floorboarding the accelerator and I had to hold onto the side of the truck as we bounced all over the road.

"Pass me another beer!" cried Funkhouser, shrugging off the attack.

"Yeah!" shouted Flynn as another shot was fired. Flynn looked back down the road and flashed his middle finger at the sniper.

"You'll never hit us, you stinkin' gook!" Flynn yelled at the top of his lungs. "We're too fast, you SOB."

"Hoo-yah!" I concurred. The rest erupted into a shout, then we passed out some more beer.

The next few miles were uneventful, unless one called beer guzzling and profane jokes an event. As we got closer to Saigon, we passed a Lambretta motor scooter with an attached platform and five Vietnamese aboard. The roof of the scooter had a luggage rack which was loaded with chickens. The two adults ignored us, but three children stared blankly as we went by.

The occasional hootch on the side of the road of a couple miles back became many hootches. Old French two- and three-story buildings increased in appearance, as did plain one- and two-story buildings like those of Taiwan and China.

Doc Brown reached into his Levi's jeans front pocket and pulled out a minigrenade. He saw me looking at him and said, "Saigon scares me more than the jungle." Then he shoved the grenade back into his pocket.

I didn't blame Doc for his nervousness. The Vietnamese were prejudiced against black people, and Doc was

black. To me, he was a friend, that was all. Not black
or white, just Doc. He was a good teammate, always
there and always ready to help. In combat, he was very
cool, calm, and collected. It was too bad, I thought, that
he had to face prejudice even in Vietnam. Facing death
in the jungle was enough burden for any man without
adding to it.

Entering Saigon, we saw people everywhere. Many
were on foot, while others drove vehicles, motorbikes,
pedicabs, or rode bicycles. The funny thing was, they
all ignored us. Why they did this, I couldn't figure out.
After all, we were there fighting and dying for their
freedoms, and they didn't seem to care one iota. Besides, I wondered how people can not notice a pickup
loaded with loaded U.S. servicemen. The mystery of it
pissed me off.

Driving carefully now, due to the heavy traffic,
Pearson took us to a main intersection, which we called
"the Y." There it was even more crowded, if that were
possible. As always, I gazed at the big painted sign
above us advertising toothpaste. It pictured a black
man's profile, and he was smiling and showing off his
very white teeth. What a paradox! I thought. The Vietnamese didn't like blacks, yet they exploited one to pro-
mote a toothpaste, certainly for the contrast of the white
teeth against the black of the man's skin. Anything for
a buck. No wonder Brown disliked Saigon.

Pearson drove down Tran Hung Dao Boulevard. The
street was lined with big trees and big French colonial
buildings. The windows in the buildings were wooden
louvered or totally open for air to circulate. Lots of ho-
tels, restaurants, sidewalk cafes, shoe shops, bars, and
laundries filled both sides of the street. Again, droves of
people flooded the thoroughfare. Workmen and peasants
were dressed in loose black trousers and short black or
white jackets. Many nonlaboring men wore Western

clothing. The Vietnamese women wore their national dress of long trousers under a long-sleeved tunic slit from hem to waist. Some of the men walked the street hand-in-hand, an ordinary mark of friendship common to many Asian countries.

Eventually we ended up in the center of Saigon at NAV-FORV, which was headquarters for Naval Forces Vietnam. The three-story building contained SPECWAR staff officers, who coordinated with SEAL platoon officers in the field, and other U.S. military personnel. That was where lieutenants Salisbury, Meston, and DeFloria gathered classified information while the rest of us drank more beer across the street at an Indian-owned tailor shop. The shop catered to GIs, serving sandwiches and beer as well as making and fitting clothes. It was also a place for trading money on the black market, an illegal practice.

Thirteen of us entered the tailor shop and took seats at the four tables. The Indian proprietor, wearing a colorfully embroidered shirt, approached my table.

"American beer?" I asked.

"No, only Vietnamese Tiger or 33 beer," he answered.

"Man, I'd rather drink piss than *Ba muoi ba*," I replied, referring to 33 beer, which was a sorry beer at best.

"Smitty's buyin'!" Funkhouser shouted. "It's his birthday so he owes us a round." Funkhouser was right. On a SEAL's birthday, the birthday boy bought a round of beer. It was a tradition that I would not be the one to break. We quickly decided on Tiger beer. The bottle was nearly twice as big as 33 beer. Quantity, not quality, had become my motto since going to Vietnam.

"Serve 'em up!" I told the Indian. And he did. As a matter of fact, two rounds came out of my wallet.

"If you keep blowin' your money like that," Katsma

chided me, "you won't be able to afford that house on the hill in Texas!"

I smiled at my friend. "You're right," I agreed. "Too bad I wasn't born on February 29. Then I'd only have to put up with this once every four years."

Kats and I laughed, then ordered another beer.

As we drank together and traded money with the proprietor, an erratic stream of Vietnamese people flowed in and out of the shop. Some bought sandwiches, others picked up clothing. Each time someone entered, we were on alert. At least we were on guard as much as it was possible for a group of inebriated men, which truthfully wasn't much. Still, we made an attempt to keep track of who-came-in-with-what, and more importantly, who-left-what. A box left behind on the counter may have contained more than just papa-san's pajamas in need of a needle.

That particular day, only one suspicious Vietnamese man entered the shop. He was carrying a shoe box and a seemingly frightened look on his middle-aged face.

As the man passed Brown's table next to mine, Brown told him, in Vietnamese, to halt. The man stopped and faced Brown with the shoe box held tightly by his left arm.

"What's in the box?" Brown asked. His eyes were riveted on the man's face.

The man hesitated, appearing confused. I heard the click of the hammer of Brown's revolver as it was cocked.

Brown barked at the man, asking if he understood him. *"Ong hieu toi duoc khong?"*

The man jerkily nodded his head up and down as he slipped the box from under his arm and into his shaky hands. "Shoe!" his voice squeaked. He took the lid off and lowered the box to show a new pair of sandals to Brown. "Shoe! Just shoe." The Vietnamese man

grabbed a sandal and took it out of the box, offering it
to Brown. "You want?"

Brown's intense glare faded and I heard the hammer
being slowly uncocked.

"No," Brown mumbled.

The man persisted. "You want shoe, GI?"

"Toi noi khong duoc," Brown said, waving the man
away. *"Di di."*

As the man backed away and jammed the sandal
back into the box, Brown shoved the revolver down inside his shirt and belt.

"Saigon scares the shit outta me," he muttered in my
direction.

A moment later, Mr. Meston entered the shop through
the open door. "Let's go, men," he said. "The PX awaits
us."

Everyone guzzled the last beer and headed for the
truck parked just outside the door. All aboard, Pearson
drove us a couple of miles to our favorite spot in Saigon, the Post Exchange in the Chinese city of Cholon.

The Post Exchange, or PX, was a big French building
where we could use our ration cards to obtain a month's
supply of hard liquor and wine, two bottles each per
man. We could also buy Japanese stereo and camera
gear on the spot, or we could order it through the PX
catalogue and have items sent directly to the States.
Good deals were found on jade objects, oriental furniture, and other things made in the Orient, such as stereo
gear, camera gear, and lens accessories.

Mr. Meston gave us an hour at the PX, telling us to
rendezvous at the main entrance at 1300 hours.
Funkhouser, Katsma, and I were the first in line for our
liquor ration.

As I waited my turn behind Funkhouser, I chuckled
to myself. Funky never outran me in anything, except

the liquor run. While I was always content to walk, albeit rather briskly, to the service counter, he sprinted.

I chuckled again when Funkhouser placed his order. "Two quarts of Early Times." Then he ordered two bottles of Portuguese wine.

"I'll take the same," I sang out. Funkhouser grinned at me.

Katsma giggled from behind me. "You remind me of the Texan who was sittin' at a bar when this guy walks in and orders a stiff drink. He drinks it and immediately blacks out and falls to the floor. The Texan says to the bartender, 'I'll have what he had, only make mine a double.' "

I laughed, collected my booze, and went shopping.

At 1300 hours, all of us gathered at the entrance to the PX to fill up the truck. Everyone had his liquor, and some, like me, had other purchased items. I carried an AM/FM radio, which I'd been wanting.

We traveled another couple of miles to the Continental Hotel, where we sat at sidewalk tables beneath beautiful mango trees and enjoyed sharkfin soup with noodles, fried rice, beer, and French coffee for lunch. Our eyes feasted on the hordes of women walking by.

Two times, Bohannon asked a particularly pretty woman to sit down with him. *"Moi co vao ngoi choi,"* he said.

Two times, he was ignored.

As the woman walked away, Bo shouted after her, *"Co o dau?"* Again, the woman was silent, not wishing to tell him where she lived.

I watched the beauty disappear into the masses. I felt a sense of loss when she was gone, as I, too, had hoped she would join us. I knew I would've enjoyed gazing into her dark, almond-shaped eyes for a little while. Instead, I was stuck with Bohannon's bloodshot blues.

Finally, Funkhouser bellowed, "Let's go back to the Quonset hut and have some fun!"

"Let me at the piano," agreed McCollum.

"Hoo-yah!" echoed down the street as the sixteen of us went for the pickup truck.

Mr. Meston told us we were making one more stop at the Saigon Central Market.

Mojica exclaimed, "Great! I wanna buy a monkey."

Bohannon hit him with the obvious comeback. "You are a monkey."

"And you're monkey puke," Mojica bettered him. The two men stared hard at one another. I stepped in between them and looked into Bohannon's red eyes.

"We're all gonna be puking before this day is done," I said with a smile.

Bo studied my grin, then said, "And it's all your fault, birthday boy!" He slapped my back, and all was well.

After a ten minute ride, we arrived at the market and started wandering through the place. There, under roofs of clean-lined buildings, a wide variety of things were for sale. All kinds of fish, squid, eels, and snails in baskets were available. Brassware, jade, cloth, and hundreds of other items were on display. The odors of fish, seashells, spices, and peppers combined to make up an oriental smell unlike any other I'd experienced.

I ambled over to the site where wild animals and reptiles were shown. Mojica was already there purchasing a young monkey. I watched as he paid fourteen hundred piaster, or about twelve dollars, for the cute little animal.

As the monkey, which was on a leash, climbed onto Mojica's shoulder, Mojica grinned at me. "I've already got a name for him," he told me.

"What is it?"

"Bo," he said with a devious laugh. I couldn't help but laugh with him.

I stuck with Mojica as he bought some bananas and

mango for the monkey, then we met the others at the truck. All of the men took an immediate liking to the monkey, and all loved his new name, except Bohannon. Bohannon swore he'd get even with Mojica, and by the look on his face, I was sure he'd try. But for then, Mojica had the upper hand and he was enjoying it plenty.

On the trip back to Nha Be, no one did any drinking. Instead, we had to hang on for dear life as Pearson gunned the truck down the narrow gravel road.

When we reached the place where the sniper had fired at us, the truck was speeding along like a roller coaster on a downhill slide. We were bouncing up and down and moving fast. The wind was beating loudly against my ears. Even so, I heard the sound of gunfire. The sniper was at it again. But again, he missed everything.

After the fifth or sixth report, Flynn waved and shouted, "Bye-bye, shithead!"

Later that afternoon, I felt like the shithead. Having consumed several too many beers, my head was splitting as I lay in my bed. My last beer at the Quonset hut I had chugalugged without pause after my teammates had sung "Happy Birthday" and the old "Chugalug" song. As the beer had gone down, my eyes had watered and I had gagged at the finish.

As I stared through the mosquito net at the ceiling, a sudden white fog overwhelmed me. Through the cobwebs in my mind, I realized that the base DDT truck was outside spraying around the barracks.

For a few seconds, I lay frozen, knowing that the insecticide, at the very least, was at any moment going to choke me up and cause more gagging. While I waited, I heard some of the other SEALs coughing and running through the barracks. One of them was cursing the DDT truck driver.

"I wish he'd stick that hose up his ass!" he screamed.

I silently agreed. Then I gagged. Happy birthday.

CHAPTER SIX
Mission Ten

"The only monuments to this war will be the dead, the maimed, the despairing and the forlorn."

Letter to President Lyndon B. Johnson from the International Voluntary Services Agency, cited by Bernard Weinraub in *The New York Times*, J September 20, 1967

DATE: 2 October 1967
TIME: 0635H to 1235H
COORDINATES: YS105771
UNITS INVOLVED: Foxtrot Platoon
TASK: Recon patrol and 48 hr. river ambush
METHOD OF INSERTION: Helo—Navy
    Seawolves (2)
METHOD OF EXTRACTION: LCM-6
TERRAIN: Mangrove and nipa palm, thick
    undergrowth
MOON: 1/4
SEAL TEAM PERSONNEL:
Lt. Meston, Patrol Leader/Rifleman, M-16
Lt. (jg) Schrader, Ass't. Patrol Leader/Rifleman,
    M-16
RM2 Smith, Point/Rifleman, Shotgun
BT2 McCollum, Grenadier, M-79
BT2 Moses, Grenadier, M-79
ADJ2 Markel, Radioman/Rifleman, M-16

HM2 Brown, Corpsman/Radioman/Rifleman,
M-16
SM3 Katsma, Automatic Weapon, M-60
ADJ3 Flynn, Automatic Weapon, M-60
LDNN Ty, Rifleman, M-2 carbine
AZIMUTHS: 160 degrees-550m, 230
degrees-100m
ESCAPE: 090 degrees
CODE WORDS: Challenge and Reply—Two
numbers total 10

The juice of a partially visible sun spilled over me as I climbed out of the mud after jumping out of a Huey slick. Nine other men had landed besides me, deep in the dangerous T-10 area of the Rung Sat Special Zone.

I quickly adjusted my web gear and the four claymore mines I was loaded down with, which had shifted after the plunge, and I assumed the point position. Mr. Meston moved in behind me and motioned for me to start for the ambush site.

The ambush site was six hundred meters southeast, where we'd set up on the Rach Bau Bong at a point where another smaller tributary joined it, creating a Y of waterways. But to get there, a jungle of nipa palm and nearly impenetrable mangrove had to be conquered.

As usual, the going was extremely difficult. Twisted roots and tightly growing clusters of vegetation impeded my progress. Every step was deep into soggy, sucking mud. Hundreds of mosquitos congregated before my eyes in the early morning daylight. A spider the size of a hardball hung on a web to my right. Biting ants crawled all over a bush to my left. In a word, the place was oppressive, but I'd been trained to handle it.

I slowly snaked my way through the brush and mud, and the nine men behind me followed my path in single file. I looked back once at the green-painted faces of

Mr. Meston and Brown. Looking forward again, I remembered the day during Hell Week in the mud flats south of Coronado, when Teddy Roosevelt IV, John Odusch, Bud Burgess, Muck McCollum, some others, and I had sat in a line on each other's laps with interlocked legs and arms, moving as one force in a backward motion through the mud. That had been the caterpillar race in which we either worked together as a team or we did not budge. This morning, I felt like a part of that caterpillar again.

During the next two hours, the temperature seemed to creep upward with every ten steps that I crept forward. The long johns I was wearing did a good job of decreasing mosquito bites, but they also did a good job of burning me up. By the time I found a small tributary we were to cross, I was wetter than it.

It being low tide, the stream bed was almost dry, but stodgy with black mud. I held up at the edge, where human tracks were abundant. I gave Mr. Meston the hand signal for "danger point." Mr. Meston directed Moses and Flynn to move forward to the creek bank. Moses set up on the left flank with his M-79 40mm grenade launcher while Flynn set up on right flank with his M-60 7.62mm machine gun. The rest of the men formed a skirmish line behind me in the brush.

When Mr. Meston signaled that my teammates were ready, I sat down on the edge of the steep, slick bank and slid on my fanny into the muddy creek bottom. My feet buried themselves in the muck. Without hesitation, I pulled my right foot out along with a shoebox-size hunk of clinging mud, and I stepped ahead and back into the morass. Then I lifted my trailing left foot, again dragging a clump of gunk.

After nine or ten difficult steps, I made it to the opposite bank. The bank was five feet high, almost straight up, and slicker than grease on linoleum. I

DEATH IN
THE JUNGLE

Above: Class 36's idea of becoming a frog-man, from tadpole to bullfrog, 1965. (Photo credit: Gary Smith)

Left: Unofficial emblem of SEAL Team One. (Photo credit: Unknown)

UDT training at the mud flats. Ensigns Odusch and McCollum entertaining the instructors. (Photo credit: Unknown)

Smitty's weapons: M16/XM-148, Swedish K 9mm submachine gun, Ithaca M39 12-gauge shotgun, CAR-15/XM-177E2, and assorted knives. (Photo credit: Gary Smith)

STAB boat used to insert and extract SEALs. Boat Support personnel in boat. (Photo credit: Gary Smith)

Gary and Seaman Hyatt about to depart on another mission. Notice Gary's M16/XM-148 40mm grenade launcher and the old black Chevy pickup truck. (Photo credit: Gary Smith)

Harlan Funkhouser carrying a Stoner machine gun. (Photo credit: Gary Smith)

Doc Brown, Gary's friend and teammate. (Photo credit: Gary Smith)

Rung Sat Special Zone. Notice the brown defoliated areas next to the streams. (Photo credit: Gary Smith)

Vietnamese being detained and questioned for being caught in a restricted area. (Photo credit: Gary Smith)

Patrolling through the Rung Sat Special Zone. Flynn with his Stoner machine gun and McCollum with his M79. (Photo credit: Gary Smith)

Gary holding a seven-foot python. (Photo credit: Gary Smith)

Navy Seawolf 2.75-inch rocket attack against a VC base camp. (Photo credit: Gary Smith)

VC bunker made from mud, sticks, and logs. They were almost indestructible. (Photo credit: Gary Smith)

Navy Seawolf dropping Foxtrot Platoon more demo to blow VC bunkers. (Photo credit: Gary Smith)

Foxtrot resuming the patrol after a short rest. (Photo credit: Gary Smith)

Dee Daigle with his weapon of preference—a Stoner—while operating in the Rung Sat Special Zone in 1968. Notice the effects of defoliation. (Photo credit: Dee Daigle)

reached up as far as I could and shoved the barrel of Sweet Lips into the lower branches of a bush. Then I grasped a branch in both hands, jerked my right foot out of the mud, and attempted to swing my leg up on the bank. There was so much mud weighing down my foot that I couldn't quite perform the feat. After three futile attempts, I simply used my arms and pulled my body upward through the mud. By the time I dragged myself out of the creek bottom, I was a smelly, shiny black mess from chin to toe. I looked thrice as bad as I used to look when, as a five-year-old, I had thought stuff like this was fun.

I slid Sweet Lips back into my slimy hands, then executed a short recon up and down the creek bank. Again, I found numerous human tracks but nothing else to concern me. I secured a position beside a nipa palm tree and signaled Mr. Meston to send over the AW (automatic weapons) man and grenadier. This was a dangerous time for us. With SEALs fighting the mud in a creek bottom, we were tactically very vulnerable.

Katsma, carrying several grenades and an M-60 machine gun with five hundred rounds of 7.62mm linked ammo belted around him, was the first to come. He crossed the muddy bottom with surprising agility considering the weight he was lugging and the awful conditions. However, when he emerged from the hole, he looked just as sloppy as I.

McCollum, the grenadier, with the M-79 grenade launcher and eighty rounds of 40mm HE, was next. He had more trouble, but made it. As he crawled atop the bank, toting gobs of mud on every limb, he looked and smelled much worse than Katsma or me. The nickname Muck certainly fit McCollum at that moment in his hitch.

Mr. Meston crossed next, with Doc Brown behind

him. Both carried M-16 rifles and various grenades and flares. Brown also packed the PRC-25 radio.

As Mr. Meston climbed up the bank successfully, Brown found himself floundering in the middle of the creek bed. He fought to free his right leg, which was sunk over the knee in the black mud. Failing in the attempt, he worked on his left leg while his right went even deeper. Again, his efforts were futile and he ended up falling and wallowing in the mud like an unpracticed hog.

All of us on both sides of the creek suppressed laughter, but lots of white teeth were showing through big grins. The only one not in the mood to laugh was Mr. Meston, who stripped his gear and slid down the bank and back into the stinking creek bottom. He battled his way to Brown, who was now up to his crotch in muck. Mr. Meston grabbed Brown's M-16, then grabbed Brown's hand and pulled until he freed him from the hold. By the time the two men climbed out of the bed, they were the dirtiest and ugliest men in the jungle.

As the muck in the creek bottom became progressively deeper and more unmanageable, Mr. Schrader's group struggled to make it safely across. When they finally did, Mr. Meston motioned for me to take the point and get us the hell out of there. I was glad to put a little more distance between me and the malodorous lieutenant and the corpsman.

I patrolled through relatively dry ground and thick, nasty brush for thirty minutes until I reached a medium tributary. This channel had water in it. Checking the bank, I saw VC footprints all over the place.

Once again, Mr. Meston signaled me to recon the area. I followed the stream to the southwest, and after fifty meters, I discovered the Y of waterways where we were to set up our ambush. Our intelligence sources had informed us that a large VC hospital complex was located approximately six to nine hundred meters south-west of that Y.

Returning to the others, I used hand signals to tell Mr. Meston what I'd found. Strict noise discipline was a must in an area of heavy enemy activity, prohibiting voice communication. Mr. Meston alerted the others, and the ten of us cautiously moved to the ambush site.

At 0945 hours, Mr. Schrader and his four men set up along the riverbank for the first twelve-hour watch. Mr. Meston's group positioned itself back in the brush as the rear security element. For me, that meant a little re-laxation from the stress of functioning as point man on patrol.

I deployed three of the four claymore mines I'd been carrying, one on each flank and one in the jungle to our rear, then dropped my own rear onto some twisted man-grove prop roots that literally made for a half-ass seat. Resting Sweet Lips on my lap, I took a drink from one of my canteens and opened a C rats can of ham and eggs, one of the finer dishes issued to us swamp war-riors. At least there was no big gob of grease in the ham and eggs entrée as there was in ham and lima beans.

As I ate, I contemplated a statement made by Mao Tse-tung, who said, "Political power comes out of the barrel of a gun." I glanced at Sweet Lips and confirmed that the end of her barrel jammed between Mao's legs would drain all the power, political or otherwise, out of his loins and would easily transfer it to the gun bearer, which I'd have loved to be me. And after the sign-over, believe me, I'd have squeezed the trigger and frag-mented the president's precious jewels.

I was distracted from these elevated thoughts by two black flies, which were flying tight circles around me. I tried to keep up with them with my eyes, and I did well until three or four more joined the merrymaking. I realized that the flies had been attracted by my brand new splash-on muddy cologne.

After a while, I ignored the little disease vectors, even though they were landing all over me. The fact that some were probably carrying malaria was an uncomfortable thought, but I took my weekly malaria pills faithfully, anyway. I closed my eyes and allowed my body to relax. It felt so good that I let my mind go blank and I fell asleep.

Suddenly awaking at 1155 hours, I shook the fuzziness out of my head, somehow gathering that I needed to regain my alertness. Something had tickled one of my senses. I glanced around my immediate vicinity. Seeing nothing besides the ordinary muck and yuck, I stopped moving my head, slowed my breathing and pricked up my ears.

In the next twenty seconds, I realized many things. The temperature had risen considerably, the mud all over my clothing had dried up, most of the flies were gone, the men around me were dozing. Then my ears told me what I needed to know. Human voices were coming from far away.

I lifted Sweet Lips from my lap and flicked off the safety. I hesitated and listened again. The voices were suddenly closer, emanating from upstream. I rose to my feet and started forward toward the ambush site. Peering through the dense foliage, I tried to spot one of the camouflaged SEALs waiting in the brush along the bank. Before I saw one, a sampan floated by on the water. I barely saw it between the nipa palm branches and leaves and the bushes. I only got a split-second look. Just as abruptly as it had appeared, the sampan vanished from my line of sight.

I heard a noise behind me and looked back to see Mr. Meston approaching. I motioned that I'd seen a sampan, and he got close and put his mouth right next to my right ear.

"See Mr. Schrader and ask why he didn't fire!" Mr. Meston commanded.

I carefully advanced toward the riverbank to the place where the center of the killing zone of the ambush site should be. Mr. Schrader, who had been watching my convergence, materialized from behind a bush. I snuck beside him and gave him a "well, what happened?" shrug.

He whispered, "Old woman and two boys. Waiting for a better target."

I nodded my head and slipped quietly back to Mr. Meston, who was waiting where I had left him. Mr. Meston told me to go ahead and whisper to him, so I quietly passed along Mr. Schrader's message. Mr. Meston whispered to me to go back and tell him that if another boat came by, he should stand up and holler "*Lai dai* (Come here!)" and try to capture the occupants.

Again I made my way to Mr. Schrader and gave him Mr. Meston's orders. He acknowledged the information with a nod, and I reversed to return to the rear. I went only a few steps before I heard more voices up the river, so I turned and joined Mr. Schrader and his men overlooking the waterway.

Several seconds crawled by. A lung fish splashed downriver. A widgeon flew toward us from out of the south. Things were existing in their natural order. I wished it were so easy.

Then a sampan came into view. Two men, dressed in the green uniforms of the NVA, were standing up in the boat, one at each end, steering the craft along with the current. Two women were seated, both holding packages or bundles of some kind. I couldn't believe they were moving through a free-fire zone in broad daylight.

As they drew alongside us just ten meters out, Mr. Schrader jumped up, compromising himself, and yelled, *"Lai dai, Lai dai!"*

My eyes darted back and forth between the two NVA soldiers, whose mouths had dropped open in shock at the surprising sight of an enemy who had the drop on them in the middle of their own swamp.

"Lai dai!" Mr. Schrader screamed again, but the four in the boat continued to stare as they gradually drifted away. *"Lai dai,* dammit!" Mr. Schrader hollered after them in frustration. "I told you to get the hell over here!"

Suddenly the two men in the sampan dove overboard and disappeared under the surface of the water. Instantly, my teammates and I opened fire. Bullets riddled the stream like a hard-driving hailstorm.

In the midst of the hellacious gunfire, one of the women dropped her bundle into the sampan and threw herself into the stream. The other woman stayed seated and leaned over as if to protect her package. In between heavy bursts of gunfire, my ears recorded a baby's bawl. My hair stood on end as I realized the contents of at least one of the two bundles.

"Don't shoot the boat!" I yelled for all I was worth. As I did, one of the gooks stuck his head up for air. I turned Sweet Lips on him and pulled the trigger. Water sprayed in front of his face as I pumped in another round and fired again. More water droplets exploded around his head, which sank underwater.

I glanced at the woman in the sampan. She was still huddled over her parcel. The boat was a lame duck, seemingly drifting in slow motion, with bullets tearing up the water behind it.

"Don't shoot the boat!" I shouted, wishing I could play God to reach out and pluck the woman and the baby, or babies, to safety. I yelled again, and the woman in the sampan turned her head and stole a look back toward me. I was sure she couldn't pick me out, but I could see even her fearful eyes. A second later, she hunched over and hid her face in the bundle on her lap.

As weapons continued to pound on both sides of me, Mr. Meston charged up from the rear and started firing his M-16 across and into the fifty-meter-wide stream. One of BT2 Moses's 40mm HE grenades exploded on the opposite bank, followed by a second loud explosion. M-60 machine gun noise banged the hell out of my eardrums. I added to the ruckus as I blasted the water where I had last seen the enemy's head.

Moments later, as the assault began to diminish, another head popped up for air near the opposite shore. Without shilly-shally, all SEAL team weapons went full bore. A fusillade of bullets drove the head back down.

Not wanting to lose the sampan, Mr. Meston yelled at me to go get it. I laid Sweet Lips in a bush and grabbed the big pair of duck fins. Quickly, I pulled them on over my coral booties and slid my body off the bank and into the stream. The water was immediately refreshing as I breaststroked toward the boat. Maybe I could play God, after all. I heard a baby crying, and I was determined to rescue it.

Heavy gunfire suddenly erupted behind me. I looked ahead across the water and saw the two male gooks trying to claw their way up the riverbank to escape into the jungle. But the bank was a nightmare, steep and slick with mud. The men slipped and slid as bullets splattered all around them. Pieces of flesh were torn from their bodies, yet they continued to scramble upward. Miraculously, after ten seconds more of all hell breaking loose, the two made it up the slippery bank and fell into the thick brush, but they left trails of blood and entrails behind them. I would have bet a year's pay that neither of them would ever see another paycheck. I knew dead men when I saw them, even if they were last seen still crawling.

I tried to catch up with the drifting boat as it rapidly floated toward a bend in the stream. When I swam to within forty feet of the sampan, I saw the woman who had jumped overboard pulling it by the bow toward the far bank. I yelled back at my teammates, and Mr. Schrader took a shot at her with his M-16. She let go and swam for the riverbank. I thought about trying to catch her, but I was too loaded down to seriously attempt it. I forgot about her and stroked for the sampan.

Just as I reached the boat, the woman in the water made it to the muddy bank. As she scratched her way up, someone shot her and wounded her, but she managed to roll into the brush and disappear.

I grabbed the side of the sampan with both hands and pulled myself out of the water and into the boat, being careful not to capsize it. I looked hopefully at the woman who was bent over onto her own lap, and my stomach sank. There was a bullet hole in the small of her back and a ring of blood surrounding it.

A newborn baby drew my attention at the bow of the sampan as it cried bloody murder. I crawled over to it and picked it up from a blanket and cradled it in my arms. The baby was naked and was a boy. He had blood slowly flowing from a leg wound in which his left calf muscle has been laid open its full length to the bone by a bullet. More ghastly still, he had pieces of someone's brain on his face.

I looked back at the dead woman, and from that angle I could see part of her head was blown open. My eyes riveted on a large piece of her skull bone lying on the sampan deck. I desperately fought to keep from crying, realizing I must control my emotions. I stared despairingly at the screaming, tiny baby held snugly against my chest, and tears fell from my cheeks and onto his. My heart slammed heavily against my rib cage, and I felt an ache inside of it. The pain intensified as my tears increased, until my whole being wanted to scream, "War is hell!"

Through my tears, I saw Ty, the Vietnamese SEAL, treading water as he held onto the edge of the boat. I moved my weight to the starboard bow to balance the sampan as Ty pulled himself over the port side. Once inside, Ty picked up a paddle from the deck and began paddling us back toward the ambush site. He also had noticed a small pile of papers on the sampan deck, which he scooped up, folded, and slipped inside his wet shirt.

I did my best to wipe away my tears and water droplets from my face, knowing I was smearing the cammo paint all over. Then I looked again at the dead woman and took heed of a bundle squashed beneath her chest. I scrambled over to her body, and while holding the baby boy with my left arm, I lifted her drooping upper torso with my right. A second newborn baby was revealed.

I allowed the torso to flop backward, then I removed the baby from the lap. As I curled my right arm around the tiny body, which also was a boy, I saw that its head was dangerously swollen. It was obvious that the baby had had too much weight crushing down on his head, and even though he was breathing, he may have been without oxygen for a while beneath his mother's body.

With the baby in my left arm whimpering, bleeding down my side and going into shock, and the baby in my right arm lying limp against my chest, I felt like the lowest bastard on earth. Here I was taking these injured three- or four-week-old babies away from their mothers, one of whom was dead and the other wounded and, no doubt, fighting for her own life. If the two NVA soldiers were the respective fathers, I knew they wouldn't be taking on any bottle-feeding duties. The baby boys, then, if they themselves survived, would never know their parents.

As Ty continued paddling us closer to shore, my sudden, sole consolation was that I knew in my heart that I hadn't wanted anything like that to happen. If I could have, I'd have prevented it. The worst thing was that deep inside my guts, I knew it would happen again, in Vietnam, to me. That was the cold, stark reality of the damnable war. God forgive us all.

Doc met us as we hit the shore, and I gave him the baby with the bleeding leg. By the time I climbed out of the sampan with the other baby, Doc was already applying a bandage to the wound. I showed him the swollen head of the baby I was holding, and Doc took the little fellow out of my arms.

I felt somewhat dizzy, so I just walked away. Most of my gear was at the rear, and since our presence in the T-10 was compromised, I had to retrieve my gear and my shotgun and "get out of Dodge" with the rest of the platoon. Mr. Meston had called on the radio for *Mighty Moe* to come and extract us, so it wouldn't be long. In the meantime, I had to reload Sweet Lips and get prepared for a possible enemy counterattack.

After slinging on my gear, I stole my way to Mr. Meston, who was using the radio to direct the extraction boats to us. I asked him to call for a medevac (medical-personnel-on-board helo) for the injured babies, then I ambled over to help Doc. Together we tried to feed the babies some water from a canteen, but neither wanted to drink. I noted with some surprise that the baby with the leg wound still had good color, as his whole body was flushed. The baby with the mashed head, however, was very pale and his breathing irregular. He needed a hospital and fast.

A few more minutes went by, then I heard *Mighty*

Moe and the LCPL busting in with their powerful diesel engines roaring. As the noise got closer, I was amazed at the courage of the crews, risking it all in broad daylight to get our bared butts out of danger. They were coming in like gunslingers, riding down the main street of town for all to see and to shoot at. They were exposed and vulnerable, but still they came, as ready to fight as a riled tomcat at a dog show.

Mr. Meston guided *Mighty Moe* right to us, and not far behind I saw the LCPL coming down the river. *Mighty Moe* eased her bow into the bank while letting down the bow ramp. As the ramp touched the shore, the ten men of Foxtrot Platoon, with Doc and me each carrying a baby, quickly boarded the boat. We boarded with confidence, believing we would not only be secure on *Mighty Moe* but that we could stand off any force that wished to confront us.

The coxswain reversed the engine and carefully maneuvered the boat away from the shore. As we backed up, he slowly turned the bow back into the current, then proceeded to accelerate forward. The LCPL hugged the far bank and allowed us to pass, then fell in behind and followed our tails out of there.

The procession traveled less than two hundred meters when some kind of a large round hit *Mighty Moe*'s starboard bow. Whatever it was, it was a dud, as it failed to detonate. Nevertheless, Charlie had shot at us from the riverbank, and he would pay big time.

All six of *Mighty Moe*'s .50-caliber machine guns immediately opened up, with three on starboard and three on portside blasting the respective shorelines. The LCPL's two gunners opened fire, one with a mounted M-60 machine gun and the other with a Honeywell 40mm, which was a Gatling-gun affair. All .30-calibers started barking and everything in our hands slammed away at the jungle. Two helo gunships appeared overhead and joined the unbelievable uproar, spraying M-60 machine gun fire and exploding 2.75-inch rockets on the river banks. In all, two dozen weapons were simultaneously raining hell on some poor, dumb slobs who had been imprudent enough to have thrown a brick at our beloved *Mighty Moe*.

Whoever the dummies were, they deserved whatever hit them. But my eardrums were getting trounced by a hurricane of sound.

Our assault on the jungle was incredible. Not only were leaves and branches being blown into the air by the onslaught, but whole trees were being cut in half and were falling onto the riverbanks and into the water.

All kinds of cartridge cases and hulls flew everywhere. They were bouncing off the deck, sailing overboard, even hitting me in the arms and legs. I glanced at the babies and saw dozens of casings all around them. The boy with the enlarged head had one resting on his chest. His slanted eyes were barely open, and I wondered if he would live to see a better day.

After another half minute of intense landscaping activity, we vacated the premises. Doc and I cleared away the empty cartridges and sat down on the deck of the boat. I gently lifted the baby with the swollen head and cuddled him against my chest. He was limp and almost lifeless. Doc held the other baby who, despite his injured leg, had looked pretty good before the heavy offensive. Now he looked colorless.

I dropped my head and closed my eyes for a minute as we sped along the stream. I heard only the ringing of a giant bell inside my head. Between every peal, I saw the brave mother on the sampan bent over and protecting her baby, and then I saw her brains scattered everywhere.

I opened my eyes and noticed the helo gunships were staying right over us. The boys in the skies were making sure we didn't run into cables tied across the stream to hang us up, to be followed by an ambush. Once again, I was grateful to those courageous men above.

When we reached the main river, a medevac arrived and hovered over *Mighty Moe*'s protective overhead. As Doc and I climbed on top of the cover over the well deck, ready to hand the two babies to the helicopter crew, one of the MST guys took off his green shirt and tossed it to me. Doc and I wrapped the babies in the shirt, then lifted the bundle up to awaiting arms.

A few moments later, the medevac flew away. I watched it go until it was out of sight.

I sat down on the deck and Doc dropped down beside me. Both of us had blood on our clothes. He put his arm around me. I looked into his eyes, and he looked into mine, just for a moment. We said nothing. The events of the day had already spoken too much.

CHAPTER SEVEN

Mission Rehearsal

"Any man's death diminishes me, because I am involved in mankind; and therefore never send to know for whom the bell tolls; it tolls for thee."

John Donne, *Devotions*

DATE: 6 October 1967
TIME: 0700H to 1930H
COORDINATES: YS023743U
UNITS INVOLVED: MST-3
TASK: Simulate method of capturing VC from sampan
METHOD OF INSERTION: LCM-6
METHOD OF EXTRACTION: Boston Whalers
TERRAIN: Flat, tall grass, underwater at high tide
MOON: 1/2
WEATHER: Clear
SEAL TEAM PERSONNEL:
Lt. Meston, Patrol Leader/ Rifleman, M-16
Lt. (jg) Schrader, Ass't Patrol Leader/Rifleman, M-16
RM2 Smith, Point/Swimmer/Rifleman, Shotgun
MM2 Funkhouser (sick)
BT2 McCollum, Ordnance/Grenadier, M-79
BT2 Moses, Grenadier, M-79
ADJ2 Markel, Radioman/Rifleman, M-16

ADJ2 Flynn, Automatic Weapons, M-60
HM2 Brown, Corpsman/Radioman/Rifleman,
  M-16
SM3 Katsma, Rifleman, M-16
LDNN Ty, Swimmer/Rifleman, M-2 Carbine
LDNN Sat, Rifleman, M-16
LDNN Thanh, Rifleman, M-16
AZIMUTHS: 190 degrees-300m
ESCAPE: 010 degrees
PHASE LINES: None
CODE WORDS: None

I ate breakfast at 0545 hours, my mind drowning in my coffee. I was still haunted by our mission of four days earlier. Mr. Meston had told me both of the injured babies were doing well, but somehow I didn't believe him. I thought he was just trying to make me feel better. And even if the babies were fine, their parents were not. All four of them found out in a big way they weren't bulletproof, let alone immortal.

The day before, I had practiced karate exercises for an hour, then had played two hours of volleyball in an effort to take my mind off thoughts of death. I had been semisuccessful until I had picked up my laundry from Nga's. While walking back to the base, the feel and smell of the clean clothes had stood in stark contrast to the feel and smell of this dirty war.

"Lighten up, Hawkeye!" Katsma cheered me as he sat down at my table. "Today's another day."

I managed a smile. "You're right," I said, shaking off the blues. Kats's friendliness always had a positive effect on me.

Katsma dug into his biscuits and gravy. "Eat good," he said. "Today's practice evolution might get long. After all, you're gonna have to try to capture me, and I won't make it easy."

We were rehearsing the capture of a Viet Cong from the T-10 area, from whom we would extract good intelligence information. We knew there were big enemy units in the T-10, and we needed to find out where they were. The area was so thick that just about the only way to find them was to be told their location.

"Don't be so competitive," I told Kats. "This is only a rehearsal. We can get serious when we're doing the real thing."

Kats looked at me with a mischievous grin, then shoved a whole biscuit into his mouth. The gravy ran out the sides of his lips, and we both chuckled.

At 0700 hours, twelve of us boarded *Mighty Moe* for the hour trip down the Long Tau River to our point of insertion. Two Boston Whalers followed us to our objective. Upon arrival, we inserted onto the riverbank, observing all security measures, leaving the boats in the main channel to await our call for extraction.

I took the point and began moving parallel to a small stream called the Vam Sat. Each step was relatively easy, as the terrain was flat and sprouting only tall grass. The ground was soggy due to being underwater during high tides.

I didn't sense the usual tension as I patroled, as I was aware this was simply a practice op in a relatively secure administrative training area; however, I still had to play everything straight because one never knew for sure where the enemy may lurk. I certainly didn't want to trip a little gookish surprise booby trap.

As we traveled the three hundred meters to our simulated ambush site, I spotted three ducks flying low over our heads. Their wings were spread and curved downward for landing. Suddenly they changed their plans, flapped their wings and soared higher. Obviously, they had spied their most feared enemy: the 12-gauge pump shotgun in my hands. I'd seen this fast-feathered reaction a multitude of times back home in Texas: the quacks had moved in, prepared to light, then up had popped the mouth of the dreaded monster from the lagoon. No duck that loved life needed more than a split-second glance before he freaked and beat the hell out of the air, bound for dizzying heights. When dealing with me, many a surprised duck had died with that "look of horror" on his beak. That morning, however, those lucky duckies got away, never to realize that strict noise discipline had saved their tail feathers.

About a hundred meters from our ambush site, I reached a creek. I signaled Mr. Meston, and he signaled "danger point" to the others. Katsma positioned himself on our right flank with his M-16 rifle. McCollum moved to our left flank with his M-79 grenade launcher. Mr. Meston, as always, moved up behind me as I stepped down into the creek bottom, which was only three feet deep with water.

The creek was five meters wide and easy to cross. When I climbed out on the opposite bank, I made a short recon, finding nothing of concern. I then waved the others across.

McCollum stepped into the water first, following my exact path, which I had found to be safe. Katsma came second. When they reached my side, they set up on right and left flanks. The rest of the men filed across in a well-spaced line.

We patrolled in a southerly direction for perhaps fifty meters, paralleling the direction of the meandering creek for that short distance. Then Mr. Meston pointed for me to go west, which meant we had to cross the creek again.

We handled the creek crossing in the same manner as earlier, then moved sixty meters to the Rach La and the ambush site. Following the previous day's briefing instructions, eight of us set up on the eastern bank of the large stream. ADJ2 Markel, with the radio, positioned himself a few meters in back of Mr. Meston. Mr. Schrader, ADJ2 Flynn, and LDNN Thanh set up as rear security.

With everyone in place, Katsma, who was going to play the part of a VC bad guy in our rehearsal, slipped down into the stream and began swimming across the twenty-foot-deep water. I admired him from my position at Mr. Meston's left side. His strokes were powerful in the swift current.

I raised my eyes from Kats and searched the opposite bank. I was looking for anything that could endanger my friend, such as the enemy or a "man-eating man-a-cheetah." Spotting nothing in the bushes, I focused on Kats as he reached the shore. As he lifted himself out of the stream and climbed the bank, water cascaded off his body and clothes.

With an M-16 in his hands, Katsma did a short recon of the shoreline. Convinced that all was well, he signaled Mr. Meston with the thumbs-up sign, then stepped back into the brush.

Mr. Meston motioned for LDNN Ty and me to enter the stream. I was carrying a haversack of ten pounds of C-4 explosives, weighted down on a flotation bladder, which was attached to a hundred and fifty feet of reinforced electrical firing wire. Ty and I were to swim the explosives about three-fourths of the way across the Rach La, stringing out the full length of the firing wire from Mr. Meston's position, then let the weighted haversack drop from the flotation bladder and sink to the bottom of the stream.

Ty and I walked upstream along the bank as far as the firing wire would reach, slipped into our duck fins, then slid into the water. Immediately, we had to swim hard toward the opposite bank, as the current was extremely strong. After a minute of all-out effort, we were directly in front of Mr. Meston, about thirty-five meters away. I looked at the lieutenant, and he motioned for me to drop the explosives. I tried to release the haversack from the flotation bladder, but the firing wire was tangled with the life jacket. While I struggled to release the explosives, Ty and I drifted farther downstream outside the kill zone of the ambush site. The wire soon pulled taut, then broke in the middle of its length.

Disgusted, Ty and I had to swim back to the ambush site, where we could repair the firing wire. This was easier thought of than done. Finding it impossible to swim directly into the strength of the current, Ty and I struck out crosscurrent for the shore. We ended up reaching the riverbank about seventy-five meters south of the others.

Crawling out of the water, I swung the heavy sack of explosives and weights over my right shoulder while Ty rolled up seventy feet of attached firing wire. We walked through the brush to Mr. Meston's position in the center of the ambush line, where he awaited with his end of the wire.

I first tied the bitter ends together using a square knot. I carefully repaired the wire, using the Western Union splice. Then I taped each wire separately, and finally together, for insulation and strength. As I finished, I looked across the river and tried to see Katsma. I couldn't find him, but I was sure he had gotten a real kick out of watching Ty and me flounder around in the current. He probably had had all he could handle in stifling his guffaws.

"Hang in there, Smitty," Mr. Meston encouraged me. Not wanting a repeat performance, I freed the weighted haversack from the flotation bladder and dropped the bladder on the ground. I planned to make sure there was no tangled mess the second time.

Ty and I again walked upstream, stringing out the

wire before dropping off the bank. Swimming was much tougher now as the weighted haversack of C-4 had nothing to keep it afloat but my arms. My arms were enough, however, tired though they were.

When I reached the drop point, I let the weighted haversack go. It sank in the water, and I was relieved of a hell of a burden. Ty and I drifted momentarily with the current as we looked to see if all was well. Mr. Meston gave us a wave that all was okay and to return to his location. As I breaststroked, my arms felt light, relieved to be free of the heavy haversack. Ty was right behind me as I climbed out of the water.

We made our way to the others and took up our positions in the ambush line near Lieutenant Meston. He gave us a couple of minutes to catch our breath, then notified all concerned that the simulated ambush was ready to happen. We were to pretend that a sampan, occupied by the VC, was floating down the stream toward us. When the imaginary boat was supposedly in front of Mr. Meston and directly above the C-4 explosives, he'd command detonate the charge, which would capsize the craft. That was when Ty and I were to jump into the stream and swim to the opposite bank and "capture" Katsma.

Suddenly the explosives blew, but forty meters farther downstream than the drop point. Obviously, the haversack of C-4 had not been weighted down enough to keep the swift current from moving it. Plus, the explosion was not big enough to capsize a sampan and stun the occupants. Next time we'd have to double the charge. But that would be next time.

This time, Ty and I had to swim across the water and tie up Katsma. With duck fins on my feet, and electrical tape in my pants pocket, I slid into the stream and went for the opposite bank. Ty was right behind me.

As I breaststroked for all I was worth, I looked for

my friend across the river in the bushes. I didn't see him. Drawing closer to shore, I really wondered where Katsma had gone. Then I remembered him saying at breakfast that he wasn't going to make his capture easy on me.

"Dammit," I muttered as I cut through the water.

Reaching the beach, I grabbed a root sprout and dragged myself out of the stream. I plopped my fanny down on the bank and pulled off my fins. Ty clutched the same sprout and heaved himself up beside me where he, too, took off his fins.

"Where Kats?" Ty whispered.

I shrugged my shoulders. Standing up, I stared into the brush around us. I figured we'd just wait a few seconds and Kats would materialize.

After half a minute, Kats did not appear. I searched the ground and found a set of fresh bootprints that must have been his. I motioned to Ty and started following the tracks.

We walked less than ten meters when we were suddenly startled.

"Here I am!" Kats popped up from behind a bush, smiling at us. I waved for him to come to us, but he shook his head, laid down his M-16 rifle, and put up his fists.

"I'm your VC prisoner," he said. "You're supposed to take me by force."

Here we go, I thought. He was gonna fight us like a real gook. I looked at Ty, raising my eyebrows. Simultaneously, we broke into a charge at Katsma. We crashed into him together, and all three of us fell to the ground. That was when the wrestling began.

Kats locked his arms around Ty's neck and held him down. I jumped on Kats's back and tried to pry him off Ty. Kats spun away from Ty and flipped me onto my back. Like a cat, Kats was on me in an instant. I threw my arms around his waist and bear hugged him with all my might. Then Ty slammed his body into both of us, sending all of us sprawling.

I sat up on my knees and barked, "Come on, Kats! You've gotta back off or we'll never take you in. Then Mr. Meston's gonna be pissed."

Katsma, also on his knees, grinned at me. "Try again," he said.

I rose to my feet and pulled the squashed roll of electrical tape from my pocket.

"We've gotta tie your hands and feet," I reminded him.

He was still grinning. "Come and get it," he said.

I glanced at Ty, who was sitting on the ground just a few feet from Kats. Ty winked at me, then whipped a handful of swamp mud in Kats's face. Instantly, Ty and I lept onto Kats as he wiped at his eyes. Half-blinded by the muck, Kats swung a wild arm and knocked Ty to the side. I dropped the roll of tape, grabbed Kats from behind and squeezed him in an arm lock.

"Come on, Kats!" I demanded. "Give us a break."

"Let me clean out my eyes," Katsma dealt, "then I'll let you capture me."

I released my grip and Katsma stumbled a few yards to the riverbank. He dropped to his knees and bent over in a reach for a handful of water. He splashed his face several times, then got up and held his hands out toward me.

"They're yours to tie," he said with a smile. "Just go easy."

I picked the tape off the ground and approached Kats with it. Ty stepped forward, grabbed Kats's left hand and walked it around behind Kats's back.

" 'Just go easy,' he says now," I smirked, twisting Kats's right hand behind his back and pressing it against his left. "I will, but you don't deserve it."

Ty and I wrapped the black tape firmly around Kats's hands at the small of his back, but only three times around. I motioned toward the ground and Kats sat down on the bank of the stream. I pulled his feet out and wrapped the tape three times around them at the ankles.

"Is that it?" Kats said sarcastically. "You guys are awful nice."

I smiled at him. "We've got orders to gag you, too," I reminded him. I pulled a dirty rag from my pants pocket and stuffed it in his mouth. Then Ty ran tape twice around the rag to secure the gag.

Less than a minute later, two Boston Whalers came shooting down the stream with their 105-horsepower engines singing. As Ty and I readied our "captive" for transport, the coxswain of the lead boat cut back on the throttle and flared the boat right in front of us. Mr. Meston, using radio communication, had directed the Whaler with the boat crew of three and the MST lieutenant right to us. The second Whaler eased over to Mr. Meston's position on the opposite bank.

The bow of the first Whaler eased up to the riverbank and I grabbed hold and pushed the boat around until it was parallel to the shore, pointing upstream. Then Ty and I hoisted the gagged-and-bound Katsma into the boat and the awaiting arms of the crew. I grabbed Ty's fins and tossed them into the boat with mine, then Ty, with Kats's rifle, and I climbed in next to the "prisoner." Without a word, the coxswain navigated the boat across the stream to Mr. Meston's position. As the bow touched the bank, I gave Katsma a pat on the head and a grin.

"Bye-bye, ol' buddy," I said. Kats raised his eyebrows at me and grunted. I moved forward with Ty, and we stepped off the boat and jumped onto the shore.

As part of the rehearsal, BT2 Moses simulated

wounds to his eyes. With a battle dressing having been applied, he and Doc Brown boarded the boat. They sat down, then the coxswain backed the boat away from shore with seven people aboard, turned into the current, and opened up the outboard motor to vacate the area. His assignment was to take the prisoner and wounded man to the Long Tau River, where the LCM-6 awaited their transfer. There the VC would be interrogated and Moses would be medevacked by a helicopter.

Lieutenant Meston, as prearranged, kept the rest of us at the ambush site to practice the use of different-size charges in the Rach La. The second Boston Whaler stayed with us to divert any sampans away from the area for security and secrecy purposes. During daylight hours, local fishermen were allowed to use their nets in the Rach La. The crew of the Whaler would keep these people from the rehearsal area.

From the mission rehearsal, we'd already learned that ten pounds of C-4 is not enough to upset a sampan. Perhaps twenty pounds would be. When in doubt, double the charge! With that in mind, Mr. Meston and I decided that we should prepare another haversack with that specific charge. I also suggested adding more weights to prevent the bag from drifting with the current.

As we readied the explosives, a call from the officer in charge of *Mighty Moe* sounded over the radio.

"Stan, this is Bill Jackson. Be advised the Boston Whaler has swamped. A petty officer is missing. We are searching for him at this time. All other personnel are accounted for and aboard the LCM-6."

Mr. Meston blurted out, "No! No!" His voice was shaky. He took the PRC-25 handset from Markel, put it to his mouth and managed to ask. "Who's missing?"

The reply caused my guts to roll: "Petty Officer Katsma."

Mr. Meston visibly slumped and muttered, "God, no." He recovered in a few seconds enough to order a Dust-off, which was the code word for U.S. casualties. By this time, I had moved right next to him.

After the transmission, he looked at me with a sickly expression. "What in the crap happened?" he asked.

Mr. Meston bowed his head and covered his face with his left hand. I felt my heart hitting hard against my chest. I gazed at the stream, wishing Katsma would appear with a big grin on his face. Either that, or I'd wake up from a bad dream.

Lieutenant Meston raised his eyes and stared at me. His facial expression had changed for the better.

"Smitty, you and I are gonna run along the riverbank to the Long Tau. Maybe we'll spot him." His voice was excited and carried a note of confidence. I, too, felt a sudden flush of hope.

"Flynn!" Mr. Meston barked. "Come with me." Then he gave Markel the radio and told Mr. Schrader to secure the rehearsal and patrol with the rest of the men back to the Long Tau.

"Keep radio communication with *Mighty Moe*," Mr. Meston directed Mr. Schrader. "Call for extraction when you reach the main river. Have the others pack Smitty's gear."

With that, I grabbed Sweet Lips from a resting place against my operating gear, then Mr. Meston, Flynn, and I broke into a run on the edge of the Rach La. Since we were less than three hundred meters from the Long Tau, Katsma couldn't be far from us. He may have been dead, but maybe not. Maybe he had made it somehow. Dammit, he had to have made it. He was too good of a man not to have made it.

We ran in single file with me in the front, picking a way along the riverbank. After the first one hundred meters, the running became easier as we entered an area

of defoliation. There were still bushes that had been
well watered by the high tide, but they weren't as dense
farther back.

All of our eyes darted back and forth from the foot-
ing to the water, eager to spot any sign of Kats. If one
of us could have but glimpsed his body, I'd have swum
through hell and high water to get him ashore. As a
matter of fact, I'd have cut off my right arm and traded
it for Kats's life if God had been in the business of
making such deals.

With no sign of our teammate, we kept pressing on-
ward, one foot in front of the other. My senses, as always when I was in the jungle, were teeming and
feeding info to my brain. My skin, drenched with sweat,
told me it was hot and humid. My ears, ever alert,
picked up my inhaling and exhaling, and even the
throbbing of my pulse. My nose drew in the smell of
fish rotting somewhere on the beach. My tongue, after
licking my dry lips, drew back inside my mouth with a
speck or two of salt. And my eyes, crying loudest, told
me that things were looking bad.

As we approached the intersection where the Rach La
met the Long Tau, I scanned the main channel for activity. *Mighty Moe* and the Boston Whalers appeared several hundred meters downstream to the east. I pointed
them out to Lieutenant Meston as we jogged.

"Let's go!" Mr. Meston said, waving his hand in the
direction of the boats. I angled to the east and ran with
urgency. We were on flat, defoliated, grassy terrain, so
cranking up the speed was the natural thing to do.

My eyes glanced along the Long Tau, looking for a
body, but I realized my searching was in vain. The
LCM-6 was far downstream, and drifting away as fast
as we were running. Certainly, a man's body would be
pulled by the strong current in like manner.

"Hurry, Smitty!" Mr. Meston called from behind me.

I looked back to see Flynn right behind me and Mr. Meston falling back and struggling. Mr. Meston's face looked pained and desperate.

I decided to race as hard as I could for the boats, to give it one more chance. After all, Katsma, I knew, would do no less for me were I the one missing.

I went hard. Leaping a small ditch, I forced my legs into high gear. My arms started pumping at a frenzied pace. I stretched out for all I was worth, trying to reel in the LCM-6.

I leapt over another ditch, feeling like I was flying. I sensed that I'd gained a bit on *Mighty Moe*. Could I catch her?

Katsma suddenly appeared in my mind. He was running beside me, going all-out. The base gate at Nha Be was just ahead. We were neck and neck, revved to the maximum. Kats looked over at me with anguish in his eyes. We were both in overdrive, both overheating. We were ready to crash and burn, but the gate and the win were just ahead.

Then something cut us apart. Something separated us. I saw a form, a shape in the way. I thought it was Nga. I blinked my eyes, refocused, and I saw a darkness. I saw Death. Katsma began flailing his arms as he crashed through the gate. There was surging black water on the other side, and I screamed as he plunged in and disappeared into the darkness.

Stop! my brain cried. *Mighty Moe* was still five hundred meters ahead of me, and I couldn't catch her. I gazed once more at the Long Tau, then bent over, put my hands on my knees for support and sucked in lots of air. Sweat beads ran off my face and fell to the ground between my coral booties. I glanced to my side, half hoping to see Katsma panting and perspiring and smiling as usual after our races, but he was not there. There was only a terrible void, an emptiness.

I looked down and watched my sweat drip to the grass below, but I could barely see. All was fuzzy as my eyes flooded with water. My sweat mixed with tears.

I heard Mr. Meston and Flynn approach, but I didn't look up.

"Forget it, Smitty," Flynn said weakly. "Katsma's gone."

Forget it. Yeah, sure. Forget Katsma. Forget one of the best men I've ever known.

Never. Never.

CHAPTER EIGHT

Mission Eleven

"Youth is the first victim of war; the first fruit of peace. It takes twenty years or more of peace to make a man; it takes only twenty seconds of war to destroy him."

Baudouin I of Belgium,
address to joint session of U.S. Congress,
May 12, 1959

DATE: 8, 9 October, 1967
TIME: 080645H to 090530H
COORDINATES: YS024609
UNITS INVOLVED: Foxtrot Platoon
TASK: Recon patrol, 24 hour river ambush
METHOD OF INSERTION: LCM-6
METHOD OF EXTRACTION: LCM-6
TERRAIN: Mangrove swamp, underwater at high tide
TIDE: 0500H High, 1209H Low, 1900H High, 0100H Low
MOON: None
WEATHER: Cloudy with rain
SEAL TEAM PERSONNEL:
Lt. (jg) Schrader, Patrol Leader/Rifleman, M-16
RM2 Smith, Point/Rifleman, Shotgun
BT2 McCollum, Grenadier, M-79
BT2 Moses, Rifleman, M-16

ADJ2 Markel, Radioman/Rifleman, M-16
ADJ3 Flynn, Automatic Weapons, M-60
HM2 Brown, Corpsman/Rifleman, M-16
AZIMUTHS: 120 degrees-500m
ESCAPE: 090 degrees
PHASE LINE: None
CODE WORDS: Challenge and Reply—Two
    numbers total 10

Mr. Meston, Flynn, and I, totally subdued, made our way back to the Rach La and Long Tau intersection. As we arrived, we saw Mr. Schrader and the five other men walking up the Rach La toward us. Mr. Meston sat down on a large root of a bush and closed his eyes for several seconds. Flynn and I stood nearby and watched the others approach.

"Anything?" Mr. Schrader inquired, even though he easily could see by our demeanor that we'd struck out.

I shook my head. No one said a thing until Mr. Meston looked up at Markel, the radioman.

"Bring the radio," he ordered. Markel moved to Mr. Meston's side and Mr. Meston used the radio to report our need for extraction. After the transmission, Mr. Meston directed us to set up in a semicircle perimeter until the boats arrived. McCollum and Flynn took the right and left flank positions, and I sat down on a clump of grass next to Flynn.

"This is a shitty day, and someone's gonna have to pay," Flynn muttered in my direction.

I put my head down and stared at my hands. The hands that had tied up Kats.

Why hadn't he snapped the tape and saved himself? I wondered. He must've banged his head when the boat had swamped, or he had gone into the water and had hit his head beneath the boat. That had to have been the answer. He had been knocked unconscious. So, who was gonna pay for that?

I glanced at Lieutenant Meston in the center of our circle. He was our leader, a part of us, yet somehow he seemed singled out and solitary. He saw me looking and returned my gaze. I stared for another couple of seconds, then I looked away, knowing that it was he the Navy would blame. I believed the lieutenant already had figured that out. And it was a shame. No one was a culprit in this. Katsma's death was just a sad, unfortunate, heartbreaking accident.

My ears picked up a distant vibration, and I recognized the whirring sound of helicopters. Checking the sky for several seconds, I finally spotted two Seawolves approaching from the west. They were flying along the Long Tau's southern bank, right over the top of us, no doubt having been called in on the search for Katsma's body.

As the helos passed by, I saw the gunner in the lead chopper give us a wave of recognition. I waved back once. The gunner in the second helo just looked. I looked at my teammates and saw Markel and McCollum greeting the Wolves' presence with waves of their hands. As always, we were glad to accept the help of our friends in the air.

A few minutes later, Mr. Meston directed two PBRs to our location. Having intercepted the Dust-off transmission earlier, the thirty-one-foot river patrol boats, each bearing five-man crews, had hurried to assist us. The ten of us split into two groups and boarded the boats for transport to *Mighty Moe*.

While we journeyed downstream, I studied the river along the southern bank for a minute. Then my eyes focused on the water splashing beside the boat. This is the water that got Kats, I thought to myself. Fifty or sixty feet deep, with a six-knot current, the Long Tau River had taken my mate. Dammit. Water was supposed to be a SEAL's friend.

"Smitty." Mr. Meston's voice broke my train of thought. I turned my eyes to the lieutenant.

"Smitty, I want you and Mr. Schrader to stay with the PBR and keep looking for Katsma's body. The rest of us will go back to the base. I'm gonna have to get with Lieutenant Salisbury over this and fill him in on the details."

I nodded my head. "Aye, aye, sir."

"I still don't know what the hell could've happened," Mr. Meston grumbled.

"Me neither," I declared.

We didn't wait long to find out. When the PBRs reached *Mighty Moe*, everyone from our platoon but Mr. Schrader and me boarded the big boat. Lieutenant Jackson immediately explained the accident to Lieutenant Meston. Mr. Meston, in turn, sent Moses from *Mighty Moe* to join us on the river patrol boat and our search. Since Moses had been in the Boston Whaler with Katsma when it was swamped, he started telling me the grim details as the PBR moved away from the LCM-6.

"When the Boston Whaler came along the port side of *Mighty Moe*, the coxswain all of a sudden cut the gas, causing the bow to dip. With seven men aboard, plus the .30-caliber machine gun and two sandbags in the bow, this was a bad move. Three of the boat support people stepped on the starboard gunnel, grabbing for *Mighty Moe*. This was the second bad move. That's when we capsized. There was no need to panic, 'cause the Whalers won't sink, anyway. I saw Doc try to hold Katsma, but he lost his grip. Kats went underwater and never came back up." Moses stared at me for a reaction.

"Shit," was all I gave him.

Moses looked out of the boat at the water and spat.

"I'm sure he smacked his head under *Mighty Moe*," he said, looking back at me.

"What makes you so sure," I wanted to know.

"'Cause we turned over right into *Mighty Moe*, and the current was sucking us beneath her. I'll bet he hit his head on the prop guards."

Moses's theory made sense. After all, in UDT training back in '65, all of us had been tied just like I had tied Katsma, then we had been tossed in deep water where we kicked and swam like porpoises in order to pop our heads above water for air. The exercise hadn't been that difficult.

"He had to be knocked out to keep him from coming up," Moses finished his supposition.

I nodded my head, then quietly said, "He'll come up sooner or later, and I want to send him home where he belongs. Keep your eyes peeled." I sat down on the starboard side of the PBR as we cruised down the Long Tau close to the southern bank. My eyes darted everywhere, as the body could be anywhere. Somewhere in that great river was my teammate, and I was determined to find him.

After twenty minutes, we'd traveled downstream about three miles. The coxswain turned the boat to the port side and crossed five hundred meters of water to the opposite shore, where we headed slowly upstream in our search.

The sun was cranked to the hilt, scorching me. I glanced at its blazing yellow face and the beast blinded me in return. Closing my eyes, I watched dancing spotlights torch my brain.

Opening my eyes again, I blinked rapidly, then squeezed my eyelids together in my fight to defeat the incessant sun spots. After several seconds, they plagued me still. But like all human beings who occasionally have been dumb enough to glare at the sun, I'd been in this position before, and I knew the little bouncing buggers would soon go back to wherever it was they had come from.

Halfway ignoring the spots, I glanced around inside the boat at the crew. All of the men seemed rather chipper. I hated that for a moment until I realized we had to work at staying lively for the sake of team morale. We couldn't allow Kats's death to destroy us.

I've got to let this go, I spoke inside myself. Kats's destiny was in bigger hands than mine now, so I had to let him go. My other teammates would be counting on me to be a hundred percent ready for the next mission, which meant being mentally "up." With these thoughts in mind, I forced a grin at Mr. Schrader, who was staring at me.

"He was a good man," I stated loudly. "Let's win this stinking war and make sure he didn't die in vain."

Mr. Schrader gave me a thumbs-up and said, "We'll kick some ass."

But for the next eight hours, our asses got kicked by stifling heat, humidity, and the tedium of doing nothing but making runs up and down the big river. Even my eyes were sunburned when we finally gave up and went back to the base.

"His body will surface in a day or two," I told the coxswain in an attempt to keep things somewhat positive.

"Yeah," he replied, "if the sharks don't eat him first."

I hadn't forgotten the sharks; I just didn't want to talk or think about them. And those giant, God-awful, saltwater rats would rip away at a gallant SEAL. Damn them. When Moses and I, sunburned and tired, arrived at our barracks just after dark, Brown informed us of a meeting in the morning at 0830 hours. We were to gather in the TOC (Tactical Operations Center) with

Lieutenant Salisbury, no doubt to hear all sides of the story of Katsma's death and for a needed pep talk.

I walked to my cubicle and found Funkhouser sitting up in his bed, protected by his mosquito net and writing a letter. He lowered his pen and pad of paper as I reached the foot of my bed.

"Did you find him?" he inquired, his voice hoarse from the flulike illness, which had kept him from the mission rehearsal.

"No," I replied, "but we will." I sat down on my foot-locker to untie my boots. I started jerking impatiently at the laces, which didn't seem to want to cooperate.

Funkhouser, observing my touchy behavior, was considerate and asked no questions, such as the natural "What happened?" He undoubtedly had been told the main details several times already.

After several more frustrating seconds, I pulled off my left boot and shoved it beneath the corner of my bed.

"You got any whiskey?" I asked impulsively, glancing at my roommate.

"Yeah. You want a shot?"

I nodded my head and bent down to untie my right boot.

"Open my locker and it's right on top," Funkhouser offered. "Pour yourself whatever you want, and give me a glass. I need something strong to kill this crud I've got."

I got my boot off, slipped it under my bed and moved to Funky's footlocker. I lifted the trunk lid, gathered the essentials, and in less than a minute, Funky and I were gulping Early Times whiskey. He was trying to cure the crud, and I was trying to sink the sharks. After several shots apiece, our conscious vexations ceased as we passed out in our beds.

The next thing I knew, someone was yelling, "Reveille!" just outside our cubicle. I rubbed my face awake and opened my eyes, groggily aware that I'd been dreaming that Katsma was dead. A few seconds later, I realized it was not a dream at all; rather, it was a dreadful truth that had slimed over my brain's control room. The cleanup process would take a while.

Looking at my Rolex watch, I saw that it was 0635 hours. I climbed out of the sack and got dressed for breakfast. Thinking about eating, I remembered Bolivar and fed him a half dozen beetles I'd imprisoned in a small glass jar. For a moment, I was tempted to reach under Funkhouser's mosquito net and interrupt the sound sleeper's snoring by shoving a beetle into his mouth. The thought was fleeting, however, and I left my sick roommate alone with his feverish visions.

At the mess hall, I ended up sitting at a table already occupied by Flynn, Brown, and Moses. All three greeted me, then returned to their conversation.

"Bucklew went back to CONUS," Flynn said, referring to the continental United States, as he chewed some food.

"What for?" Moses asked.

Flynn smacked his lips. "A death in the family, I guess."

"That's goin' 'round," Brown commented.

I stabbed my fork into a link sausage and poked the whole thing into my mouth. Having eaten little the day before, I was famished.

Moses set his fork on his cleaned plate and picked up his coffee cup. Before drinking, he said, "It's supposed to rain like hell today."

"Great," Flynn grumbled. "Another one of those days where you gotta jump in the river to dry off."

Moses chuckled. "And we'll prob'ly be out there gettin' soaked to the bone." He sipped from his coffee cup.

"What makes you think so?" asked Brown.

Moses swallowed, set down his cup, and replied, "It's called 'gettin' right back in the saddle after you've been thrown.' The officers aren't gonna let us sit around and stew. They're gonna put us back out there."

Flynn nodded in agreement. "First Lieutenant Salisbury is gonna grill us."

"He'll go easy," I interjected softly. "It was an accident, and nobody needs a browbeating over it."

No one said anything for a few seconds. Flynn finally retorted. "We shall see."

Two hours later I found myself in the briefing room with Flynn, Moses, Brown, McCollum, Markel, and Dicey from second squad. Lieutenants Meston and Schrader were also present as we listened to Lieutenant Salisbury's pep talk. His words were encouraging and inspiring, giving all of us a sense of relief.

"However," Mr. Salisbury said, and the tonal change in his voice alone was enough to cause instant apprehension, "there's one more step you will all have to endure."

I glanced at Mr. Meston, whose face looked pale.

"All Foxtrot, PBR, and MST personnel involved in yesterday's exercise will speak individually with the XO at the officers' club, beginning at 0900 hours. The XO will be handling the internal investigation."

Flynn looked at me and raised his eyebrows. He had been right about the grilling; he just had had the wrong guy heating up the coals. Still, I thought an investigation would only show that Kats's death was nobody's fault. That was the truth of the matter, and the truth is the truth. No doubt, all of our stories would correlate, and this tragedy would be put to rest.

I was called in to the Lieutenant Commander's office at 0950 hours, after Lieutenant Meston and the Boston Whaler crew. The XO, sitting at his desk, had me sit in a chair across from him. He said he wanted to know, in exact detail, how I had tied Kats in our rehearsal. I told him, then took a couple of minutes to write the account on a piece of paper.

"Is tying personnel during exercises, while being transported over water, a frequent occurrence for UDT and SEAL teams?" the XO deliberately and pointedly asked me.

I sensed this question was possibly the biggest one of all, so I ran the answer through my mind for a few seconds before engaging my tongue.

"Yes, sir," I replied steadily. "On the Colorado River, during the escape-and-evasion course, the UDT instructors tied me the same way I tied Katsma. This is routine, sir."

The XO studied my face for a moment, then said, "Add that information to your written report."

As I wrote, he told his yeoman via his intercom to send in five crewmen of the PBR. In less than a minute the office door opened and the five men entered. The lieutenant commander told them to stand behind my chair.

"Are you finished, Smith?" he asked me, sounding impatient.

"Yes, sir," I answered as I wrote my last two words and punched a period at the end.

"All right," the XO said, opening his top desk drawer and lifting out a roll of electrical tape. The tape was identical to that which I had used in the mission rehearsal.

"I want you to tie all five of these men's hands in the precise manner you tied Katsma's hands," the XO instructed me as he reached the tape out to me across his desk.

I took the tape and stood up. Turning around, I glanced at the faces of the crew of the PBR, with whom I had searched for Kats's body. Their faces were as red and sunburned as mine.

"I'll be tying your hands behind your backs," I informed them, then I walked around the first man, who happened to be the coxswain. He cooperated by moving his hands behind his back for me. Just as I had done Kats, I wrapped the tape three times around the coxswain's wrists.

After taking a couple of minutes to tie the other four men's hands, I looked at the executive officer and nodded my head.

"All right," he said, sitting forward in his chair, "I want all of you to attempt to break loose, right now." Simultaneously, the men strained and pulled, and in a matter of a few seconds, all five snapped the tape and displayed their freed hands. The XO stared for a moment, then sat back in his chair. I could almost see his mind going a hundred miles an hour.

"Thank you," he finally said. "You're all dismissed."

I walked back to my barracks, glad that the quizzing was done.

At 1400 hours, Lieutenant (jg) Schrader gave Foxtrot Platoon a warning order. The warning order was a "heads up" that a mission was imminent. At 1900 hours, Mr. Schrader would brief us on a twenty-four-hour recon and river ambush.

I gathered my gear for the op, then checked out Sweet Lips from the armory. I hadn't cleaned and oiled her as well as usual after the mission rehearsal, so I took her to the cleaning table outside my barracks. Using diesel fuel and a couple of firm bristle brushes, I gave the shotgun a real good scrub. When I finished, Sweet Lips looked pretty enough to kiss, which I did in front of two of my teammates.

"You must be awful horny," McCollum said with a chuckle.

"I just wanna keep my lady happy," I replied, wiping the stock once more with a cloth. "After all, she never complains, does everything I want, and smells and looks better than you do."

"I agree!" Moses guffawed, pointing a teasing finger at McCollum. I laughed with Moses, and Muck finally broke a smile. He slowly unzipped his pants and dropped them to his knees. In true SEAL tradition, he was wearing no skivvies.

"Smell and look at this," he smirked as he turned around and bent over, sticking his bare rear end at us. We just laughed harder.

I took Sweet Lips with me to my cubicle, where I intended to crash for a couple of hours before supper. As I crawled into bed beneath my mosquito net, I looked at my Rolex watch to check the time. The watch registered 1405 hours, which had passed at least an hour earlier. I tapped on the glass face with my right index finger, but the watch was dead. I shook it on my wrist to no avail.

Looking at Funkhouser, who was still sick in bed and lying on his back, I found him staring at me.

"What time is it, Funky?" I asked him. He raised his left arm in front of his face and gazed at his Rolex.

"Fifteen-fifteen hours," he reported, then dropped his arm on his chest. "What's up?"

"Got a briefing at nineteen hundred hours," I told him, giving my watch another shake. The face stared back at me, showing no life. "Wake me up at seventeen hundred hours if you're awake."

I closed my eyes and relaxed my body. After only a minute, I got my mind slipped into neutral. I began drifting into another world.

". . . funny your watch quit today," printed out in my brain. For a few seconds, I didn't know where this had come from. It was maybe part of a dream. "Of all days, it quits just after Kats dies. You think that's an omen of some kind?"

Suddenly, I was awake and focused on Funkhouser's voice. I opened one eye and rolled my head toward my roommate.

"No," I flatly stated. Funkhouser just stared back at me.

I closed my eyes and turned away. I breathed deeply, let my muscles relax and looked for slumber. But it was too late. Sleep had run away without me. Funkhouser's interruption had shifted my brain into reverse and I flashbacked to the day before. It was there I drowned until Funkhouser told me it was 1700 hours.

"How'd you sleep?" Funkhouser asked as I climbed out from under the mosquito net.

"Like a baby," I lied, not wishing to discuss the things that had kept me awake. I slipped into my coral booties and asked Funky if he wanted me to bring something back for him from the mess hall.

"Yeah," he muttered, "a nice breast."

I ignored him and headed for the latrine. After doing my duty, I went to the mess hall and loaded up on steak and potatoes.

At 1900 hours, I gathered with McCollum, Moses, Markel, Flynn, and Brown in the briefing room above our barracks. Mr. Schrader came in and told us about a twenty-four-hour patrol and ambush scheduled for early in the morning. We were to board *Mighty Moe* at 0400 hours. Echo Platoon was going to insert about two thousand meters east of our insertion point on the Song Dinh Ba. Since the three VNs who were supposed to go with us had left for Saigon the previous day without checking out, there would be only the seven of us going on this mission. That was no big deal to me.

When the briefing ended, McCollum and I walked to the Quonset hut for a beer. I had only one, as I didn't like to drink a lot on the night before an operation.

There was a good chance of dehydration out there in the hot sun when a person's veins were floating in alcohol.

McCollum swigged a couple of beers before sitting down at the piano. As he started clunking the keys, my attention centered on the human skull resting on top of the piano. It was the skull I had found in the jungle several weeks before and had "loaned" to the bar to spruce up the decor. Someone had secured a candle inside it, and now the flaming wick glowed eerily behind the eye sockets.

McCollum suddenly erupted into song:

> "The ship goes sailing down the bay,
> Good-bye, my lover, good-bye!
> We may not meet for many a day,
> Good-bye, my lover, good-bye!
> My heart will evermore be true,
> Tho' now we sadly say adieu;
> Oh, kisses sweet I leave with you,
> Good-bye, my lover, good-bye!
> The ship goes sailing down the bay,
> Good-bye, my lover, good-bye!
> 'Tis sad to tear my heart away!
> Good-bye, my lover, good-bye!"

The twenty men in the bar applauded politely as McCollum did his usual big ending. The moment the clapping quieted down, Muck sang the song again, this time substituting vulgar words in strategic locations. And this time when Muck finished singing, the applause was thunderous.

"Thank you!" McCollum shouted, waving a hand in the air. "Now here's a song for the other woman in your life!"

After a fancy introduction across the ivories, McCollum started singing more soberly:

" 'M' is for the million things she gave me,
'O' means only that she's growing old,
'T' is for the tears were shed to save me,
'H' is for her heart of purest gold,
'E' is for her eyes, with lovelight shining,
'R' means right, and right she'll always be,
Put them all together, they spell 'Mother,'
A word that means the world to me."

As McCollum sang the last word, the ovation was greater than ever. Everyone clapped and cheered for his dear old mom, including me. My mother's weekly letter, usually with a few lines from Dad, was always an uplift, as was her occasional package of candy, magazines, and books.

McCollum's song reminded me that I owed Mom and Dad a letter, so I left the Quonset hut for my cubicle. When I arrived there, I saw that Funkhouser was gone. I suspected he was at the mess hall, trying to eat his way back to health.

Taking a pad of paper and a pen from my footlocker, I kicked off my coral booties and crawled into my bed. I wrote an upbeat letter to my parents, choosing to mention Katsma's death only in passing. I didn't want to upset my parents and cause them to worry, so I wrote mostly of pleasant and humorous things, like Muck's mooning me. McCollum, I was sure, would be happy to hear me say his moon-job was something I considered pleasant, but there in the Rung Sat Special Zone, it was, comparatively speaking. Compared to the sight of someone's blown-out brains, a healthy, bare ass looked damn good.

After half an hour, I finished the letter. I felt sleep touching my eyes with his invisible hand, so I decided to catch him this time around.

The next thing I knew, Flynn was waking me. "Hawk, it's 0330. We board the LCM in thirty minutes."

"My watch quit," I sputtered, thrashing at my mosquito net with my arms. I stumbled out of bed and got dressed in my cammo clothing. Then I made a head call and washed my face and brushed my teeth.

As I swished a mouthful of water, I looked at my face in the mirror over the sink. I was wide awake now, ready to resume my profession as a swamp warrior. I had no smile for the mirror, only a glare. Guerilla warfare brought out the ferocity in a man. Confronting the enemy deep in his own territory demanded a bastard, not a good ol' boy. Believe me, my face that morning did nothing to bolster the image of a young and handsome gentleman.

My gear was ready, so I gathered everything in my arms and carried it to the dock. I boarded *Mighty Moe* with my teammates.

At 0400 hours, we moved down the Long Tau. The sky was black. No moon or stars were visible. With nothing to see, I lay down against the starboard bulkhead and closed my eyes. If I could manage to fall asleep, I would get two and a half hours of shut-eye before we arrived at our insertion point.

The hum of *Mighty Moe*'s engines seemed loud at first, but the more I relaxed, the less distracting was the sound. After a few minutes, I even relished the steadiness of it. Steady, even, solid, consistent. Just like I someday wanted my life to be. Like I *hoped* it would be. For that kind of life, though, I would need to change, and I wasn't sure I could. I'd need to give up the risks and life-threatening dangers that I'd always gone for. The only cure, I supposed, was to grow up. I was finding that the Rung Sat Special Zone had a way of expediting the process.

I gradually slipped into semiconsciousness. While I

was visiting there, worrisome things took a back seat to delightful visions of Scotland, Texas. I saw myself riding a black horse in front of my little house on the hill. It was a splendid sight.

When I awoke from my dreaming, I found I was riding black waves in a black world. Hello, Vietnam. Yes, it's you again.

With nothing for me to do, my choice was either to go back to sleep or to stay awake. I chose sleep, but I stayed awake. That's how it went sometimes.

After what seemed a long while, the sky started to glow ever so slowly. Dawn had never missed an engagement yet. She'd been late a few times, like the early morning I had heard a whitetail buck horning a small tree right in front of my blind, and I couldn't see squat until he was gone, but she always showed up eventually. Eventually became then as our squad prepared to insert.

We made a fake insertion first, then a second. The third time was the charm. As usual, I jumped off the boat ramp first, plopping into the mud of the Song Dinh Ba riverbank. The mud felt cool on my left hand, which I'd stuck out to avoid a nose dive, but I didn't pause to savor the experience. Instead, I scrambled ahead into the thick brush. My six teammates followed.

I went ten meters into thick nipa palm and waited in an expanse of skunkweed. Lieutenant (jg) Schrader came up beside me, and we waited a while. My ears were tuned to the jungle, listening for sounds of human activity.

Ten minutes later, after hearing nothing but distant birds greeting the rising sun, Mr. Schrader motioned me to lead out. The going got tough immediately. Thick, tangled brush clawed at my every move. The ground was a mire, sucking at my boots. Mobs of mosquitos sucked at my blood.

After only a hundred meters, Mr. Schrader wanted

me to stop. He whispered to me that Flynn, who was lugging the heavy M-60 machine gun, was having a hard time. He needed a rest.

I knew from the previous day's briefing that we had another 450 meters of that dense vegetation before we reached our ambush site on a small tributary branching off the Song Dan Xay. At the slow rate we were advancing, that meant another two hours on patrol. Two hours that would feel like twenty.

As we waited, I looked at the hog tracks that were everywhere around me. A stick cracked ahead of me and I automatically pointed Sweet Lips in the direction of the sound. The safety was already off and my index finger lightly caressed the smooth trigger.

Another twig broke. My heart stepped up its drumming. I glanced at Mr. Schrader, who had his M-16 aimed toward the oncoming mystery.

The snapping hurried closer, and I saw movement in the brush only thirty feet away. A low-standing, dark-colored shape materialized, and another appeared beside it. As the objects came closer, I recognized them to be wild boars. Five or six more followed the first two. Appearing to weigh fifty to sixty pounds, they looked a lot like the javelinas back home.

When the hogs closed to within ten feet, the lead boar stopped and stared at me. His nose lifted slightly and I watched the nostrils flare as he sniffed the air.

Suddenly, the hogs panicked and started running in frenzied circles and chaotic zigzags. One almost brushed my pant leg as it streaked by at a hundred miles an hour. Had it crashed into me, the animal easily could've broken my leg.

After twenty seconds of disorder, the herd disappeared, leaving behind some screeching birds and some hammering hearts. I looked at Mr. Schrader, who was wiping his brow and grinning at me.

"That one almost took off your nuts," he whispered, then motioned for me to take the point and resume the patrol.

We reconed about a hundred meters when Mr. Schrader stopped me. He had us rest again for ten minutes, which irritated me. The area we were in was supposedly not hot for enemy activity; therefore, we should have moved a little faster. Thank goodness we didn't have three or four thousand meters to recon that day because we'd have never gotten it done at that slow rate.

Three pit stops and almost two hours later, we finally reached the Song Dan Xay, a river that was five to six hundred meters across. I moved another forty meters south along the bank and found a small stream branching off to the west. This was where we were hoping the VC would float a sampan or two sometime in the next twenty hours. If they would cooperate, we planned to detonate twenty pounds of C-4 explosives beneath them and flip all boatmen into the water. Moses and I, the designated swimmers, then would enter the stream, with our K-bar knives at the ready, to capture one or two prisoners.

While the others held back, I slowly reconed the bank of the stream. I found lots of deer tracks, but no signs of humanity. When I made my way back far enough so Mr. Schrader could see me, I waved him on.

It took but a few minutes to set up our ambush overlooking the stream. Flynn, with the M-60 machine gun, took the right flank, and McCollum, toting the M-79 grenade launcher, positioned himself five meters from Flynn. Mr. Schrader settled in next, with Markel dropping a few meters behind him into a thicket with the radio. Both of them had M-16 rifles. Brown found a hiding place just off the bank with his M-16, followed by Moses, also carrying an M-16. I secured the left flank position with my steady girlfriend in my arms.

Once we were well situated, Mr. Schrader signaled to

Moses and me to plant the haversack of explosives in the water. As we'd rehearsed, Moses and I walked down the bank opposite the flow of the stream. I hoisted the haversack, which was much heavier with weights than during our practice, while Moses strung out the electrical firing line that extended to Mr. Schrader's location.

When the firing line reached its full length, Moses and I put on our fins and slipped into the water. We swam until we ended up smack-dab in front of Mr. Schrader, in the middle of the stream, where we dropped the weighted haversack and watched it disappear as it sank toward the bottom. Then we swam back to shore and retook our places on the bank of the stream.

For a short while, I felt refreshed and invigorated, as I was soaked with cool water. But as the temperature rose, my wet cammo clothing and long johns warmed and bonded tightly to my skin. I became itchy and uncomfortable, but there was nothing I could do but sit through a long drying-out period.

As the daylight hours slowly passed, I got pretty bored. Dark clouds had moved in and the day was dismal. Nothing interesting happened to speed things along. Due to habit, I found myself looking at my watch about every hour, but each time, I was reminded that the watch had stopped working the previous afternoon. I was forced to guess at the time of day.

Sometime around 1600 hours, a greenish-blue duck flew by just above the water. I followed it with my eyes until it disappeared. A minute later, the duck came back and landed in the stream just twenty meters out from my position. It quacked six times, sounding comparable to a dinner bell to me. I took a can of C rats and a canteen from my backpack, and I ate while watching the duck bob for fish.

During the next couple of hours, Mamma-san Nature did her thing. She slowly hung a curtain of darkness while gently easing the tide in on us. At 1930 hours, according to Moses's watch, we were sitting in two feet of water. Then it started raining hard. For two hours, the tiny missiles buffeted our bodies.

Just as the rain finally began slacking off, I heard voices fifty to seventy meters upstream. I alerted the others, but when the rain stopped a couple minutes later, so did the voices. Dead silence dropped on us like the closing of a coffin.

With no visible moon providing light, I couldn't see very well. I did my best to look over the dark water, seeking the black shape of a sampan.

Suddenly my heart leapt into my mouth as an elongated object floated in front of me. Sampan! I thought. I was just about to jerk three times on the communication line between me and Moses when I realized I was seeing only a big log. I slumped back a little from my stiff, upright posture and took a deep breath.

Just as I was feeling relief over the fact that I hadn't sent out a false alarm, the line tied to my right wrist was pulled three times. Moses had mistaken the log for a sampan. Before I could do anything about it, Mr. Schrader set off the charge in the water, which erupted right where we had dropped it. I couldn't see how the explosion affected the log, as it was too dark.

In the few seconds of silence following the blast, I shouted, "It's only a log!" Regardless, someone down the line opened up with his M-16. A moment later, the M-60 spewed dozens of rounds across the small stream. I watched the tracers streak through the night.

As everyone else started shooting, I cursed as loud as I could, yet I couldn't hear my cry. The ruckus was too much. Disgusted, I pointed Sweet Lips upstream and let her scream for me. Once, twice, thrice—she belted out my frustration.

A grenade went off on the opposite shore, then another blew in the water. I felt like swearing, but I started laughing instead. The fact that seven grown men were shooting the hell out of nothing struck my funny bone.

"Hoo-yah!" I yelled, then Sweet Lips echoed me three more times.

As I reloaded, someone down the line sent up a pop flare over the stream. In the sudden light, I saw a massacred log drifting away. Behind it floated a multitude of splinters from its wooden anatomy.

"It's only a log!" I shouted again. A couple of seconds later, the noise ended. My eardrums, though, didn't stop reverberating. The resounding ring of another assault snaked around inside my head like a dentist's drill gone wild.

"It was only a damn log!" Mr. Schrader's voice stabbed my ears.

"Yeah," said Moses next to me, "but it's just a stick now."

I chuckled at the remark.

The pop flare died in the black of night as Mr. Schrader took the radio handset from Markel and reached the LCM-6.

"Barracuda Seven, this is Dogfish One. Be advised, mission is compromised. No enemy contact. Request extraction as soon as possible."

After the transmission, I heard the others moving toward my position. I rolled up the parachute suspension line between Moses and me and slipped it into a pant pocket, then I stowed my gear and put on my backpack. When everyone was ready, Mr. Schrader told me to head for the Song Dan Xay just thirty meters to the east.

With the tide having edged out, we didn't have to walk in water; instead, we walked in mud. The stuff sucked at my every step, but the struggle lasted only a couple minutes. When I reached the Dan Xay riverbank,

I felt like I was home free. I could hear the sweet sound of *Mighty Moe*, coming to steal us away.

Mr. Schrader directed the boat to us by using brief radio communication and a red-lens flashlight. *Mighty Moe* drew closer and closer while we waited in the heavy vegetation on the riverbank for the boat ramp to drop down. Seconds later, as the ramp lowered, it hit the branches of a tree and broke apart a large red ant nest. Thousands of ants were scattered all over the ramp and all over us. Nevertheless, we hurried across the ramp and onto the boat, stepping on the ants as we went. I doubted if many of them died, as they were as tough as pit bulls. I was reminded that they have jaws like mad dogs, too, when one of them chomped into my neck. I took immediate revenge by grabbing the little gook and biting him in half with my teeth. I spit his ass into the night, then found a seat at the other end of the boat, as far away from his comrades as possible.

Mr. Schrader sat down next to me a couple minutes later as we headed back to Nha Be. I made out his eyes looking at me in the dark.

"I just found out they found Katsma's body," he said. His words slugged into me like a heavyweight's fist.

"Where?" I blurted.

"Washed ashore near where he went down," Mr. Schrader said, his voice shaking a little. He paused a moment, then added, "His hands were free, but his feet were still tied. Part of his face was eaten."

I crumbled inside. Tears welled up in my eyes, and I fought to hold them.

Mr. Schrader kept going. "Some of the flesh on his hands was gone, too. The Vietnamese found him first and took his Rolex watch."

I couldn't hear anymore. I rose up and walked into a darkness like I'd never known before.

CHAPTER NINE
Mission Seventeen

"I have seen children starving. I have seen the agony of mothers and wives. I hate war."

Franklin D. Roosevelt,
Chautauqua, New York,
August 14, 1936

DATE: 4, 5 November 1967
TIME: 041830H to 050530H
UNITS INVOLVED: Foxtrot 1, MST-3, PBR
TASK: Overnight river ambush
METHOD OF INSERTION: PBR
METHOD OF EXTRACTION: LCM-6
TERRAIN: Thick water palm
TIDE: 1720H-12.5 feet, 2240H-7.5 feet, 0400H-13.1 feet
MOON: 1/4
WEATHER: Heavy rain
SEAL TEAM PERSONNEL:
Lt. Meston, Patrol Leader/Rifleman, M-16
Lt. Flynn, Ass't. Patrol Leader/Rifleman, M-16
RM2 Smith, Point/Rifleman, Shotgun
MM2 Funkhouser, Automatic Weapon, Stoner
BT2 McCollum, Ordnance/Grenadier, M-79
HM2 Brown, Corpsman/Radioman/Rifleman, M-16
LDNN Ty, Ass't. Point/Rifleman, M-16

AZIMUTHS: 190 degrees-50m
ESCAPE: 000 degrees
CODE WORDS: Insert-Yale, Ambush Site-
   Harvard, Extract-Dartmouth, Challenge and
   Reply—Two numbers total 10

The early morning was dark and quiet as our squad walked across the naval base to our barracks. The mobile support team followed behind us. No one seemed in the mood for talking, but we had to debrief.

We went upstairs to the briefing/intelligence room, and Mr. Schrader quickly reviewed the mission. When he asked for suggestions or comments, there were none. The recommendation that came to my mind was, "Next time, let's not bark up the wrong tree," but I didn't say it. The guys may not have been able to grasp such sophisticated humor at that early hour. The second suggestion I had was, "Let's patrol a little faster next time," but I didn't mention that either, because next time Mr. Meston would be back in charge, not Mr. Schrader. Mr. Schrader had been just a substitute while Mr. Meston had filled out reports and met with the XO about Katsma's accident.

When Mr. Schrader dismissed us, I went straight to the showers. I stepped into the shower with my cammo clothing still on my body and Sweet Lips in my hands. The water felt good as it cascaded off the top of my head and down my back. As always, I gave my shotgun a good rinsing, then I peeled off each article of clothing as it got cleaned.

When I finished, Brown was ready to take my place in the shower. I scooped up my wet clothes and my gun and moved out of Brown's way. I then hung the clothing in the dressing room before heading for our berthing space and my cubicle. I knew I was a sight to see, stark naked and carrying a 12-gauge pump shotgun. If my past girlfriends could have gotten a glimpse of me then, they'd have realized what they were missing. On the other hand, the manic depressive, schizophrenic, serial-killer look wasn't playing too well in Abilene.

Once at my cubicle, I stood Sweet Lips in the corner and slipped into my blue-and-gold T-shirt and UDT swim trunks. In a flash, I climbed into bed and fell asleep when my head hit the pillow.

Sometime around 0700 hours, I awoke and looked at my watch. It was working again, but it showed 1827 hours, and I knew that was nowhere near the correct time. I pulled on my coral shoes, then walked to the mess hall for breakfast. Funkhouser, already there and pretty much recovered from his illness, was eating with McCollum. I grabbed a plate of "shit on a shingle," which was ground beef mixed with gravy, and some peaches and coffee and sat with the two men.

I wolfed down my food and finished when Funky and Muck did.

"What time is it?" I asked Funkhouser as we left the chow hall.

"Zero seven twenty-four," he informed me, and I set my watch.

"Let's run around the base," I suggested. Both men looked at me like I'd just turned into a moron.

McCollum snorted and said, "I want my shit on a shingle to come out my ass, not up my throat."

I knew I wouldn't push myself hard enough to vomit, so I broke into a jog and went off by myself. The morning air was cool and tonic. I enjoyed every step of the easy run.

I ended my exercise at the armory, where I checked out Katsma's M-16. I carried the weapon to my cubicle and grabbed my shotgun, then walked back outside to the cleaning table.

Upon inspection, I found Katsma's rifle somewhat

rusted. The rifle had been submerged in saltwater during our mission rehearsal, and it was obvious that no one had cleaned the weapon after Kats's death.

I tore down the M-16 and dunked every part of it in the tub of diesel fuel. I used the stiffest brushes to clean away the light rust. After drying each piece with a towel, I lubricated them and reassembled everything. The rifle was then ready for a new swamp commando. Whoever that man would be, he would have huge shoes to fill.

I gave Sweet Lips the ultimate cleaning, too, then I returned both weapons to the armory.

Continuing my chores, I took my half-dried cammies and other dirty clothing from the dressing room hangers, folded them, and carried the load to Nga's. When I entered the establishment, two old Vietnamese men were sitting at one of three wicker tables drinking tea. They nodded at me as I passed and walked toward Nga, who was working behind the laundry counter.

"How you, Smit-ty?" the middle-aged woman greeted me. She smiled big, not a bit self-conscious about the three gaps in her grin where teeth were missing.

"Toi manh gioi," I responded, telling her that I was fine. I set the pile of clothing on the counter.

Still smiling, Nga said, "Be ready, two day." She held up two fingers.

I nodded in acknowledgment. *"Chao,"* I said with a little hand wave for good-bye.

"Bye-bye, Smit-ty," she called after me as I walked out of her shop.

Back on the base, I gathered up our platoon's radios, including the PRC-25, a French radio, and two Motorolas. I toted them to the newly built maintenance building, which was a three-story structure with numerous rooms and departments for repairing everything from small equipment to large boats. I entered a compartment for electronic parts maintenance where I took each radio apart. I dried several pieces in a special oven, cleaned them thoroughly, then reassembled the radios. After testing each radio for its workability, I wrapped them individually in clear plastic and sealed them with duct tape in order to waterproof them.

Just as I finished the two-hour duty, Funkhouser walked in and gave me some butt-breaking news. "Plague shots at 1300 hours."

I looked at my watch. "That's in fifteen minutes," I moaned.

Funkhouser bobbed his head up and down. "My ass hurts just thinkin' about it."

Half-petrified over what we would get when we got there, we made the long walk to the barracks as long as possible. I'd rather have reconed a thousand meters of enemy-controlled jungle than have faced Doc Brown's monstrous hypodermic needle and syringe charged with five c.c.s of bubonic plague serum.

"Line up, ladies!" Brown shouted as we walked through the open door of the barracks. Twenty other men were already in line, which Funkhouser and I joined. At the other end operated Brown, teasing and chastising as he stuck one behind after another.

"Drop the skivvies and bend over!" I heard Brown direct. "Let me shove this where the sun never shines."

Mojica, my boat support pal, was two men ahead of me in line. He turned around and looked at me with a sickly grin.

"Doc is makin' me sick," he muttered. "I thought doctors were s'posed to make you well."

I didn't know what to say, so I attempted a smile. My lips felt awkward, though, and the smile fell apart on my face. Mojica shook his head and looked away.

When Mojica's turn came, I watched him as he pointed at the long needle and exclaimed, "Holy shit!"

Doc chuckled. "This'll give you a holy shit, all right."

"What d'ya mean by that?" Mojica demanded in a squeaky, high-pitched voice.

"I mean that the next time ya sit on the john, it'll be a painful experience. You'll be a-callin' on Jesus's holy name, believe me. Now bend over."

Mojica's usual dark complexion was gone as he slowly slid down his skivvies. He stole one more hopeful glance at me as he reached for his ankles, looking like death warmed over.

Doc Brown, milking the suspense for all it was worth, aimed the point of the needle, then hesitated. For five unbearable seconds, Mojica waited for the hurtful poke. He flinched, but before he bolted, Doc froze him by asking him a question.

"Right cheek or left?"

A visible shiver ran through Mojica's body. He closed his eyes, then blurted, "Right."

Instantly, the needle was plunged into his left buttock. Mojica let loose with a bloodcurdling scream that shook the barracks and almost caused me to wet my pants. The boat support person in front of me, whose name I didn't know, fainted and fell to the floor.

Without missing a beat, Doc jerked the needle out of Mojica, loaded a new syringe, and pulled down the passed-out sailor's skivvies. He was in and out with the shot in ten seconds, then looked up at me.

"You're next, Hawkeye," he told me, as if that horrible fact could possibly have escaped me.

Mojica, having hoisted up his own skivvies, pulled up his teammate's skivvies and dragged the unconscious man a few feet out of the way. As Mojica patted the man's face to revive him, Doc readied a dose of serum for me.

"Bend over," he bellowed for the umpteenth time.

I looked him in the eye with a hard glare, sending a message I knew he understood: treat me right or payback will be hell on you.

"Bend over," he repeated, softer this time.

Feeling brave and in control again, I dropped my swim trunks and gave Brown a nice rear view.

"You're pretty," he said.

I glanced back at him and his needle. "That's what they all say."

"Pretty ugly," he finished.

I looked away, anticipating the poke.

"Right or left cheek?" Brown asked.

I smarted off. "Just miss the lovely sack hangin' down in the middle."

A sudden, sharp sting pierced my right buttock. As Brown shoved in the serum, the pain increased. A five-c.c. dose was a big one, and I felt my flesh bulging. Unconsciously, I hung my mouth open as the syringe was emptied, and I realized it only after a string of saliva fell to the concrete floor at my feet.

"Damn!" I muttered as Doc finally extracted the needle.

"Next!" he barked after I pulled up my swim trunks and stumbled away. I managed a look back at Funkhouser, who was next, and he was watching me with terrified eyes. My own pain was so great that I felt no sympathy or care for my roommate. All I wanted to do was lie down in my bed for a few minutes.

Just as I reached my cubicle, Funkhouser emitted a horrendous howl. But that was his problem. That was one time I had to worry about my own ass.

Three and a half weeks later, I was on point and back to worrying about my own as well as six other asses. This was our sixth mission since all of us had received the plague shots with the screaming and moaning that went with them. In contrast, no one was hollering now.

The peacefulness of the jungle was in evidence, and yet, a battle could have erupted at any second. Seven guerrilla fighters looking for trouble on an enemy's travel route amounted to a war waiting to happen. And if one enemy didn't show, you could bet your soaked and shriveled hind end that the other would be there: greetings, Culicidae family, you bloodsucking, disease-carrying bastards.

We were moving at first light, back into the brush, away from our overnight ambush site on the Rach La and Cu Lao Ca Xuc intersection of waterways, since there was not enough cover to have stayed on the stream in the daylight. We'd heard nothing over the long night's downpour. The sky, gray and ugly, threatened overhead. A sinister atmosphere pervaded the swamp.

After wading about 125 meters away from our ambush site, Lieutenant Meston motioned for me to stop. We were at a point where we were well concealed by nipa palm, and it was here where we'd hang out until nightfall. Then we'd move back into position on the stream for another all-nighter.

Mr. Meston signaled for us to form a circle and settle down in the water. He gestured to me to take the first two-hour watch. I walked to one of the more prominent trees outside the men's circle and leaned my back against the trunk. The others got comfortable, if sitting in water up to the armpits could be described as comfy.

Over the next hour or so, the water level went down considerably until it was but a couple inches deep. I kept my eyes and ears open all the while as the others attempted to ignore the mosquitos and sleep.

Glancing at my watch, I saw that it was 0835 hours, then I looked up at the sky, which was very gloomy. Before I looked away, I heard rustling in the brush directly outside the perimeter from me. I clicked off the safety on my shotgun and found the trigger with my shooting finger. A twig snapped, and I slowly swung Sweet Lips toward the sound.

For the next few seconds, I heard nothing. My eyes scanned the brush, but I saw nothing. Sweat trickled down my forehead and into my left eye. The sting forced me to close it. No matter, as I needed only my right eye to take aim.

A sucking noise reached my ears, and I knew there was someone walking in the mud. If that someone was a VC, I intended to shoot him when he broke through the vegetation and came into view.

While I prepared myself for killing, a sudden chopping noise shattered the stillness. A second chop followed and I pinpointed the sound as coming from a mere ten meters away. Then a series of chops rang out and awakened a groggy Lieutenant Meston, who climbed to his feet with a curse.

I waved my arm, getting Mr. Meston's attention, then placed a finger vertically in front of my lips and whispered, "Shhh." Mr. Meston immediately lost the cobwebs and grabbed his M-16 from its resting place in a bush. The chopping, however, had ceased. My brain told me we were compromised as the woodcutter had heard Lieutenant Meston's voice.

I stared at Mr. Meston, waiting for him to give me directions. Flynn stood up beside Lieutenant Meston and they whispered to one another. As they conferred, another chop resonated. Good, I thought to myself, the man had not been spooked off.

Mr. Meston listened for several seconds to more timber slashing, then motioned for me to go get the woodcutter. I waved at Ty to follow me.

As fast as I could, I crashed through the thick vegetation with Sweet Lips at the ready. The woodchopper didn't have time to flee as I was on his case in an instant. He was standing next to the tree he'd been cutting, wearing baggy, rotting, black-pajama-type clothing and holding a makeshift ax.

When the middle-aged woodcutter saw me, all painted up and with my weapon aimed at his guts, he sank to his knees and began pleading in Vietnamese. I moved to within ten feet of him, never taking my eyes or my gun off him.

Ty stepped up beside me. *"Ong co so linh My khong?"* he snapped, asking the woodcutter if he was afraid of American soldiers.

The man, visibly shaking and obviously petrified, bowed up and down like a Buddhist in fervent prayer, babbling as fast as his lips would move.

"Shut him up!" I told Ty.

"Dung noi! Dung yen!"

The man grabbed a rag, which was protruding from his pants pocket and shoved it into his mouth. He bit on the rag to stop his teeth from chattering and to quiet his tongue. Even so, squeaks and squeals emanated from him. Ty had to threaten to slap him three times before he shut up completely.

I picked up the man's ax as Mr. Meston, Brown, and Flynn came through the brush behind me.

"Does he have personal identification papers?" whispered Lieutenant Meston when he reached my side.

"The can-cuoc cua Ong dau?" Ty asked the woodcutter. The man, his eyes wider than ever at the sight of three more commandos, shook his head. He then noticed my K-bar knife before dropping his head and staring at the watery ground.

I felt I could read the woodchopper's mind. He was expecting to be killed, probably soon and silently with my knife. But instead of facing death, he faced me as I stooped down next to him. I grabbed his right arm, felt it quivering, and pulled him to his feet.

My four teammates and I escorted our "prisoner"

back to McCollum and Funkhouser. Mr. Meston radioed
TOC and asked if they wanted the woodchopper for
interrogation. They did. Lieutenant Meston then called
for extraction via LCPLs.

Since we were 125 meters from our ambush and extraction site, we began moving toward it in single file,
with the woodcutter between Brown and Flynn. The
walking was easier than earlier, as the water had re-
ceded to its lowest level, only an inch deep. I wove a
different pattern through the nipa palms in case someone was sitting in wait on our old, water-filled, muddy
tracks.

As I went, a sprinkle of rain tap-danced on my floppy
cammo hat. A wait-a-minute thorn bush grabbed at my
shirt sleeve, then let go as I pulled away. A green pigeon with his beak buried under a hunched-up wing ignored me as I walked past the branch he was perched
on. He was just too cozy to get off his seat, or the dark
sky appeared too unfriendly for that particular flyer to
lift off right then.

A couple minutes later, the unfriendliness turned severe as the rain came hard. The bird knew, I told myself. His instincts had warned him. He hadn't reasoned
it out, because only man reasoned. Instincts, then. Listen to your instincts, Smitty. It may save your life someday.

I maneuvered through the mud and the rain, glancing
back at Mr. Meston every thirty meters, until I reached
the Cu Lao Ca Xuc. As Mr. Meston and Brown approached my position just shy of the riverbank, I sensed
a presence on the water to my right. Trusting my instincts, I quickly turned my head in that direction.
Through the driving rain I made out an oncoming sampan.

Shit! my brain screamed. I wheeled Sweet Lips toward the sampan in a manner that Lieutenant Meston

couldn't mistake. I knew he was reacting to my move and was reflexively raising his M-16 to his shoulder.

"*Lai dai!*" pounded my ears as Meston hollered for the two occupants of the sampan to come to us. At that point, they were but twenty meters away. I saw two young boys, drenched like we were, looking my way with mouths wide open in astonishment.

"*Lai dai!*" Mr. Meston yelled again. The boys obeyed and paddled the sampan right at us.

"Get 'em, Smitty," directed the lieutenant. "Brown, keep your eyes on the prisoner."

As the sampan drew close, I couldn't help but notice the extreme filth of the two boys. Their wet clothes looked as if they were about to rot off their bodies. Their faces were caked with dirt. But I forgot about their poverty and stared at their eyes—the almond-shaped eyes that were focused on the barrel of my shotgun, which was pointed right at them.

"*Gio tay len!*" I shouted as I grabbed the bow of their sampan. Instantly, they raised their hands high above their heads.

The sampan hit the bank and I grounded it onto the beach. Ty helped me give the sampan one hard pull.

"*Dung len!*" barked Ty, and the two boys stood up. "*Di di!*" Ty spit. The boys stepped out of the boat, and Ty ushered them to the older prisoner. Mr. Meston wanted their identification cards, and Ty asked for them. Like the woodcutter, they had none.

Suddenly I saw another sampan drifting toward us. Again, I aimed Sweet Lips at the boat. I glanced back at my teammates, who were concentrating on our three Vietnamese captives.

I knew there was one way to draw their attention.

"*Lai dai! Lai dai!*" I yelled at the top of my lungs. This time there were three people in the sampan, and one of them jumped to his feet. I could see that he was a small boy, and I refrained from shooting him, even though his quick action brought me close. The other two occupants were females, one old and one young.

Out of the corners of my eyes, I saw the barrel of a weapon on each side of me. I looked right, and there was Mr. Meston. I glanced left. Flynn was aiming his rifle at the sampan.

"*Mau len!*" I shouted, telling the Vietnamese people to hurry up.

"There's another boat coming behind them!" Flynn informed us.

Raindrops were running off my hat in front of my eyes. I gave my head a quick, hard shake, then I stared upstream. Sure enough, there was a third sampan with three more occupants.

The lead boat was a few meters from shore when Lieutenant Meston hollered at the other, "*Dung Lai!*" I made out an older boy with two old women in the sampan. They, like the others, showed surprise and fear. What else would you show? I thought. When you were a flick of a finger away from termination, a little fear may just reach up and grab you by the throat. And believe me, fear was working overtime that day on the Cu Lao Ca Xuc.

Both sampans hit the bank before Lieutenant Meston ordered the six people to step ashore. As they stood and followed directions, I saw that their clothing was as rotten as the boys'. They moved quickly to demonstrate compliance, gathering into a tight group beside Lieutenant Meston.

Mr. Meston had Ty ask them for identification, but none of them could produce anything at all. I checked their sampans for papers and found nothing.

"Take 'em to the other three while I find out what TOC wants me to do with 'em," Lieutenant Meston said, looking at Ty and then me.

"Re tay Phai. Di truoc," commanded Ty, pointing his rifle where he wanted the women and children to go. The group moved toward the other prisoners, who watched us approach. The woodchopper's face lit up at the sight of the others, but he refrained from speaking.

When the nine detainees were gathered together, Ty told them to sit down. *"Noi!"* he barked. All obeyed immediately.

"Ong co thay Viet-Cong khong?" Blank faces stared at Ty. Again Ty asked if they'd seen any Viet Cong.

"Da khong," the woodcutter answered negatively.

"Da khong," echoed one of the old women.

Ty looked at me. "Bullshit," he muttered.

As we waited for the LCPLs to arrive, I noticed the small boy who had hopped to his feet in the sampan watching me. He appeared to be about eight or nine years old, and when I looked away, he scooped up a handful of mud and started painting his face like mine. Of course, the hard rain quickly washed his cammo-job away since he had no hat.

"TOC wants the woodcutter for interrogation," Lieutenant Meston informed me when he got off the radio. "The others we'll let go."

The LCPLs were almost upon us before I heard them over the beating rain. Mr. Meston told Funkhouser to hold the woodcutter while Ty and I directed the other Vietnamese people back to their sampans.

As the eight walked ahead to their sampans, the small boy glanced at me several times. When he reached his boat, he gave me a quick smile before climbing aboard.

"Em!" I called to him from the bow of the sampan. He turned and stared at me. I dug into my pants pocket and pulled out a round tin of Skoal chewing tobacco. I dug deeper and found a pack of Wrigley's Spearmint chewing gum, which I held out toward the boy. He grinned and took the gum from my hand.

"Chuc may man," I wished him good luck. He turned to the old woman who had joined him in the sampan and displayed his prize. She looked at the gum, then at me, showing no emotion. I gave her a slight bow, then hurried away to my teammates.

Funkhouser and Ty escorted the woodcutter onto one of the two LCPLs. Lieutenant Meston and Brown followed. McCollum, Flynn, and I stepped onto the other steel-hulled landing craft. The two boats backed away from the shore, the bows swung downstream, then the engines kicked into forward gear.

I took a final look at the small boy. He was still standing in his sampan, peering my way, and I saw him stick a piece of gum in his mouth. He flashed another smile as the rain tore at his tattered clothing.

We pulled away, and I threw a sharp salute at the boy. I froze his image in my mind, then closed my eyes and turned around.

"Chao, little fella," I whispered into the wind.

At the Nha Be base, I escorted the woodcutter to Marine First Lieutenant Winsenson, an old mustang (an officer who came up through the ranks), who was to handle the interrogation. After telling Mr. Winsenson the details of the man's capture, I ate at the chow hall, grabbed a shower, then stretched out in my bed until 1630 hours.

The rest felt good but it was not very long. We were to board an LCPL at 1700 hours and head for another ambush site on the Tac Ong Nghia River about eight hundred meters southwest of the previous site.

I put on fresh long johns and camouflage clothing, fed Bolivar some insects, then grabbed my gear and walked to the dock. The rain had stopped, thank goodness. If it didn't start up again, I'd stay dry for another hour before we inserted. Then I'd be up to my neck in water, as we were inserting at high tide. That's when I'd wish I were a duck and not a schmuck weighted down with tons of gear.

We boarded the LCPL with the same personnel, along with the addition of PR1 Pearson and his M-79 grenade launcher, BT2 Moses, and ADJ2 Markel, both carrying M-16s. That gave us ten men this time. I welcomed the added firepower since we were going back fairly close to a compromised area.

The late afternoon was muggy, and I was glad when the boat got going. I took off my hat to let the air rush over my head as we sped along the Long Tau River. During the hour-and-a-half ride, I contemplated the usual preinsertion topics: life and death. The topic sentence for the first was "Gary Roger Smith is alive and well right now." For the second, "Gary Roger Smith may be dead within the hour."

Since I liked the first topic sentence much better than the second, I'd prepared well to keep the truth of it perpetual. Sweet Lips was my companion, and I was loaded down with ammunition, grenades, claymore mines, flares, food, and water. I was prepared for living. Other people would have to die from time to time for me to live; so dictated a thing called war. I had a strong feeling someone would die that night. My instincts told me this. But my will to live told me it wasn't gonna be me. And I intended to help make sure it wouldn't be any of my teammates.

Since a dry boat ride was a lot more enjoyable than a waterlogged recon, the scheduled hour-and-a-half trip seemed to end in half the time.

Mr. Meston called out for us to lock and load. That meant the fun was over and the ferocity would begin. As the LCPL slowed, I moved to the starboard side of the bow. When the coxswain cut the engine to just above an idle, I got ready to insert. Lieutenant Meston,

Brown, and Flynn collected behind me. The other men grouped on the port side.

As the bow touched into the branches of a nipa palm tree, Lieutenant Meston told me to go. I tossed the cargo net over the bow and climbed down it. I let go and dropped into almost five feet of cool water, and my first thought was, "Thank God I made the riverbank!" If I had fallen short, I would be blowing bubbles where the barracuda and stinging jellyfish played.

Without pause, I waded several paces ahead, making room for the other men to enter the deep water. I heard them splashing behind me as I moved around nipa palm branches, keeping my eyes on the swampland before me. Feeling my way with my legs and feet, every part of me was underwater except my head and neck. All of my gear, and even Sweet Lips, took the wet route. But I'd done this before: I'd gone where no ordinary soldier would go, and that was the key to our success as SEALs. No one was expecting us in the places where they ran into us, which gave us the greatest weapon of them all: the element of surprise.

Our objective was to set up an overnight ambush just a hundred and fifty meters northwest of our point of insertion. That was where a small stream branched off the Tac Ong Nghia. Mr. Meston, using his compass, pointed the way. I looked at my wrist compass for a rough azimuth and eyed the top of a tree standing higher than the rest. With this for my landmark, I headed out. The others fell in line behind me.

Walking in the water was tough. The palms were thick, making for slow going. I found no high spots at all, which kept the water lapping from our waists to our Adam's apples without relief. Darkness was coming fast, bringing with it the eerie atmosphere I'd experienced in the early morning. A ghoulish, ominous ambience surrounded me, and it was beautiful in a swampy sort of way.

Since we discovered no high ground on which to stop and rest, Mr. Meston kept us going until we reached the spot where the small stream should have been. We could see a thirty-meter-wide finger extending through the swamp where no vegetation showed above the deep water. In the trees overlooking this open space, we positioned ourselves for the night watch. I settled in on the left flank, while McCollum took the right. In between, Lieutenant Meston, Brown, Funkhouser, and Pearson set up. Flynn, Moses, Markel, and Ty dropped several meters back for the sake of rear security.

With the water still up to my neck, I was forced to stand as the night descended. Sweet Lips, however, got a break as I lifted her over my head, dumped the water out of her barrel, and propped her up in the branches of a small tree. Then I gave Pearson one end of my parachute suspension line when he waded a few meters to get it. He waded back to his position, stretching the communication link between us. The last thing I saw before the swamp was totally black was Pearson tying the line around his left wrist.

The area was quiet except for the droning of a couple dozen mosquitos that had discovered my head. None of them was brave enough to stake a claim, though, thanks to the working power of a large gob of repellent I had applied while back on the LCPL. The stuff was so effective that the bloodsuckers went away in ten or fifteen minutes, just before the water started receding and my back became a juicy target.

A bit later, I felt some tiny fish biting at the hair on my wrists. It was irritating at first, and I attempted to swish the fish away. They were persistent, however, and I eventually gave up, hoping they'd tire of their game soon. About the time I started enjoying their playful antics, they departed, leaving me alone with my thoughts.

I relished the peace only for a couple of hours. At 2230, the tide was at its lowest level. I was sitting on the bank of the stream in slimy mud and a tiny puddle of water. The mosquitos were back. I believed the two dozen had spent two hours recruiting ten dozen enlistees. I couldn't see them in the dark, but their relentless noise told me the story: parts of me were getting stuck like a pin cushion.

After an hour of torment, rain started falling. This was good in that the mosquitos dissipated; it was bad in that I quickly felt chilled to the bone. Having trouble stifling a sudden cough, I dug the remedy out of my backpack: a small plastic bottle I'd filled with Early Times whiskey. I unscrewed the cap and took a snort. The stuff went down smoothly, and a couple seconds later I felt fire from my throat to my gut. I took another swig, and while enjoying the warmth inside my chest, I put the bottle away.

The rain softened in a few minutes. As it became quiet again, I heard voices upstream to my left. I tugged the suspension line connected to Pearson twice as I brought Sweet Lips up off my lap. I rolled onto my knees in the mud and looked hard over the dark expanse of water in front of me.

The sound of a paddle hitting the side of a boat reached my ears. It was close. I jerked the line three times.

Suddenly I made out a sampan in the glimmer of moonlight. I saw the silhouettes of two people; one was seated and one was standing aft. They were right in front of me for a few seconds, then they were slightly past me and sitting ducks in our kill zone.

Before I could say, "Make your peace with Buddha, boys," Funkhouser's Stoner machine gun shattered the stillness. I reacted instantly by firing my shotgun at the dark figure in the rear of the sampan. In less than a second I fired again. Then I heard M-16s blasting away.

I fired three more times before a grenade exploded in the water. As I reloaded Sweet Lips in the dark, somebody sent up a flare. The sky lit up with a brilliancy comparable to the sudden turning on of all the house lights in a dark theater at the end of a play. The only difference of significance that time was that the lights were coming on at the end of two lives.

Now that I could see clearly, I shoved a sixth shotgun shell into Sweet Lips and looked out at the sampan. The boat had drifted to the other end of our kill zone, but I saw no people in it. Funkhouser took advantage of the light and sprayed the water on both sides of the boat with the Stoner, then Lieutenant Meston tossed a concussion grenade into the stream. It blew a few seconds later, sending an eruption of water into the air.

"Smitty!" hollered Mr. Meston. "Go get the sampan!"

His words were not music to my ears. The last thing I wanted to do was swim away from my teammates in the middle of the night now that we had been compromised. If an NVA detachment found our location before I got back out of the water, I'd be in a hell of a mess. But that was beside the point right then. I'd been given an order, so I quickly pulled my duck fins over my coral booties. I grabbed Sweet Lips and carried her a few meters along the riverbank to Pearson.

"Hang onto my baby," I told him, then I slipped down into the water. I swam for the sampan, but I went only fifteen or twenty meters when shooting spewed forth. The sudden burst of gunfire scared the you-know-what out of me.

In the fading light of the descending flare, I treaded water for several seconds while my teammates shot toward the drifting sampan. I could see bullets tearing up the water near the boat, but I couldn't see who was there that needed killing. One thing was certain: I hoped the guy was dead before I got there.

"Okay, Smitty! Get the sampan!" Lieutenant Meston yelled when the firing stopped. I took my K-bar knife, which I'd had in my hand, stuck the blade between my teeth and struck out after the sampan. I took a last look at the runaway boat before the flare extinguished and I was left in total darkness. Actually, I was in the worst of conditions, as my night vision had been wiped out and I saw only white spots before my eyes. In other words, I was swimming blind.

Continuing my strokes regardless, my nose picked up the strong odor of blood on the surface of the water. Obviously, that told me that somebody was bleeding. Because I was sucking on a very large and very sharp knife, I hoped it was not my own blood.

Taking the knife out of my mouth with my right hand, I immediately felt better. Too many movies had depicted some gallant hero paddling away with a dagger between his lips, but now I knew what a sham I'd been handed. Knives and lips and teeth were not made for one another, I could assure the world.

A few seconds later, I assured myself that the blood in the water was not mine. It was definitely someone else's. At the moment of my relief, a second flare burst in the sky over my head, and there was light in my tiny world again.

I saw the sampan hung up by overhanging branches alongside the opposite riverbank. After swimming forty meters to the craft, I grabbed the bow and looked inside. There I saw the bullet-riddled body of a man dressed in the green uniform of the NVA.

I didn't look twice. I freed the sampan from the low tree limbs and started back toward my teammates with the boat. The going was not impossible as the current was laggard. Still, I was swimming against the flow of the water, and that made it tough enough.

By the time I reached the riverbank, McCollum and Funkhouser pulled me and the sampan with the dead body ashore. I took off my fins and climbed to my feet as the light from a third flare died out.

"One confirmed kill and one probable," Lieutenant Meston told me. "Get your gear and get ready for extraction."

I couldn't see spit again, but somehow I managed to find my backpack and web belt. Pearson walked with me back to the others and gave me some news that broke my heart.

"When we fired when you were in the water, I fired your shotgun. Only thing is, I accidently got mud jammed in the barrel somehow before I fired. The barrel's blown apart." Pearson handed me the shotgun. I slid my hand down the barrel and found the end expanded and split apart. The gun was ruined.

"Sorry," Pearson muttered an apology.

Sweet Lips was only a gun, I told myself. There were other guns. Don't get melancholy over a gun.

I heard the hum of the LCPL in the distance. It was a sound I'd been in love with ever since my first extraction. When I heard one of our boats coming, I was reminded of my mother's humming me to sleep when I had been a little boy. It was a sound that said, "Have no fear. All is well."

As I waited with the others for the boat, I touched Sweet Lips's barrel again. For some reason, I reflected back a half dozen years to when Barbara, the love of my youth, had left me for a truck driver. I had told myself then that it hadn't mattered, and that there were many girls. But Barbara had been one of a kind. When I lost her, I lost a piece of my heart. I'd never before had a gun like Sweet Lips. Yes, I'd need to choose another companion now, but nothing would replace my faithful, tried-and-true shotgun. Somehow, she had not been just a shotgun to me. She had been my nerve and my spirit, my link to the living. "I got his weapon, papers, and documents," I heard Ty tell Mr. Meston, referring to the dead enemy lying in the sampan.

"Good," Lieutenant Meston replied. "Let's get the hell outta here."

The LCPL cruised up the stream toward us, and it was a sight for tired eyes. When the boat bumped against the riverbank, I climbed aboard with Sweet Lips for our last trip home together.

Two dead bodies were left behind for whoever or whatever found them first.

CHAPTER TEN

I left the mess hall after a hearty breakfast and walked to the base armory. I walked past a couple of armory personnel and went to our platoon's cubbyhole where the weapons were stored in cabinets. Only the members of Foxtrot Platoon had access to this particular area. I'd stored Sweet Lips there after cleaning her every part, unusable though she was. The shotgun would be shipped back to the States eventually, and the receiver with the serial number would go to the Naval Weapons Center in Crane, Indiana.

Next to Sweet Lips rested my new weapon, an M-16/XM-148 combo that I'd used on the past three missions. This weapon consisted of a basic M-16 rifle with a grenade launcher installed below the barrel. The trigger for the XM-148 was easily adjusted to sit an inch forward of the M-16 trigger on the right hand side. Having been trained on the use of this versatile combination, which I liked, it was my first choice as a replacement for Sweet Lips. I favored the shotgun in the thick jungle for close range encounters, but the shotgun, I kept having to remind myself, was dead.

I'd fired about seventy 40mm HE rounds through the XM-148 into the Dong Tranh River for practice, and I shot very accurately with it up to two hundred meters. I intended to increase the distance of precision shooting to 350 meters.

"Whatcha doin'?"

I looked up from making a minor adjustment on the grenade launcher's trigger and saw Funkhouser entering the room.

"I'm all done," I answered, turning away from my teammate and propping my new weapon back up in the gun cabinet. "I just moved the 148's trigger a little more forward. No biggie."

Funkhouser and I left the armory and walked toward our barracks.

"Some of us are makin' a run to Saigon at 1100 hours," Funky informed me. "You in?"

"What's the plan?" I asked.

Funkhouser told me with a grin, "The usual! We'll hit a couple bars, wink at the women, eat lunch at the Continental Hotel, go shopping at the PX in Cholon. Sound good?"

I pondered the offer for all of two seconds.

"Yeah," I said, slapping my roommate on the back, "I'm in."

Funkhouser chuckled. "What convinced you, Smitty, the women, the bars, or both?"

"Neither," I lied, keeping a straight face. "It was the lunch."

Funkhouser guffawed, causing me to laugh, too.

"Lunch?" he cracked. "Lunch with who? Nga, or Chi, or that sweet young thing that hangs around the Continental Hotel?"

We entered our barracks, laughing. Doc Brown heard us and met us as we approached our cubicle.

"What's so funny?" he wondered aloud.

Thinking fast, I responded, "The sight of you sticking a plague shot in your own ass!"

Funkhouser gave me a wide-eyed look, then almost died laughing. I just grinned at Brown, who didn't crack a smile. He simply watched Funkhouser carry on for several seconds before sticking a hand out in front of my face, with the palm up. What I saw wiped the grin off my face.

"Time for your malaria pill," Brown told me as he shoved the large, yellow pill closer. I stared at the thing, fully aware of the diarrhea that accompanied it.

Funkhouser's laughter suddenly died when he spotted the unwelcome pill in Doc's hand. "For cryin' out loud, Doc! You're the biggest pain in the ass I've ever known, and I mean that literally. It's Thanksgiving Day, for cryin' out loud!" Grabbing the pill out of Brown's hand, Funky tossed it into his mouth and swallowed it.

"There!" Funkhouser spit. As he walked away and into our cubicle, he called back, "When the thunder starts rumblin' in two hours, Doc, I'm comin' to your cubicle! And when the lightning strikes in three, I'll be sittin' on your bed!"

Funkhouser disappeared, and I was left staring at a second pill which Doc had placed on his upturned palm.

"Your turn, Smitty," he said.

I grabbed the pill. "You really enjoy makin' us suffer, don't you!"

"Suffer?" he said with a mischievous grin. "Hell, I'm constantly savin' your mangy lives around here! Now, swallow the pill!"

"I will," I grumbled, walking away with it in my hand.

"You better!" Brown barked after me.

I entered my cubicle. Funkhouser was standing next to our new apartment-size refrigerator, which we had bought together in Saigon, chugging a shot of whiskey. He gulped it down, burped once, then looked at me. "I'm tryin' to kill that pill before it kills me," he muttered.

I nodded my head, fully understanding what he meant.

"Did you take yours?" Funkhouser inquired of me.

I held out my hand and showed him the yellow monster. Then I took the pill between my thumb and index finger of both hands and snapped the pill in two. "Will you pour me a shot?" Without hesitation, Funkhouser opened the refrigerator and took out the bottle of whiskey. Filling the same shot glass, he held it out to me.

"May you outrun the runs," Funky said as a salute.

I took the glass, popped a half of the pill in my mouth, and swallowed it along with the whiskey. Smacking my lips, I gave the glass back to Funkhouser.

"What about the other half?" he questioned.

I stepped beside my bed and slid Bolivar's wooden cage out from beneath it. I unlatched the mesh-wire lid and swung it open. The boa constrictor struck suddenly and bit at my hand, just missing.

"Why, you little ingrate!" I growled at my pet. "You shouldn't bite the hand that feeds you." I flipped the half pill into the cage, then closed and latched the door. Funkhouser started chuckling as I shoved the cage back under my bed.

"Don't want him to catch malaria," I quipped, smiling at my roommate.

Funkhouser laughed harder. "This should prove interesting. I've never seen a snake with the squirts before."

"And you prob'ly won't this time, either," I countered. "You'll be too busy takin' care of your own."

We spent the next couple of hours staying close to the latrine, lying in bed and listening to country-and-western music, courtesy of Armed Forces Radio, on my portable radio. I was enjoying the music immensely when I heard, "Oh, no." Funky crawled out of his bed and broke into a run for the john. I laughed so hard I cried, knowing that Funkhouser, like all true SEALs, wasn't wearing any underwear to "detain" the problem.

Twenty minutes later, I wasn't laughing anymore. I

was perched on the pot in the john next to Funkhouser. Next to him on the other side sat McCollum, another victim of Doc's "cure." The smell was intolerable, but there was nothing I could do but bear it. A bad case of diarrhea greatly limited one's travel options.

"Hey, Smitty!" My roommate got my attention. "Is half a pill any easier on you than a whole one?"

"Not hardly," I replied. "Next time I'm gonna try just a quarter."

A few seconds of silence slid by, then Funkhouser said, "Let's dissolve the other three-quarters in Doc's coffee."

I thought I heard Funkhouser giggling, but the sudden sounds erupting in my own stall demanded my total concentration.

An hour later, we found ourselves in our black Chevy pickup truck and on our way to Saigon. Pearson was driving fast, as usual. Flynn and Brown were seated in the cab with him. McCollum, Moses, Ty, Funkhouser, and I were drinking plenty of beer in the box. Brown, Moses, and Ty were packing pistols for our protection.

"No snipers today!" Moses announced after we reached the outer limits of Saigon.

"Not on the way in," agreed McCollum, "but this is a round-trip excursion. We might run into trouble on the way back."

Funkhouser finished a can of beer. Then he said, "Let's have fun first, and we'll worry 'bout the trouble later."

As we progressed into downtown Saigon on a tree-lined avenue, I studied the sea of humanity. The sidewalks were crowded with hucksters peddling their wares. Vendors with two-wheeled carts full of coconuts and bananas seemed to be everywhere. Many people rode bicycles that were stacked high with boxes and sacks. Young men on motorbikes zigzagged through intersections, ignoring stop signs. Simply put, the place was clogged.

The first place we went on that day was to the Continental Hotel for lunch. Pearson parked the truck in a luckily found spot a block away, and all eight of us bailed out and walked to the open-air terrace cafe. We confiscated two small tables beneath the veranda and sat down, four men to a table. The cool, shaded area under the roof quickly revived me, as the stifling heat of the city had caused me to feel faint just a minute earlier. So many people, so much traffic, so much carbon monoxide was in this place.

Soon, a waiter came to take our orders. All of us wanted a cheap, cold Tiger beer, except Funkhouser, who decided to splurge and drink a Heineken.

"I've had a rough morning," Funky declared, giving Doc Brown the evil eye. "I've had enough cheap shit for one day, so I'm gonna put something of quality into my system."

I looked at Doc, who was smiling. Don't worry, Doc, I said to myself, we're going to pay you back. And payback can be hell.

I caught the waiter before he left and ordered a Chinese soup with noodles, pork, and red peppers.

"Easy on the peppers," I told him. "It's hot enough today without burning up my throat."

"*Da,*" agreed the waiter as he imitated the wiping of sweat from his brow. "Very hot."

"Also, I want some fried rice," I added.

"*Com,*" he said, writing it on his pad as he walked away.

The eight of us kidded around for a few minutes until the waiter returned with a tray full of bottles of beer and glasses. He set four bottles and four glasses on each table, making sure the Heineken went to Funkhouser.

"I've got a Thanksgiving Day toast to make," announced Funkhouser, holding up his bottle. The rest of us lifted our bottles in the air. I glanced at McCollum, who saw my look and shrugged.

"This is a toast to the three sins of stealing, lying, and drunkenness," Funkhouser stated with a smile. "If you must steal, steal away from sin. If you must lie, lie with one you love. If you must drink, drink with me, for I am your friend."

Funkhouser tipped his bottle into his mouth and drank.

"Aw, shit," muttered Brown, "wasn't that nice?" I gave him a hard look, but he was smiling. When he sipped his beer to honor the toast, I drank mine, too.

"Where'd you get a toast like that, Funky?" asked McCollum after a long swig from his bottle.

"Out of a toaster." Funkhouser grinned.

"Very funny," McCollum retorted sarcastically.

"Actually," returned Funkhouser, "I made it up."

Everyone chuckled and hooted at this apparent lie.

"Made it up, hell," spat Brown, who was sitting at the other table. "A moron couldn't come up with something that good."

We laughed. Funkhouser didn't. Instead, he raised his beer bottle before his eyes and stared at it. After a moment's reflection, he said, "Then let me offer another toast from a moron's perspective." The rest of us hoisted our beers as Funkhouser continued slowly and carefully, "What goes around, comes around, and no one can escape this rule." He paused to think, then added, "So here's to one who thinks he will, but he won't, I assure you, to Doc Brown, the fool."

"Hoo-yah!" I whooped, and everybody laughed except Doc this time. Then down the pipes went the beers.

Two dozen beers and ten dozen laughs later, we were all done with our lunches and headed to the post exchange in Cholon. As we traveled there, I studied the masses of people on the sidewalks and crossing the street. As always, I was amazed that we were totally ignored. No one waved or smiled at us. No one uttered, *"Chao"* or *"Cam on ong."* No one yelled "Good afternoon," or even "Kiss my ass." Yet Katsma had given his life for these people's freedom. And I might even have to give mine. Or Funkhouser. Or McCollum. Or one of the others. That was why a smile would have been nice. Just one to have given me a little peace. But as I watched the hundreds and thousands of faces, I saw not one.

At the PX, all eight of us collected our month's supply of liquor and wine. I picked up Early Times whiskey and some Italian wine. Then, while the others paged through mail-order catalogs and perused the floor merchandise, I decided to take a walk by myself outside on the street. Perhaps, I thought, the people would greet me if I was alone and on foot.

It took but a block of walking to realize that only the hawkers would address me, and they only in an attempt to get at my money.

"GI, buy naked virgin very cheap?" a young male peddler called to me from behind his little table on the sidewalk as I stepped past. I glanced at the statues of nude maidens he had stacked before him and shook my head.

"No, thank you," I pronounced over my left shoulder while accidentally bumping into someone with my right arm. I turned back to apologize, but no one acknowledged the slight collision. No one looked at me; everyone just kept walking.

Continuing my journey, I traveled a couple more blocks as an insignificant part of a maze of pedestrians. I walked past the peddlers and their wares: the hanging parrot cages, ceramic elephants, cheap jewelry, watches, seashells, and Chinese herbs.

An old woman shoved a tin cup under my nose and begged, "Please?" I reached into my pants pocket and pulled out a ten-piaster coin, which I dropped into her cup. She smiled at me, revealing broken teeth. The teeth were stained reddish brown, which was common among the Vietnamese who chewed betel nut.

There! I thought. I had gotten a smile. Of course, I had paid for it, but what the hell.

I decided to walk back to the PX on the opposite side of the street, so as I reached the next intersection, I started across the roadway. I dodged a boy on a bicycle and moved around a slow-moving old man wearing a black Chinese Mandarin robe. While passing the man, I looked at him out of the corner of my eye. He had a yellow, wrinkled face with a long, thin, white goatee. His eyes were bloodshot, and overall he looked sickly.

Not wanting to stare and thereby give insult to the fellow, I looked away and kept walking. But after a few steps, I heard a "thud" behind me. I took a peek over my shoulder and saw that the old man had collapsed onto the street. The sight caused me to stop in my tracks.

I tried to move back toward the stricken man, but the steady stream of people walking by bumped into me and pushed me back. I couldn't believe it. Everyone was ignoring the crumpled body, walking around it and even showing some displeasure at the inconvenience. One man stepped right over the top of his fallen countryman without so much as a break in his stride. Seeing that, I spun around and went with the flow until I found a place where I could watch from afar.

What I saw was baffling. The old man received no attention or assistance. Perhaps he was dead. In that case, it appeared to me that he'd lie there until some street sweeper scooped him up later in the day. Until then, the only interested party may be a party of flies. Under the strange circumstances, I chose to protect myself from a possible sticky situation and walked back to the PX.

As I approached the entrance to the big French building, my teammates were filing out. Their hands were full of booze and gifts.

"Where you been, Smitty?" asked Flynn, sounding as if he had a right to know. His question irritated me since he was the one I had told I was going for a walk. It was obvious to me he was setting me up for some teasing from the others. Sure enough, they let me have it.

"He's prob'ly been with some red-hot, sexy lady," piped up McCollum. The others chuckled and murmured their approval.

"That's right," I spouted without hesitation, "your wife was good." The chuckles became cackles as we walked to our pickup truck.

"Actually," chimed in Funkhouser, "I think the Hawk set up a rendezvous with Nga. She's let it be known that she's interested in more of Smitty than just his laundry."

Above the howls and catcalls, I shouted playfully at Funkhouser, "You traitor!" Then I laughed with the others.

We climbed into our truck and Pearson drove through Saigon until he found a bar advertising strip shows. He parked close, then bailed out of the cab with a grin on his face. Flynn and Brown crawled out the passenger-side door.

"Flynn asked me to stop!" Pearson announced to the rest of us. "He needs a pick-me-up before we go back to the base."

The five of us in the box jumped out and joined our teammates on the sidewalk.

"We need one of us to stand watch over our booze and other items," Pearson reminded us. "Do we have a volunteer?"

"I'll stay with the truck if someone will bring me a beer," I answered.

"All right, Smitty," replied Pearson as he turned to go into the bar. He saw several Vietnamese children running along the sidewalk toward our group. Knowing what a nuisance the street urchins could be, Pearson and the others hurried inside the bar, leaving me to deal with the mischievous kids.

"Shoe shine, GI, shoe shine?" barked the first little boy to reach me. His almond-shaped brown eyes glowed with expectancy.

I looked down at my gray coral shoes, which were made of canvas. Pointing at them, I replied, "*Da*, go ahead." The boy stared at my coral shoes for a moment, then looked up at me with a sudden grin. He shook his head.

"Funny, GI," he said as four more boys brought their running to a halt right next to me. They were a ragtag bunch.

"Give me American cigarette," said the tiniest one, holding out a hand. This was a common request of Vietnamese city children, as they sold all they could get on the black market.

"No cigarettes today," I stated.

The little hand remained outstretched. "Buy me gum," the boy persisted.

I noticed two of the older boys slipping behind me. Wise to their pickpocketing abilities, I moved a couple of steps closer to the pickup truck. When I turned to face the boys again, my backside was flush against the truck door, thereby protecting my wallet.

"Buy me gum," repeated the small boy with his hand still out. I dug into a pants pocket and found a fresh pack of Wrigley's Spearmint. I tore open the pack and distributed one piece of gum to each of the five boys. While the other boys wasted no time in getting the gum into their mouths, the oldest-looking boy held his piece in his hand and stepped right in front of me.

"American cigarette?" he asked curtly. I stared into his eyes, looking for a sign of hostility. There was none to see; rather, I sensed sportiveness.

"American cigarette bad for lungs," I stated, then I coughed twice in the boy's face. He stepped back from me, then opened his gum wrapper and popped the gum into his mouth.

As the boy began chewing, he looked at me and said, "American gum bad for teeth." He smiled big, showing me his crooked and decayed set. Then he spun around and ran away, with the other boys in hot pursuit of him.

Five minutes later, as I waited in the oppressive heat and wondered which of my teammates was going to bring me a beer from the bar, all seven of them approached me.

Funkhouser handed me a bottle of beer and said, "We're gettin' outta here."

"What's wrong?" I asked, taking the beer. Everyone began piling into the truck.

"We don't like the atmosphere," McCollum told me. "There's some questionable characters in that bar, and we don't feel secure."

As I jumped into the box, Moses continued, "We've only got three weapons, just pistols. I got a feeling that in another twenty minutes we'll need a lot more firepower than that!"

"Besides," added Funkhouser, "there's no striptease show until tonight." He grinned at me as Pearson cranked up the engine.

CHAPTER ELEVEN
Mission Twenty-one

"They are surely to be esteemed the bravest spirits who, having the clearest sense of both the pains and pleasures of life, do not on that account shrink from danger."

Thucydides, *The Peloponnesian War*

DATE: 24, 25, 26 November 1967
TIME: 240615H to 260600H
UNITS INVOLVED: Foxtrot 1, 2, MST-3
TASK: Recon patrol, two overnight ambushes
METHOD OF INSERTION: LCPL MK-4
METHOD OF EXTRACTION: Boston Whalers
TERRAIN: Nipa palm, very thick undergrowth
MOON: 3/4
WEATHER: Cloudy, then clear
SEAL TEAM PERSONNEL:
Lt. Meston, Patrol Leader/Rifleman, M-16
Lt. (jg) Schrader, Ass't Patrol Leader/Rifleman, M-16
PR1 Pearson, Point/Rifleman, M-16
RM2 Smith, Ass't Point/Rifleman, M-16/XM-148
BT2 McCollum, Ordnance/Grenadier, M-79
BT2 Moses, Grenadier, M-79
ADJ2 Markel, Radioman/Rifleman, M-16
ADJ3 Flynn, Automatic Weapons, M-60
SN Dicey, Automatic Weapons, Stoner

AZIMUTHS: 100 degrees-600m, 075 degrees-200m
ESCAPE: 225 degrees
CODE WORDS: Insert-Tijuana, Ambush Site-San
   Diego, Second Ambush Site-Los Angeles,
   Extraction-Bakersfield, Challenge and Reply—
   Two numbers total 10

We arrived back at the base at 1515 hours. Funk-houser and I walked together to the barracks and found a Vietnamese woman sweeping up the dried mud in front of our cubicle. Her presence was not a surprise, as she cleaned for us almost every day. We addressed her as mamma-san, and each man who resided in our bar-racks chipped in and we paid her four hundred piaster per day.

As Funky and I tarried for a few moments short of our cubicle entrance, allowing mamma-san time to fin-ish sweeping the area, I noticed her little boy and girl staring at me from the other side of the aisle, just ten feet away. They were but four and five years old and were always very clean. I smiled and winked at them. The girl smiled back, but the boy lowered his eyes and turned away in an obvious display of shyness.

I felt around inside my pants pockets, looking for gum, but I'd already given my pack away. When mamma-san's cleaning removed her from our doorway, I stepped inside our living quarters and grabbed two sticks of gum from my footlocker.

"Gum," I announced as I walked back into the aisle. The girl saw the sticks in my hand and stepped forward with her hand outstretched. The boy hesitated, but when he watched his sister take a piece, he raced to me and grabbed his own. Then both ran away to the other end of the barracks.

"Follow me, Smitty!" said Dicey with some urgency as he headed for the barracks door.

"What's up?" I asked, not willing to move until I knew. I'd watched too many of my gullible teammates walk into traps, ending up the butt of a prank, for me to blindly follow Dicey.

"One of the support personnel guys has a nine-foot python outside," Dicey told me over his shoulder, then he stepped through the open door and was gone.

I called my roommate. Funkhouser stepped out of our cubicle and gave me a look.

"Let's go see a nine-foot python," I suggested, pointing to the door. I allowed Funky to walk outside first, just in case there was a setup, then I followed. Lucky for Funkhouser, no one was waiting with a bucket of water or anything like that; instead, around the corner of the barracks, we found a group of men surrounding a sailor who was holding a large snake. Funkhouser and I joined the swelling crowd of gawkers, some of whom had cameras and were taking photographs.

"He's as docile as can be," stated the owner as he cradled the middle of the reticulated python's body in his arms. "Somebody grab the two ends." There was a moment of hesitation among the onlookers, so I took advantage and hoisted the tail off the ground. Someone else could fool with the head, I thought, and someone soon did.

As I held the thick, ropelike body of the snake, Funkhouser jogged back to our cubicle to get his camera. He returned a minute later and snapped a couple pictures of his roomie and the python. Then we traded places and I took two of him.

When Moses assumed Funkhouser's position with the snake, Funky and I thanked the owner for the chance to take some pictures, then we walked back to our cubicle.

"It's a good thing Bolivar isn't that big," Funkhouser told me in the privacy of our abode. "I'd quit being your roommate in an instant."

I laughed. "Didn't you like holding that python?"

"Not a bit."

"But," I reminded him, "you sure were grinning for the camera!"

Funkhouser grinned again. "Gotta keep up my image for the ladies back home in the States!"

Pearson stuck his head inside our cubicle and reminded us we were to be in the briefing room at 1630 hours. We were going on a forty-eight-hour mission early in the morning deep in the T-10 area of the Rung Sat Special Zone. The specific op area contained two large enemy base camps, a hospital, and from two to six hundred VC.

For the next forty minutes, Funkhouser and I prepared some of our gear for the next day's operation while listening to my radio. Then we reported to the upstairs briefing room where Lieutenant Meston awaited us. When all nine SEALs from Foxtrot Platoon and eight members of the LCPL and Boston Whaler crews were assembled, the room was sealed off.

Mr. Meston began the briefing, explaining the mission step by step. Insertion off the Dong Tranh River would be at 0615 hours, followed by a 750-meter patrol through thick nipa palm and brush. The patrol would take most of the morning, as we would have to move very quietly. Pearson and I would alternate as point men until we reached the ambush site on a small stream just five hundred meters from two enemy camps. The hospital complex was but 150 meters farther. Our job was to intercept any boat traffic moving to or from the camps, capturing or killing the enemy occupants. I was the designated swimmer who would bring in any wounded VC and floating gear. Following SOP, we would attempt to preserve all intelligence data that was gathered.

We examined air recon photographs and pictomaps of the area of operation. The latest weather report indicated cloud cover with a chance of rain, then a gradual clearing. There would be plenty of moonlight both nights after the clouds dispersed.

The point men were cautioned to beware of booby traps.

Finally, we were given the mission's call signs and code words, then we sterilized the briefing room. All photographs, maps, charts, and notes were removed, and not a trace of the forthcoming op was left behind.

Since the base CO had ordered the Seabees to work half of the day, even though it was a holiday, the cooks had scheduled the Thanksgiving meal for 1800 hours. I decided to retrieve my laundry from Nga's before I went to the chow hall, and while I was in the village I bought three brass vases to send home.

At 1740 hours, I dropped my clothes off at my cubicle, then, desirous of a holiday trim, walked to the base's new barber shop, where haircuts were free. Knowing that Thanksgiving was Thanksgiving only to Americans, I hoped the Vietnamese barber, whose name was Nguyen, was still at the shop so late in the afternoon. A minute later, I found that he was.

"Moi ong vao ngoi choi," he welcomed me, asking me to sit down in his chair. I sat. He immediately started in on my head with his electric clippers. After a few minutes on top, he spent a couple of minutes spreading shaving cream on my ears, nose, and cheeks and shaving these parts with a razor. Next, he had me remove my T-shirt and lie back in the chair. He had me close my eyes while he shaved my neck and shoulders, handling the razor so deftly and gently it was as if he'd been born with it in his hand. I relaxed almost to the point of falling asleep.

When Nugyen was finished, he tapped my shoulder with a finger. I opened my eyes and focused on his smiling face.

"Het roi," he said, telling me he was done. I slid out of the chair and pulled on my T-shirt.

"Cam on ong," I thanked him. I took a twenty piaster coin from my pocket and gave it to the barber as a tip. He bowed and thanked me. I returned the bow, then left for the chow hall.

The cooks had pulled out all the stops on the Thanksgiving dinner, preparing hot turkey, dressing, sweet potatoes, mashed potatoes, green beans, cranberry sauce, salad, and pumpkin pie. I stuffed myself until I felt like I couldn't eat another bite, then I gobbled up some more. The food was so good that, if I'd have closed my eyes, I'd have thought I was sitting at my mother's table back home. Of course, I'd have had to have closed my ears, too, because people didn't talk at Momma's table the way they did in a Navy mess hall.

After dinner, I finished preparing my gear for the forty-eight-hour mission. Since I was the designated swimmer, I gathered my duck fins and coral booties. Of course, with my shotgun having been replaced by the M-16/XM-148 combo, which I'd dubbed Bad Girl, I was toting different ammunition. I'd taped three 30-round magazines together for the M-16, and I'd carried four magazine pouches: two were each filled with three 20-round magazines for the M-16, and two contained six 40mm HE rounds apiece for the XM-148 grenade launcher. I'd also stuffed two of my quart canteen pouches with eight rounds each of 40mm HE. A claymore mine and two fragmentation grenades were attached to my web belt. My drinking water was stored in two collapsible canteens that were packed with a first aid kit in a rucksack, which I'd carried at the top center of my H-harness. With my C rations stowed to sustain me, I was ready for the op.

When McCollum was finished with his preparation, around 2030 hours, he stopped by my cubicle and asked me to go to the Quonset hut to listen to a visiting band and drink a couple of beers. I declined the invitation, as reveille was scheduled for our platoon at 0315 hours and I wanted to get a good night's sleep. Besides that, Funkhouser was in bed feeling sick with a recurring flu bug and I didn't want to disturb him at a later hour; instead, I turned out our light and crawled into my bed.

For several minutes, I pondered the upcoming mission, then my thoughts turned to some of the principles by which Navy SEALs lived. We seemed to be unique, in that we understood our strength as a team was based on togetherness; nonconformity was not tolerated. When a teammate became morose or temperamental, we showed empathy and compassion, when needed, or we harassed until he snapped out of it. A standard maxim directly applied to us: "You're only as strong as the weakest man and only as fast as the slowest man." The bottom line was that introverts generally didn't survive in the Teams. Everyone was an extrovert and we fed off each other's bravado. For the career guys, "the Teams" represented not only a career, but also in many ways, satisfied family, social, and even religious requirements. "The Teams" was indeed a unique way of life.

I finally fell asleep around 2130 hours, and I slept well. After almost six hours of rest, I awakened to someone's announcing "Reveille" outside the cubicle. Then I heard Funkhouser stirring in the darkness. I opened my eyes and saw his figure dashing into the aisle. I knew by his quick actions that he either had the runs or he was going to vomit.

I crawled out of the sack, turned on the light, and got dressed for breakfast. When I was ready, Funkhouser, wearing UDT trunks and a sweat-soaked T-shirt, stumbled back in.

"The runs or the heaves?" I questioned as he fell into bed.

"Both," he groaned, burying his head underneath his pillow. In a muffled voice, he said, "Turn out the light ASAP."

I flicked the light switch and walked to the chow hall where I drank coffee and ate oatmeal, eggs, sausage, and toast. Since I firmly believed the only way to begin a forty-eight-hour mission was with an exceedingly full stomach, I grabbed seconds of everything. By the time I left the chow hall, I was far from worried about the excess weight, as I was aware that a two-day diet of nothing but C rats and water would put the kaputs on my bulk.

After breakfast, nine members of Foxtrot Platoon, including me, gathered our gear and met at the dock. Minus Funkhouser, we boarded the LCPL MK-4 with the four-man crew. With all aboard, the coxswain started the 300-horsepower engine, then steered us into the black of the early morning. I watched the base perimeter lights gradually disappear behind us.

As we traveled down the Long Tau, I sat on the steel deck between Pearson and McCollum. Looking up, I saw no moon or stars, which indicated heavy cloud cover. The breeze over the boat was cold. The engine roar seemed louder than usual. But even though it was chilly and my ears hurt, my head drooped and rested on Bad Girl, which lay across my lap. In a few minutes, I dozed off.

I dreamed about hunting. The woods were alive with chirping birds, and chattering squirrels. The fall leaves were rattling their loosening chains. I was stalking a big buck, which looked nervously aware. He stepped into an opening in the post oaks and briars, then froze. I slowly raised my rifle to shoot. Then I woke up and the deer got away.

I lifted my head and felt Bad Girl with my fingers. She reminded me that I had become a manhunter. I'd hunted man with the M-16/XM-148 three times since Sweet Lips's demise, but I'd yet to kill with the weapon. It would have been nice if the North Vietnamese Communists would have given it up and gotten out of South Vietnam; the warring would have ceased and the dying would have ended. I would have retired Bad Girl without ever having shot a human being with her. Yes, that would have been nice. Right then, however, I realized I was thinking wishfully. In actuality, I was riding a boat so deep into enemy territory that there was a fair chance I'd have to cook some gooks, which is the way I had to think about it, so I wouldn't think about it when the time came. If I were to dwell on the thought of an enemy having a wife and children waiting for him at home, I might hesitate in squeezing the trigger and give him an opportunity to kill me or a teammate.

The coxswain cut the throttle back on the engine to slow us down a bit. We were on the Dong Tranh and getting close to our insertion point. The coxswain employed the boat's radar while Mr. Meston used his Starlight Scope to find our way and check the shoreline. Both men were looking for the small stream we were to bypass by five hundred meters, then we'd insert and work back to the stream at a point deeper in the jungle.

Mr. Meston suddenly gave the signal to lock and load. The sounds of cocking weapons filled the air as the LCPL continued moving alongside the dark shore. When the boat slowed to just above idle, I moved forward to the portside bow. Four of my teammates grouped behind me while four others crouched down at the starboard bow.

As the coxswain turned the bow of the LCPL toward the shore, I prepared myself for the jolt of boat striking land. When it came, I jumped off the port bow and onto the shore. To my delight, the ground beneath my feet was soft but not wet and muddy.

The nine of us ended up a few meters inland, waiting and listening in the brush. The LCPL backed away from the riverbank, then moved farther down the river where the coxswain would perform a couple of fake insertions.

With my ears peeled, I observed the silhouettes of my teammates in the dark. The outlines of the weapons projecting out of each body were a sight to behold—the M-16s, the M-79 grenade launchers, the M-60, and the Stoner machine guns. My courage cranked up a couple notches as I was reminded of our firepower.

After fifteen minutes, the dark sky showed the first traces of the coming of dawn. Meston had us hold for another few minutes, then he signaled Pearson to take the point position and start through the thick brush. The rest of us strung out behind Pearson and began moving east, back toward the stream we had passed in the LCPL. I fell into the fifth slot behind Pearson, Meston, Markel, and Schrader. Behind me walked Flynn, Moses, Dicey, and McCollum.

The going was slow for several reasons. The nipa palm and undergrowth was heavy. Prickly stems and branches grasped at our legs like octopus arms. The brush was noisy, and noise was a major no-no for U.S. Navy SEALs in the T-10 area. Also, the possibility of booby traps was great, as we were assuming the VC and NVA had taken appropriate measures to protect themselves and their base camps and hospital.

We covered the first two hundred meters of our 750-meter patrol in an hour. The mosquitos had acted as a sour uninvited escort since just after daybreak, oblivious as always to the killing power of our weaponry.

Mr. Meston had us halt when Pearson signaled that he had found a well-worn trail. Several sets of VC tracks, no older than forty-eight hours, were imprinted in the ground. Pearson was sent to recon a portion of the trail alone, checking for more sign. After going about forty meters, Pearson returned and informed the lieutenant that there were several diverging trails ahead. To give Pearson a break from the stress, Meston motioned for me to assume the point position. Pearson and I exchanged places, then I started down the trail with the others strung out behind me.

Walking on dry ground along a cleared pathway was a pleasant change from the normal watery muck and dense vegetation. I had to focus on my job, though, and not allow my concentration to lapse because of the luxury. After all, I couldn't afford one careless step. I, for one, intended to meet death on a golf course at an old age, not death in the jungle at twenty-six.

After we traveled about two hundred meters, the human footprints became intermingled with lots of deer tracks. Having seen thousands of deer tracks in my life, I estimated that the biggest tracks on the trail had been made by a deer weighing around two hundred and fifty pounds. My heart hammered a little faster as I anticipated the sighting of a monster buck, and once again I had to apply myself to the task at hand, which was guiding the squad carefully to our ambush site.

My attention was undivided over the next three-quarters of an hour as my teammates and I covered another two hundred meters. The numerous human and deer tracks continued underfoot, and I avoided stepping in some scattered deer droppings, but no other signs of humans or deer were manifested. I was somewhat surprised by this, as we'd moved to within seven hundred meters of the enemy base camps.

When I finally came to the designated stream, I knew our position was 250 meters inland from the mouth of the stream where it intersected the Dong Tranh. I signaled Mr. Meston, who signaled back that I should recon the bank while the others waited.

I slunk up and down the riverbank for several minutes, discovering the same old thing: voluminous tracks. I reported my findings to Mr. Meston, who decided to proceed with our game plan, which was to patrol 150 meters alongside the stream to our preplanned ambush site. That location would put us less than five hundred meters from scores of enemy troops.

It took thirty minutes to reach the ambush site, which I identified when I noted a second stream that branched off to the southwest from the main stream. At that fork we would lie in wait to capture or kill soldiers who would attempt to do the same to us. But this I knew: capturing a SEAL was out of the question; as long as breath remained, a knocked-down, wounded, and dying SEAL would continue shooting holes in enemy hides. And the rest of the team wouldn't leave until he was carried away or dead. Such was the confidence we placed in each other.

Mr. Meston signaled for half the squad—consisting of Schrader, Pearson, Moses, Markel, and Dicey—to position themselves overlooking the stream. Meston, McCollum, Flynn, and I set up as rear security several meters back in the bushes. While the other three men catnapped, I took the first two-hour watch for rear security.

As the time went by, I heard nothing except the mosquitos. I observed the still jungle and enjoyed the peaceful morning. The skies were overcast, but it didn't rain. It was a nice feeling to be high and dry on an ambush site, which was a rare experience. Even my rump was comfortable, settled down in a soft, dry pad of moss.

At 1130 hours, McCollum relieved me on watch. I stood my M-16/XM-148 against a sturdy branch of a bush, then lay my head against the trunk of the nipa palm behind me and closed my eyes. A light breeze licked at my face for half a minute, refreshing me, then it was gone to wherever it was that breezes went.

I left the war to the others for a while as my mind ran through many thoughts of a different place and time. I dreamed about the field-rat plague in the summer of 1959, when North Central Texas had been infested with millions of rats at the end of a seven-year drought. The rats had been eating up all the grasses and even the bark off mesquite trees. Day after day, Chuck Toliver, Jimmy Harbis, and I had traveled a couple of miles out of Wichita Falls on the Archer City road with our .22 rifles to shoot at the rats. We'd killed them on the ground and knocked them off mesquite branches where the rats had perched like vultures. When our ammunition had run dry, we'd picked up sticks and clubbed or stabbed the varmints to death, howling and laughing all the while.

I remembered my 1960 Harley Sportster, a souped-up motorcycle that could do 110 miles per hour in third gear. When I had wanted to show off, I would lift the front wheel off the ground when I shifted to fourth. The speedometer had stopped at 120, but I often had taken the bike to 150 in fourth gear. At top speed, the wind blast had been so strong I could barely hang onto the grips. I had even felt my fingers slipping on many occasions. As a twenty-year-old, I'd drag race at night on the boulevard in town, beating the hottest Corvettes and everybody else, then I'd escape from the converging cops in the nick of time.

In the same time period, I had owned a red convertible MG-A which could hit 120. I'd cruise town with a black-cloth top or a fiberglass red top or no top at all. The Pioneer 3 drive-through restaurant had been a primary hangout for college kids, and it was there I'd hustle the girls in my flashy sports car. One night in 1962, I had floorboarded the MG all the way between

Jacksboro and Mineral Wells on Highway 281, a trip of approximately thirty-five miles.

Suddenly my mental drifting was ended by a sound similar to the uncorking of a wine bottle. I opened my eyes and sat up, reaching for Bad Girl in the same motion. Mr. Meston, sitting on the ground a few meters to my left, slipped the safety off on his M-16. McCollum, sitting off to my right, raised the M-79 grenade launcher from his lap. Flynn, propped against a tree trunk next to McCollum, was asleep. We left him be while we listened for another clue.

A minute went by. Then two, and three. Nothing happened. I looked to the front line on the stream, but no signal was given.

A rustling of brush occurred behind Mr. Meston and my heart bolted inside my chest. I turned my head to look as the noise came again, only to spot a squirrel dart through the ground vegetation and climb into a nipa palm. I watched it for a few seconds, noting that it looked like our gray squirrels back home, then I looked at Mr. Meston. He rolled his eyes, letting me know that he, too, had been freaked by the squirrel's racket.

After another few minutes, Dicey slipped off the front line and quietly approached us. I could see by the look on his camouflaged face that something had happened.

As Dicey reached Mr. Meston, the lieutenant motioned me over. I half walked and half crawled a few yards to the two men. Dicey whispered to us that he had seen a gook come to the edge of the trees on the opposite side of the stream, carrying two water jugs. The man had peered up and down and across the stream while motioning and whispering to a comrade or comrades hidden behind him in the bushes. I asked Dicey why he hadn't shot the man, and Dicey said that if he had reached for his Stoner machine gun the VC certainly would have seen him, that's how close he had been. The stream was only twenty-five meters wide and the VC had been directly across from Dicey and had been all eyes.

I told Mr. Meston that the VC could have faked not seeing us and that he and his comrades might counter ambush us.

"Dammit," the lieutenant whispered, then he told Dicey to be extremely alert and motioned him back to the stream. I moved back to my mossy seat, knowing in my guts that some people were going to die before we got out of there. I just hoped that all of the dead had slanted eyes.

Luckily, there was no attack from the VC and no one died during the next five hours. Instead, things got real pleasant as the clouds broke up, the sky became blue, and a waft of a breeze meandered through the leaves. Most of the mosquitos took a siesta, and I, too, drifted in and out of sleep throughout the afternoon. Occasionally, I awoke and drank some water from one of my two canteens, or I dipped a little Skoal tobacco. At 1600 hours, I ate a can of C rations, more out of a need for something to do than to satisfy my appetite.

At dusk, Mr. Meston, Flynn, McCollum, and I moved to the riverbank, relieving the others, who shifted to rear security for the night. I took the left flank while McCollum assumed the right. Flynn was next to me, with Meston positioned between him and McCollum. I sat on a dry pile of sticks that Dicey had stacked and sat upon just off the riverbank between two cycads, palm-like trees with short, thick stems. Just in front of me, growing at the edge of the stream, were several water chestnut plants, tufted and grasslike plants standing a foot and a half high. As I settled down for the night watch, I liked Dicey's spot selection, which was high and dry, fairly comfortable, with a good view of the water. The only negative was a slight lack of cover, which was why Dicey couldn't reach for his machine gun when the enemy had appeared straight ahead of him. For me, that would not be a problem, as I was already being blanketed by darkness.

When the night fully descended, I could still see the outline of the opposite bank, thanks to a clear sky and a three-quarter moon. A crocodile blowed downstream to my left, then made a whistling sound, drawing air. A nearby frog answered the croc with a couple of *ribbits*. A fish splashed in front of me in the stream, and the ripples glittered in the moonlight. The jungle was coming alive with creatures, and it was possible that humans would soon join the party of noisemakers.

Sure enough, an hour after dark I heard faint talking downstream, but only for a few seconds. I listened intently for another hour; nothing made a peep except a shrew in the brush behind me. And so went the rest of the night: quiet and uneventful.

At first light, we got our gear ready to travel and we moved upstream as soon as we could see well enough. We crossed one large stream on the way, which ticked me off because I was so enjoying being dry for a change.

After crossing the stream, we found fresh VC tracks all over the place. I had never seen so many before. With me at point, we patrolled at a snail's pace, knowing the enemy was close. Soon I smelled the faint odor of *nuoc mam*, a strong-smelling fish sauce, on the breeze. A few steps later, I smelled smoke.

I motioned my discoveries to Mr. Meston by pointing at my nose. He sniffed a moment, then shook his head and shrugged. That was discouraging because he seemed not to believe me. To me, this episode confirmed once again that my senses of hearing and smell were extraordinary, as others couldn't hear or smell the inconspicuous things I could. I attributed my superior, attuned senses to my having been a country boy and a hunter. In comparison with the boys from the city, I was the one who was "practiced up."

We ended up sneaking 250 meters closer to the enemy base camps where two more streams forked from ours. The vantage point was better, but the terrain was lower and wetter, both on the riverbank and in the bush at rear security. That promised us a watery day and night.

While Schrader, Pearson, Moses, Markel, and Dicey set up overlooking the streams, I took the first watch at the rear, positioning myself to keep my eyes on a well-worn trail behind us. I sat in mud and a few inches of water, hidden between two wild fig trees and a small bush.

The long night on the first ambush site had taken its toll on Mr. Meston, Flynn, and McCollum, who fell fast asleep a few meters from me. Their having taken Dexamil pills during the early morning hours hadn't helped them because the short-term "high" had left behind an abnormal drowsiness. I was happy that I'd avoided the use of the drug, as I had to remain extremely alert, especially since we were camped less than three hundred yards from men who would have loved to have slit us from neck to nuts.

I kept watch until 1115 hours, drowning a half dozen more ants to pass the time, when McCollum woke up and took over. That was when I could finally let go and relax. The stress of playing hide-and-seek in the VC's backyard had worn me out. I propped the M-16/ XM-148 against a fig tree, hung my head, and took a few long, slow breaths. Before I knew it, I was asleep.

When I awoke three hours later, I discovered a dozen red ants crawling on me. Three of them were on my face. Quickly, I started brushing the little monsters off. Before I got them all, one of them bit my neck. That pissed me off, and I took revenge by catching the culprit and tearing him in two. I discarded the pieces and immediately felt much better.

For the next three hours, I daydreamed and catnapped while Flynn had watch. At dusk, Mr. Meston signaled for us to relieve the front line. The four of us at the rear moved to the stream. As we approached our teammates, only Mr. Schrader and Moses desired replacement. Pearson, Dicey, and Markel asked permission from Mr. Meston to stay on during the night. Meston granted their request. This gave us seven men on ambush and two at rear security.

I sat down in the mud and water on left flank, to Dicey's left. Darkness dropped, but the moon was unobstructed and bright. I was easily able to see across the thirty-five-meter-wide stream. No way could a sampan slip by unseen.

At 2100 hours, the tide came in. I was forced to stand up as the water rose to chest level. A few minutes later, I heard an airplane coming. As it drew closer, a voice resounded over a loudspeaker from the sky, telling the VC in the Vietnamese language that they were losing the war and should give themselves up. The voice spoke of the humanitarian things the South Vietnamese forces were doing to help the people. Then it said, "Number one, number one." This went on for two hours as the plane flew back and forth over the T-10 area.

I was glad when the plane finally left, as I had been unable to concentrate on listening for faint noises while the recordings had blared. Now that all was quiet again, I felt like I was back in control of the night. Mamma-san Nature, however, had her input on the situation, and she raised the water up to my neck. Then she lowered the temperature to the sixties, which was awful cold for one who was acclimated to eighties, nineties, and above.

I remained in water until the tide began to recede at 0330 hours. Even though the water level dropped, my clothes were soaked and I was freezing. My teeth were chattering; my face was numb. I thought of Funkhouser, back at the base in bed, and I suddenly wished I could trade places with him, even if only for ten minutes.

About 0400 hours, Mr. Meston used the radio to let the boat support personnel know we wanted to extract at 0600. Only two more hours of shaking like a leaf, I told myself as a pep talk. Two more hours. At the same time, I couldn't quite believe we'd spent the past twenty hours just one long golf shot from Victor Charlie, and he hadn't poked his nose out of the clubhouse. What the hell was he doing? Where was he? I cursed through tap-dancing teeth. Hell, he was staying warm next to his brown-eyed lady while I was clutching the most frigid Bad Girl the jungle had ever known. Dammit, anyway!

But Victor Charlie didn't let me down. He must've finished with his woman at 0500 hours, because at 0515 I heard his paddle smack the side of his sampan outside of our right flank position. I tugged the communication line between Dicey and me two times. He answered right back. Then I listened hard, anticipating the telltale *splash* of a paddle. Several seconds dragged by, then I heard a splash, followed by many more in a perfect rowing rhythm.

I jerked the line three times: "the enemy is here!" Raising the M-16/XM-148, I saw the sampan passing through the middle of our kill zone, coming toward me on the left flank. With my finger on the M-16 trigger, I anxiously waited for Mr. Meston to initiate the ambush. Precious seconds went by, and nothing happened. The sampan was now in front of Dicey to my right, and I could clearly see the figures of three men in the boat. Three seconds later, they were in front of me and leaving the ambush site.

"Shit!" I barked, then I squeezed the trigger. All I heard was a loud click. The hair stood up on the back of my neck at the hollow sound of the dud round.

Dicey and Flynn, upon hearing my attempt at commencing the ambush, suddenly opened up with the Stoner machine gun and the M-60. I slipped my finger onto the XM-148 trigger and fired a 40mm canister round at the sampan. I then extracted and ejected the dud 5.56mm round, recharged the chamber with a fresh cartridge and shot an entire 30-round magazine at the three VC. My rapid fire was joined by all of my teammates to my right as we collectively sent close to a thousand bullets over the stream.

In the moonlight, I could see the shape of the sampan. No human silhouettes were visible in the boat any longer. Still, we continued blasting the sampan and the water around it for several more seconds.

As the shooting died down, Mr. Meston lifted a hand parachute flare above his head and pointed it at the sky over the sampan. Once he was sure he could fire it through the canopy of trees above us, he slammed the base of the flare with his right palm and set it off. The thrust was so powerful that the twelve-inch cylindrical casing slipped over Meston's muddy hand and came back and hit him squarely in the mouth, splitting his lower lip completely in two and knocking out several teeth.

The para flare rocketed to a height of about one hundred feet, then the parachute opened and the illuminating charge caught fire and lit up the stream below. It was suddenly "daylight in the swamp."

I easily spotted the sampan drifting toward the opposite side of the stream. The three VC were nowhere to be seen. Quickly, I fired two 40mm HE rounds over the sampan and into the trees on the bank, just in case one

of the enemy had made it that far. The grenades blew
branches and debris into the air.

I looked at Mr. Meston, who had his hands cupped
over his mouth. Blood was oozing between his fingers.

In a muffled voice, I heard Meston say, "Pearson,
take over! Take charge!"

Pearson wasted no time in telling me to swim after
the sampan. I handed my weapon to Dicey and began
pulling my duck fins over my coral booties. As I finished, I heard Pearson calling for the Boston Whalers to
"get us out of here!" I seconded the motion in my mind,
remembering all too well that there were hundreds of
VC in easy hailing distance, and we sure as hell had
hailed them.

I entered the cool water with my K-bar knife in hand
as the para flare started to flicker and die out. Using underwater strokes in order to keep a low profile, I swam
without making splashes or lots of ripples beneath the
light of the flare and the moon. Unfortunately for me,
the flare quickly extinguished, and I couldn't see anything but the water directly under my nose. My night
vision was lost.

I continued swimming in the direction of the opposite
bank, trusting that one of my teammates would send up
another flare. My nose was barely out of the water as I
went, and my nostrils burned with the smell of blood;
someone had crawled out of bed too early for his own
good in the Rung Sat Special Zone.

I blinked my eyes hard a few times in an attempt to
regain my vision, but things got even darker as I swam
into the shadows of the trees lining the shoreline. I
tightly grasped my knife in my right hand, aware of the
fact that I could bump into a gook at any moment. And
no matter if he was still alive or already dead, I planned
to stick him twice before I inquired as to his well-being.

Suddenly, a flare ignited high over my head, and in

the bright light I saw the sampan hung up next to the riverbank. I swam to it, and as I reached for the bow I saw a gook lying on his back inside the boat. His knees were up and his arms grotesquely pointed skyward. Bullet holes were evident from his head to his feet. His heart protruded halfway out of his chest.

I also noted that there was a large water jug sitting in the middle of the sampan, full of bullet holes but still standing upright. The sampan, too, was bullet-riddled. I grabbed the two and towed my catch back to my teammates as the para flare extinguished above me.

When I made it across the stream, Pearson extended a hand and helped me out of the water. I hung onto the bow and pulled the sampan partway out of the water with me. Pearson explored the sampan and discovered some papers and a Chicom SKS semiautomatic rifle underneath the dead man. He salvaged the loot, then together we turned over the sampan and dumped the lifeless body into the stream. Under the circumstances, it was the closest we could come to an honorable burial at sea for the misfortunate fellow.

As the body floated away and quickly disappeared below the surface of the water, Pearson told me that he had seen a second body rise up and then sink in the middle of the stream as I had been towing the sampan. That gave us two confirmed KIAs. The third VC's whereabouts was officially unknown, but unofficially I'd have bet my Bad Girl that he'd smiled his last smile.

Speaking of smiles, Mr. Meston wouldn't have much of one for quite a while, I thought to myself as I gathered my gear and waited uneasily for extraction. In the moonlight, I watched him dabbing his mouth with a handkerchief. He had to be disgusted, as a self-inflicted punch in the mouth was no SEAL's fantasy when he dreamed about ways in which he could be wounded and shed blood for his country to receive a Purple Heart.

But what was done was done, and at least Mr. Meston still had a heart, unlike a couple of gooks I'd run into shortly before.

A minute later, I thanked God when I heard the power props of the Boston Whalers whirring downstream. Some of the bravest men in the world were brazenly entering this hellhole to save our butts from an inevitable counterattack.

When the coxswains of the two Whalers located us, they rammed their bows into the riverbank so the nine of us could jump aboard. Nothing had ever felt better to me than the fiberglass deck of the boat where I plopped my rear end, even though it was as cold as, well, steel. Cold, but safe, and being safe was at the top of my priority list right then.

The Whalers roared away from the ambush site, dramatically rescuing the good guys as they were paid to do and prayed to. We left behind two or three dead enemies, depending upon who was counting. Oh, yeah, and Mr. Meston's teeth.

CHAPTER TWELVE

Mission Twenty-seven

"Life without the courage for death is slavery."
Seneca, *Letters to Lucilius*

DATE: 23 December 1967
TIME: 1445H to 1745H
UNITS INVOLVED: Foxtrot 1, 2, Army UH1B
TASK: Recon patrol, destroy VC bunkers with demolitions
METHOD OF INSERTION: Army slick UH1B helo
METHOD OF EXTRACTION: Army slick UH1B helo
TERRAIN: Nipa palm, partly defoliated
TIDE: 1340H-3.3 feet, 2130H-12.1 feet
WEATHER: Clear
SEAL TEAM PERSONNEL:
Lt. Meston, Patrol Leader/Rifleman, M-16
Lt. (jg) Schrader, Ass't Patrol Leader/Rifleman, M-16
PR1 Pearson, Point/Rifleman, M-16
RM2 Smith, Ass't Point/Cameraman/Rifleman, CAR-15
MM2 Funkhouser, Automatic Weapons, Stoner
BT2 McCollum, Ordnance/Grenadier, M-79
BT2 Moses, Grenadier, M-79
ADJ2 Markel, Radioman/Rifleman, M-16

ADJ2 Flynn, Automatic Weapons, Stoner
HM2 Brown, Corpsman/Rifleman, M-16
SN Dicey, Rifleman, M-16
Gieng (LDNN SEAL), Rifleman, M-16
AZIMUTHS: None
ESCAPE: 270 degrees
CODE WORDS: Insert-Ford, Bunker Site-Chevy,
  Loading Charge-Blast Off, Extract-Buick

Over the next three and a half weeks, we went out on five missions. On the first, I spotted a large deer that ran from beneath the helo when we inserted. Then on ambush at dusk, a large buck appeared just twenty-five yards away from me. He was fat and sleek and had a rack similar to an elk's with five points on each antler. He foraged around for about ten minutes, barked a few times, then disappeared into the jungle. The week before my sightings, Mr. Meston had seen an enormous deer walk to the edge of the river where we had been positioned on an ambush site. I believed that to be the first sighting ever by a SEAL of a deer in the Rung Sat.

On the second mission, Foxtrot Second Squad killed two VC and expropriated two weapons and a sampan. Before the hit, I had discovered a booby trap, a pine-apple-type hand grenade secured in a tree, with a trip wire running across the trail from the grenade to another tree. Fortunately, I had found the booby trap with my eyes and not my feet.

In between these missions, the fourteen members of Echo Platoon had invited the rest of us to their going-away party at the chief's club, where the SEALs, helo crews, and boat support personnel consumed steaks, baked beans, French fries, and salad along with twenty cases of beer and two cases of hard liquor. The next day, Echo Platoon flew to Subic Bay on the first leg of its journey home, and four days later, 10 December, the twelve men of Bravo Platoon replaced Echo at Nha Be. The Bravo Platoon members were Lt. (jg) Van Heertum, WO1 Casey, EM2 Lou DiCroce, RMSN McHugh, GMG3 Jewett, HMC Blackburn, SA Keith, AN Klann, ETNSN Luksik, TM1 Payne (because of wounds Payne was later replaced by EM2 Puckett), SN Antone, and FN Hyatt.

On our last mission, which was my twenty-sixth of the tour, we patrolled to a VC base camp, which the occupants had left in a hurry before our arrival, leaving behind hot ashes in their kitchen. We blew and burned several huts and four sampans with incendiary grenades, keeping some papers and M-79 ammunition we found at the scene.

The next day was Friday, December 22, 1967. Some VC swimmers struck back at us in the early morning hours by floating a contact-detonated mine into one of the civilian tankers anchored at the naval base. The tanker suffered some damage but did not sink.

In the spirit of tit for tat, Lieutenant Meston passed a warning order early in the day, then led our briefing at 1800 hours. We were to insert by helo into an area close to the Vam Sat River where no enemy was then supposed to be. With information provided through an intelligence system run by Marine First Lieutenant Winsenson, we knew that a huge bunker complex made out of logs and mud existed in the area, and our job was to destroy the bunkers before the VC came back.

After the briefing, all of us got very busy preparing our gear. Since the area of operation was not hot, I left Bad Girl behind and carried a lighter Car-15 instead. Like the other men, I would tote ten pounds of C-3 explosives. In addition, as the designated photographer, I was to carry a Nikonos camera and take slide pictures of the op.

The next morning, reveille came at 0515 hours. After

a hearty breakfast, Foxtrot 1st and 2nd Squads assembled at the helo pad at 0630 hours. The army helos, however, didn't show up from inserting Alpha and Bravo platoons in the T-10 area, so our mission was canceled until 1400 hours.

At 1300 hours, we had a rebriefing, then we boarded the slicks and headed for the Vam Sat. The flight took just forty minutes, and with no reason for concern over close proximity of the enemy, we were dropped in a partly defoliated mangrove swamp just outside the bunker complex boundary.

We moved into the complex area and were amazed at the sight. I counted eight bunkers and they were the biggest I'd ever seen, with each one measuring at least ten feet by twenty feet. The bunkers were made with mud and logs and were built on muddy ground, designed to absorb the shock of aerial bombings and ground vibrations. Craters from U.S. bombs lay within twenty-five yards of some bunkers but appeared to have done little or no damage to them.

Foxtrot 1st and 2nd Squads were divided into four teams of three men apiece. Funkhouser, McCollum, and I were assigned two bunkers on the eastern edge of the complex. We were to enter the bunkers with flashlights, looking carefully for booby traps. After placing C-3 explosives at strategic reinforcement points within each bunker, we were to detonate the charges to destroy them.

As the three of us approached our first bunker, Funkhouser halted in his tracks and pointed at a crater just ten meters from the bunker entrance.

"Oh, my gosh," he said, his mouth agape, "look at that ten-foot hole!"

I looked. "That's what a thousand-pound bomb will do for you."

McCollum stopped beside us, gazing at the crater. He

snorted, then said, "Maybe we got lucky and a dink was standin' there takin' a leak."

I chuckled. "That's what I'd like to think. Another slopehead became a dead head." Ignoring noise discipline, we all laughed. With the enemy far away, we were not being real tactical about security.

"You go in first, Mr. Point Man," McCollum said to me at the entrance to the bunker.

I clicked on my flashlight and aimed the beam inside. "No sweat," I told him, happy to lead the way.

"Just watch out for a cobra," warned Funkhouser, half seriously.

"Or a man-eating man-a-cheetah," added McCollum quickly.

I looked back at my teammates before stepping inside the bunker.

"Anything else, fellas?"

Funkhouser glanced at McCollum, who shrugged his shoulder and said, "Don't forget the booby traps."

I nodded my head, pointed the flashlight and my rifle into the bunker and stepped inside. My flashlight beam probed every nook and cranny of the large chamber. After a minute of exploration, I was sure that no gooks or goblins awaited me.

McCollum and Funkhouser entered the bunker and all of us looked for the best place to position our breaching charges. McCollum checked out the roof and quickly made a suggestion.

"Right here is the main log in the overhead," he said, pointing at the beam. "What do you think?"

Funky and I agreed with Muck's assessment. "Let's do it," Funky affirmed.

I took the ten pounds of C-3 that I'd been carrying and fastened it to the log with a piece of parachute suspension line. At the same time, McCollum attached five pounds of C-3 to a corner support post. I then ran sensitized detonation cord from my charge to McCollum's. Funky handed me two six-foot lengths of safety fuse. On one end was a nonelectric blasting cap and on the other was an M-60 fuse lighter. We double-primed our charges, as always, in case one of the nonelectric caps was a dud. McCollum helped me tape the two nonelectric caps to the center of the det cord.

Just before we lit up our handiwork, Funkhouser went outside to make sure no other SEALs were nearby and yelled, "Fire in the hole," three times. A few seconds later, he stuck his head back into the bunker and called to us, "The coast is clear!" Then McCollum and Funky left and walked seventy meters to where a convenient crater, courtesy of the U.S. Air Force, welcomed us.

I pulled the two M-60 fuse lighters, and as the safety fuse started smoking, I hustled out of the bunker and followed Muck and Funky.

"The charges should go off in five minutes and ten seconds," stated Funky. We hid down in the hole, peeking over the top so as not to miss the fireworks.

After five minutes had passed, McCollum gave a verbal five-second countdown. "Five, four, three, two . . ." Before he could say, "One," the C-3 blew.

"You're one second off, Funky!" Muck commented.

"Eat your heart out!" barked Funky from deep within the crater.

I saw little of the blast as my natural reflex action was to duck my head, especially when the charge was but seventy meters from our cover. The detonation, however, was muffled, and when I raised my head, I saw that the bunker was still standing. There was a sizable hole in the roof and a smaller one through a side wall, but that was all. Top-notch design and construction of the bunker had enabled it to shrug off most of the effects of our modified breach charges.

"Hoo-yah!" shouted Funkhouser, waving an arm over his head in a celebratory gesture.

"Whoa-yeah!" McCollum yelled in my ear, then he slapped me on the back. "I love playin' demo man!"

"Me, too," I told him, "but we didn't play too well. The damn bunker's a long way from being destroyed."

McCollum climbed out of the crater, chuckling. "Hell," he said, "that don't matter. We'll just blow the son of a bitch again!" He waved five pounds of C-3 under my nose. "This should be good for bustin' another air vent through the roof." He grinned at me, and I grinned back.

As we set the next charge, several blasts were heard from other areas of the bunker complex where our teammates were taking care of business. We wasted little time in adding to the ruckus. Back in the crater again, we kept our heads up this time and watched as sticks and mud blew into the air. The roof of the bunker was now half gone and the remaining portion was ruptured and loose enough for us to tear apart by hand.

After pulling apart the ceiling and knocking down the bunker walls, we used Funkhouser's ten pounds of C-3 on the second bunker to rip a huge hole in the roof. Another charge or two was needed to wreck the sturdy bunker, but the three of us were then devoid of explosives.

I located Mr. Meston and told him of our predicament. He cussed the strength of the VC bunkers and said all four of our groups were experiencing the same problems. He immediately radioed Nha Be TOC requesting more C-3 to be delivered by helos. While we waited, I snapped several pictures of the bunkers. Then I took a picture of one of the helos as four haversacks containing twenty pounds each of explosives, safety fuse, and M-60 fuse lighters were dropped down to us.

Mr. Meston gave me one of the sacks, which I toted back to McCollum and Funkhouser. We utilized ten pounds of the C-3 to punch a couple more big holes through the die-hard bunker walls, then we physically forced the conquered structure down.

"Hoo-yah!" I cried as the last logs fell, releasing my frustration by throwing up my fists and pummeling the air. "It went down hard, but it went down!" We all laughed.

Several minutes later, after a few more explosions, Mr. Meston called everyone together in the center of the bunker complex.

"The helos have sighted several large bunkers about three or four hundred meters to the west," he informed us. "We'll patrol there and use the remaining C-3 on 'em." Using the azimuths the helo crew had given, he fixed our direction with his compass. Then glancing around at every face, he said, "Let's get it done before it gets dark on us."

With Pearson at the point, we began patrolling through the nipa palm toward the distant bunker complex. My position in line was behind Markel, who was carrying the radio behind Lieutenant Meston, and ahead of Lieutenant (jg) Schrader. With no enemy in our area of operation, we moved quicker than usual through the jungle. The ground was muddy, but the mud was not thick and clingy. We were able to proceed at a steady pace, which was essential in order to reach the bunkers and have time to blow them before nightfall.

After three hundred meters of relaxed, easy going, I spied something to give me pause: fresh bootprints along an intersecting path. I stopped and stared at them, pointing them out to Mr. Schrader.

"Looks like several people walked through here today," I declared. Mr. Schrader nodded his head in agreement. We both looked up at the backs of our teammates ahead of us, who were continuing on without hesitation.

"Surely they saw these tracks," I said, my voice becoming quieter as my concern escalated.

Mr. Schrader turned and faced Flynn, who was hurrying toward us with a look that told me he had something urgent to report.

"There's a VC bunker on our left flank to our rear," he told Schrader.

I got a queasy feeling in my stomach, comparable to the sick sensation I had gotten back in the fifth grade when I had discovered the school bully waiting in the bushes for me on my way home one day. I had known he had wanted to jump me, but I hadn't been expecting the attack in the security of my own backyard.

I looked at the fresh tracks again, and I knew in my gut that the enemy was close. I gazed ahead thirty meters at Mr. Meston's back, and I wondered what was in his mind. I wished he would look back so I could signal to him.

No sooner wished than done. Meston turned around. Our eyes met and I motioned for him to wait. Schrader went ahead to tell the lieutenant about the footprints and the bunker. The rest of us held our positions, eyeing the brush around us. I was fully aware that our easy op could suddenly evolve in an unexpected direction.

While Schrader and Meston discussed the situation in whispers, I held my CAR-15 a little firmer. At the same time, because of her added firepower—the 40 mm grenade launcher—I wished I were holding Bad Girl instead. Making a quick mental inventory, I knew we had two Stoner machine guns and two M-79 grenade launchers among us, which wasn't too shabby, unless we stumbled into a company of two hundred slopeheads, who were a bit perturbed at our treatment of their bunkers. In that case, we were undermanned and undergunned.

I looked again at the many human tracks crossing through the area, and I believed, in fact, that an encounter was a surety. An instant later, an abrupt burst of gun-fire scared the living shit out of me.

I dropped to my knees and swung my rifle toward the rear where the shooting was taking place. I saw Dicey firing his M-16 into the brush beside him as Moses fired two 40mm HE grenades into the same patch of jungle. The grenades blew, then the two men held their fire and stared for a moment at I-don't-know-what. A few seconds later, I did know what as Moses signaled that they had shot at two VC. One had dropped and the other had crawled away wounded.

Suddenly I heard excited male voices in the jungle to my left. The language spoken was clearly Vietnamese. This convinced me that we'd walked right into an en-emy unit.

"Recon by fire!" Meston yelled at us. All twelve of us sprayed the surrounding brush with our weapons. The shooting spree lasted only ten seconds due to the fact that we'd brought less than half of a normal load of ammo on this op and had to conserve our resources.

Mr. Meston signaled for Dicey and Moses to recon what was now our right flank, and Pearson and I moved to recon the left. After a short exploration, during which we found more human footprints but no human beings, we returned to the others. Dicey and Moses came back with two weapons that had been dropped by the VC they had drilled.

We were totally compromised. Every enemy soldier within a mile or two knew we were there, having had the pleasure of listening to our weapons emphatically bid them to go to hell. Uncomfortably aware of this, Mr. Meston gave a circular hand motion which told us to set up a hasty defense, a 360-degree circle, while he radioed for extraction via the choppers. I picked out a good spot of concealment in the brush where I sat down.

Ten minutes passed by. The only thing happening

was it was getting darker. I looked at the sky, and I realized the severity of our situation. If we weren't rescued within one hour, the black of night would have us, the helo pilots wouldn't be able to land, and we'd be left to fend for ourselves until morning. The thought of spending the night was not comforting, as we'd be stuck in a most vulnerable position: in enemy territory with inadequate firepower, and the enemy knowing where we were. If there were a couple hundred gooks in there, as I believed, then our chances of surviving through the night were virtually nil. At dawn, many dead bodies would greet our pilots. VC bodies, that was. And there would be twelve dead SEALs, too, in need of laudatory tombstones and posthumous awards.

My fears grew darker when Mr. Meston passed word that Bravo Platoon had been ambushed by the Viet Cong in the T-10 area and the helos were trying to save their butts. There was nothing that could be done for us at that time. We had to simply hang on and wait. And hope, and pray.

I kept my eyes moving, searching the brush for any sign of movement. Several minutes crept by, but nothing and nobody crept into view. All was quiet except my breathing and my heartbeat. Both sounds were abnormally audible to me.

My level of stress heightened as a half hour passed. My head ached. I was sweating profusely, mostly due to high anxiety. I felt as though I'd soon sweat blood. Our status was more than critical. We were in desperate need of some intensive care. We were in need of a life flight.

It became dark enough that the helo pilots would have trouble with their depth perception and may be forced to abort an attempted landing. Of course, if they didn't show up in a few minutes, we wouldn't concern ourselves with such trivialities. Instead, we'd focus our attention on a thing called impending death.

I heard a twig break in the brush in front of me, which was the last thing I wanted to hear. I raised my CAR-15 to my shoulder. More rustling occurred, then I glimpsed something white. My right index finger curled loosely around the trigger. I refused to blink, peering relentlessly at the white object as it moved toward me in the shadows of the nipa palm. It looked like a ghost, like walking death, and that image startled me for a moment until my eyes convinced my brain that it was only an egret—a tall, white heron.

I relaxed my grip on the rifle and slowly lowered it to my lap. Then I didn't move, as I didn't want to flush the bird so that enemy eyes could pinpoint our exact position. The long-necked heron stepped precariously closer, however, and looked right at me. I stared squarely into its eyes, again denying a blink. I hoped my camouflage face paint and clothing would be enough to keep the giant wings still if I just didn't flinch.

As we gazed at one another for a seemingly endless half a minute, my ears picked up a distant sound—a *whir*. I heard it for a few more seconds before I allowed myself to believe that helicopters were approaching. Fifteen seconds later, I didn't care about the heron anymore. I turned my head and looked above the eastern treetops, eager to lay my eyes on much bigger birds that were capable of giving me a ride out of there.

I heard the heron flapping its wings and lifting off the jungle floor, but I didn't glance back at it even once. My eyes remained glued on the darkened sky where the crescendo of chopper music was playing. And my eyes were rewarded with the sight of two Army Cobras flying in to put the VC in their place—the grave.

Mr. Meston had directed the Cobras right to us with the radio, and our position was identifiable from the air by our blue strobe lights. With this knowledge secured, the helo crews opened up on the surrounding jungle with mini-guns and rockets. Flying low, they swooped in and around in a tight racetrack pattern, firing all kinds of shit on the straightaways. The thunderous roar hurt my ears, but it was the kind of hurt I'd been praying for.

"Give 'em hell!" I shouted as a Cobra passed directly over my head and blasted the nearby masses of vegetation. "Hoo-yah, baby!" I found myself smiling. My whole being was overflowing with joy. Just like in the movies, a last-minute rescue was taking place, and I was one of the lucky, mud-sucking swamp rats who was being snatched from the bite of the Grim Reaper. I hollered again as the second Cobra went by, pounding the liberated jungle.

Two army slicks flew in behind the Cobras's last run. They hovered over a clear area at our left flank, preparing to land. Mr. Meston yelled at us to head for the choppers. Without a moment's pause, we did.

As I hurried toward the clearing, I saw the slicks hanging in the sky, hesitating from descending, like a couple of huge hawks that were unsure of themselves. I knew the problem: a lack of depth perception for the pilots in the dark. I silently prayed that there was enough light left for our rescue. It would have been a real bitch to have gotten this close to a reprieve only to have lost it at the last minute.

Fortunately, the most beautiful sight I'd ever seen occurred as first one slick, then the other, set down on the ground. Twelve happy SEALs jumped aboard, six on each helo. The slicks lifted off the jungle floor and climbed into the sky, joining the wonderful Cobras for a euphoric trip back to Nha Be.

"Hoo-yah!" The cry rang out with more heartfelt sentiment than I'd ever heard before.

"Hoo-yah!" I echoed, feeling a flood of relief. I looked at Moses and Dicey and could barely see their grins in the darkness. "You two deserve a medal!" I told them. They didn't say anything. And what was there to say, really? They had killed a man, probably two, out of necessity, for there was a war going on. The two had been our enemies, they had rifles, and they would've shot at us if they had had the chance. Cut-and-dried. Yes, in a war it was cut-and-dried. But it was not for medals that Dicey and Moses had pulled their triggers: it had been for their lives.

After a couple of minutes, the exuberance inside the helo was quelled by Mr. Meston's yelling for our attention. I stared at his dark figure sitting on the deck across from me, having a difficult time seeing his face. He turned his head once away from me, presenting his profile, and one of his eyes gleamed momentarily, reflecting a bit of light from somewhere. Perhaps the moonlight.

The rest of us were quiet for several seconds as we waited for him to speak. Only the sounds of the helo penetrated our space.

Finally from the darkened lieutenant came some dark, dark words. "Bravo Platoon got hit bad," he said, his voice cracking. "Antone was point man and never knew what hit him. The VN was killed, too. He was gutshot and bled to death before he could be medevacked." My own guts sank inside of me. My joy over living was slain at the news of my teammates' dying.

Meston cleared his throat, then added, "Lieutenant Van Heertum, Payne, and one other, I'm not sure who, were wounded. They were lucky to get out alive. The VC had 'em trapped in an L-shaped ambush on a trail." I lowered my head, weighed down by the heavy details. My senses were dulled. My body was weak. A feeling of exhaustion drained into my limbs. Then a thought flashed in my mind that caused me to see red. Bravo Platoon was a new platoon that had no business being in T-10. They weren't ready for it. Hell, Foxtrot Platoon had been in Vietnam for a month before we had been sent into the T-10. Bravo had just gotten there twelve days before. Damn! I hated mistakes, especially when they were unalterable. For Frank Antone, there would be no second chance.

I looked out the open doorway at the black sky. Many stars were glimmering, and I wondered if Antone was anywhere near one of them. I wondered what he now knew that I didn't know.

For the remainder of the trip back to the naval base, my teammates and I kept quiet. Each person was left to his own thoughts and sense of loss. When we finally touched down on the helo pad, I was the first one out the door. I walked directly to the showers to refresh myself and rinse the dirt from my clothes.

As I started to enter the shower, I noticed a pile of cammo clothing on the ground near the head. In the light emanating from the latrine, I saw blood stains on the clothes. I saw bullet holes, too. I could smell the odor of blood in the air. I could taste it in my mouth. I stood momentarily frozen, stunned by the sight. The evidence of Bravo Platoon's day of dissolution lay before me. The cold facts were revealed.

I stepped to the clothing and bent down to pick up the shirt on top, but as my fingers touched it, I changed my mind and pulled my hand way. Death was better left alone, I thought, and I wiped my fingers on my pant leg. I returned to the shower, stepped inside and turned on the water. It was slightly cold, but the water felt good as it splashed against my head and ran through my clothes. I turned my face into the spray and opened my mouth to rinse it out. Then I turned away and dropped my head, allowing the stream of water to pound against the back of my neck.

After a few minutes, the water had washed away all of the external grime and dirt. I only wished it could have washed away the pain and misery inside my heart.

CHAPTER THIRTEEN

Sitting in a new EM club and drinking a few beers seemed to be the best antidote for the depression that hit when a teammate died. Of course, sometimes the alcohol drowned me in a deeper depression; therefore, it was probably not the best remedy, after all. But on a tiny naval base in the middle of freakin' nowhere, it was the only remedy in which I had any faith, flimsy though that faith was.

I had attended a Catholic Mass a couple of days before, where a priest had said something about putting one's faith in God. I believed he'd had the right answer, but God was hard to find in Vietnam, unless His name was Buddha. In that case, God had a lot of problems of His own, starting with several too many pounds around the middle. Anyway, I'd maybe give God a real chance in my life someday, because I'd gotten this notion He could help me. Right then, though, the beer in my hand needed tending.

As I glanced around the bar, I noticed that the base personnel were giving all the SEALs a wide berth because of the deaths. Each of my teammates gathered around me had a weird look on his face, sort of a shocked expression, but no one was shedding any tears. Instead, some were even laughing, but the laughter was forced and had a hollow ring to it. Everything seemed so strange.

"Man, did we ever walk into a pile of shit today," Funkhouser mumbled. He was perched on a bar stool to my right, nursing a glass of branch-and-bourbon.

"Right up to our noses," agreed McCollum, sitting to my left, drinking a beer.

Between sips out of a can of Black Label, I said, "We're lucky we're not still out there."

Funkhouser nodded. "Two or three minutes later, those pilots couldn't have landed. Damn, that was close!"

"Close isn't the word for it." I declared. "How 'bout gut-wrenching?"

"How 'bout ball-breaking?" said McCollum, bringing the dialog down to the level at which SEALs seemed to be most comfortable: rock bottom.

"Ball-breaking it is!" asserted Funkhouser, raising his glass of whiskey-and-water in the air in mock salute. "Here's to the Nutcracker Suite."

I hoisted my beer can upward. "And to whoever the hell wrote it, may his balls rest in peace."

Two hours later, I was certifiably drunk. Somebody I could barely see kicked me out of the club. I stumbled and wove my way to a bed and fell into it, not even sure it was mine. I thought for a moment about getting up to check, but a sudden rush of booze flooded my cerebral circuit board. I visualized myself falling off a cliff, spinning and whirling into a dark chasm with sparks spitting all around me. Everything went totally black when my body plunged into a pit of water and my life was washed away.

Reveille came at 0600 hours on the morning of Christmas Eve. My head felt like it had been detached from my neck and rented out overnight for use as a volleyball. It had been heavily spiked, I knew for sure.

I took a minute to try to get my bearings, and recognition of Funkhouser, waking up in the next bunk, told

me I had at least gotten the right roommate if not the
right cubicle. I sat up, and a few quick glances assured
me that all was as it should have been. I had not passed
out last night in the XO's bed as I had dreamed, thank
goodness. Then another alarming thought struck me:
maybe I had, and I was carried to my rightful place in
my sleep.

"Let's get Doc Brown," Funkhouser muttered beside
me. I rubbed my eyes and stared at my buddy.

"What do you mean?" I asked.

"I mean we owe Doc for all the crap he's pulled on
us, and now's the time to get him." Funkhouser slipped
out of bed and started dressing. "Brown was twice as
drunk as you were last night, so there's no way he's
awake yet. Let's pay him a nice visit."

I figured my roommate had a plan, and I was suddenly anxious to find out what it was. I hurried to get
dressed, then I realized that I already was. I had slept
with my clothes and shoes on.

"That's the quickest I've ever seen you get ready,"
Funky joked. He zipped his pants, grinned, and said,
"Let's keep our appointment with the doctor."

We walked into the aisle of the barracks and headed
for Brown's cubicle. Along the way, Funkhouser re-
cruited Dicey and Moses to join in the fun.

"Come on, you two," appealed Funkhouser, tugging
on both of the men's T-shirts. "You'll earn a couple
more medals on this mission, I guarantee it!"

"Oh, yeah?" Dicey snapped playfully, trailing along
with us. "What kind of medal?"

Funkhouser thought a moment, then chuckled. "The
Vietnamese Cross of Toiletry."

"I'm in!" said Moses with a snicker.

Funkhouser cautioned us to keep quiet as we approached Brown's cubicle. I was still unaware of the
gag we were going to pull, but I was good at follow-

the-leader. Funky was our leader in this prank, and it was obvious he knew exactly what he was doing.

Funkhouser peeked inside Doc's cubicle, then looked back at me with a devious grin on his face.

"Each of us will lift up a corner of his bed," Funkhouser informed us in a soft voice. "We're gonna carry him to the head." With that much said, he motioned us to follow him into the cubicle. The four of us tiptoed inside and positioned ourselves around the bunk. Brown was sprawled out in it and snoring, something he also did well on ambush site. When Funkhouser nodded his head, we raised the bed off the floor and maneuvered it into the passageway and toward the john.

As we carried the bed and its hungover occupant down the aisle, a half dozen other SEALs saw us and decided to follow along. Markel and McCollum each grabbed hold of a side of the bed and helped lug it. Doc quit snoring but didn't change his position.

"The frame's too big for the john door," I whispered as we halted before the entrance to the head.

"Let's put it down," Funkhouser directed, and the six of us lowered the bunk to the deck. He continued, "We'll have to lift out the mattress."

Two more SEALs hurried to assist us, and eight of us successfully hoisted the mattress into the air without disturbing Doc's sleep. We worked our way inside the john by curling up the sides of the mattress and sliding it through the door.

We toted our cargo to the middle of the concrete bathroom floor, where we set it down between the toilet area and the sinks, over the top of the central floor drain. As we backed away, I was surprised, although pleasantly, that Doc hadn't awakened. I was positive there was no way this shenanigan would work on me, drunk or not, as I was such a light sleeper. But there was Doc, snoozing like a baby.

"Now let's plug the sinks and turn on the water," Funkhouser said, revealing the finale to his caper. He wanted to flood the floor and wet the mattress.

It took but a minute for us to stuff paper towels down the drainpipes of each of the half dozen sinks and turn on the faucets full blast. Quickly, the sinks filled to the tops with water, then began overflowing onto the floor. I chuckled as the six puddles of water rapidly expanded, united with one another, and rushed Doc's mattress as a menacing pool.

"Let's get outta here!" I suggested as the water splashed my coral booties.

"Just one more thing," declared Funkhouser. He slipped a folded piece of paper out of his pants pocket, unfolded it, and set it on the mattress beside Doc's head. It read, "DO NOT CALL FOR EXTRACTION. NO ONE WILL RESPOND TO YOUR WET DREAM."

Funkhouser looked at me, his face beaming with delight.

"We got 'im!" he rejoiced.

As all of the pranksters filed out the door, Funkhouser couldn't resist turning around for one more look at Doc. I turned back, too, to fix the scene in my memory: Doc Brown, sleeping on his wet mattress on the floor of the latrine with gallons of water cascading out of the sinks and lapping at his "skiff."

Repressing a burst of laughter, Funkhouser wheeled around to hurry outside with me on his tail. We ran into the barracks with our teammates, where everyone was rolling in the aisle. Lewd comments were fired fast and furious.

"That'll teach the son of a bitch!" Moses chortled.

"Hoo-yah!" several men agreed.

"This oughta make him be more careful when he sticks the next needle in my ass." Markel smiled broadly.

"If it doesn't, next time we'll dump him and his mattress into the Long Tau River!" cried Funkhouser. Again, everyone cheered.

Continuing the banter, the men headed for the chow hall and breakfast. On the way, I got a distant look at the latrine and saw a torrent of water flowing out the door and onto the ground. There was no sign of Brown, and a tinge of worry washed over me.

"You think Doc's all right?" I asked Funkhouser as we walked together.

Funkhouser grinned at me. "I hope not," he said.

I chuckled, but my concern remained the same until Funkhouser pointed a finger at the latrine. I glanced back and saw Doc upright, slipping and splashing as he tried to exit the john. He fell and ended up on his butt in the stream of water running out the door.

Funkhouser laughed. "He who laughs last, laughs best!"

The other men looked back at Doc in the water and joined in the laughter. I cracked up, too, but I wondered what Doc would do in retaliation.

"The last laugh could still be Doc Brown's," I warned my roommate as we entered the chow hall.

"Well," said Funkhouser, "he'll have to come up with something pretty quick 'cause my tour is over in three weeks, you know."

The truth of Funky's statement smacked me hard: this tour of Vietnam would be finished in twenty-one days for all the guys of Foxtrot Platoon except Martin and me. When everyone else left, the two of us would be assigned to Bravo Platoon for four weeks of an extended tour. I knew this would be a tough transition for me. I'd trained so long with one platoon, and we'd gone through hell together, and we knew each other so well. Accepting a bunch of inexperienced and shell-shocked guys with a different type of leadership might be hard, especially when I was so close to getting out of here. The fact that I may never see some of my current team-mates again saddened me. Many of them had been like brothers to me, and soon I would have to give them up to go their separate ways in life. I just hoped I wouldn't have to give any more of them up to death during the final three weeks.

Funkhouser and I had the cooks stack plenty of pancakes and sausages on our plates, then we sat down with Dicey and Moses to eat. A minute later, Mr. Meston entered the chow hall and approached our table.

"Good morning," he greeted us. We greeted him back. He looked at Moses and Dicey and said, "Just wanted to tell you two that I'm recommending you both for a Bronze Star for yesterday's action."

I looked at Moses and Dicey, who glanced at each other, then they looked at Mr. Meston.

"Thank you, sir," piped up Dicey.

"You did what had to be done, and you did it well," the lieutenant said before excusing himself and walking away.

Dicey gave Moses a poke in the ribs. "Hear that, Mo? A Bronze Star!"

Moses calmly took a bite out of a sausage. "It beats the hell out of a bronze tombstone, doesn't it?" he said while chewing, showing no emotion.

The mention of a tombstone subdued everyone, as we were all well aware that Frank Antone's reward for serving his country would be a posthumous Purple Heart and a nice grave marker. For the next couple of minutes, we ate in silence.

Finally, Funkhouser changed the mood at our table by bringing up Doc Brown. "You know, we should get McCollum to write a song about Doc floating on his bed in the wild waters of the latrine."

I chuckled. "That's a good idea. We could sing it with some Christmas songs tomorrow."

"McCollum's over there at that far table," Dicey informed me, pointing with his thumb in the general direction.

"I'll go ask him," I said, sliding my chair away from the table and standing up. I walked to McCollum's side and asked him for a minute of his time. Taking him several feet away from the others at his table, I told him about our proposal. He agreed to write a song just as Doc Brown entered the chow hall.

"Speak of the devil," whispered Muck, nodding at Doc. We walked back to our respective tables while Doc loaded up a tray full of food.

"Where do you think he'll sit?" Dicey wondered aloud. His question was answered a half minute later when Doc selected an empty table in a corner of the hall.

"I should ask him how he liked his morning swim," giggled Funkhouser, winking at me.

I shook my head. "No way. Let him cool off until McCollum sings about his escapade tomorrow."

"Yeah," said Dicey, "he might even laugh with us by then."

Funkhouser smirked. "Or fight with us."

"Whatever," I said, smiling. "Time will tell."

Time dragged the rest of the day. I spent the hours reading the *Stars and Stripes*, working on my gear, and wishing I were home for Christmas with my parents. Being stuck on a base without family on special days gave me a real empty feeling. Every tick of the clock seemed to get slower and slower, making me almost believe that some powerful demon was working me over to make the passage of time as painful as possible. I was unable to think about the meaning of Christmas at all as I dwelled on my loneliness.

I decided to escape the blues through the bottle. At 1630 hours I went to the club to drink a couple beers before supper. Martin and some of the MST guys were there, and several rounds were bought for me. I drank and drank and never made it to the chow hall; instead, I got drunk along with everyone else.

Around 2230 hours, my drinking buddies and I were kicked out of the club, so we took the band with us back to the SEAL barracks. The band played and we sang Christmas songs that I hadn't sung since I was a boy. Some of the guys jumped around and clapped their hands like kindergarten kids. There were no parents, no wives, no relatives to hug, but plenty of brothers.

At 2400 hours, the party ended. I made my way to the chow hall, where a priest was conducting Mass. I sat in a chair in the back, behind a couple dozen other men in attendance. The priest was speaking, but I was in no shape to absorb much of what he was saying. My head hurt too much. And yet, I was there, and that was enough for me on this special occasion. To be in a place where God was spoken of—that was important to me that night. Why? Because I knew there had to be a God. I ran away from Him most of the time, but tonight I needed to be near Him. Or at least hear about Him. For me, that had always been a part of my family's Christmas. So, I sat and tried to listen, failing for the most part but trying, nevertheless.

When the service concluded, I outran sleep to my bed, but just barely. My head hit the pillow and that was that.

When I awoke at 0730 hours on Christmas morning, the hurt in my head was so sharp that I considered downing a bottle of whiskey to kill the pain. My better judgment stopped me, however, and I downed three aspirins instead.

I made my way to the chow hall and ate breakfast, all

the while wishing I could pour the bowl of thick oatmeal into my brain to act as a buffer against the banging going on inside. Every time I closed my eyes for a few seconds, I could see a miniature man running around in my skull wielding a sledgehammer. And there was no way for me to ambush the little devil and cut him down. My training, extensive though it had been, had offered no course of action on handling hangover situations, so I had to rely solely on my years of frontline experience.

I returned to my cubicle with a towel wrapped around a dozen ice cubes. After swallowing another aspirin, I flopped into bed and lay on my back, then draped the cold portion of the towel across my forehead. As the cubes gradually melted and the towel got wetter, the pounding lessened, and I fell asleep.

At 1115 hours, I woke up to the faint sound of singing and laughing. My towel had slid off my face, but my pillow was soaked with water. Feeling well, I sat up. I closed my eyes for several seconds, and there was no man or hammering. Only the singing.

I crawled out of bed and started walking toward the noise, which led me out of the barracks to a large mound of sand. A half dozen of my teammates were sitting on the mound, drinking beer and singing Christmas carols to the PBR sailors as they walked by. McCollum saw me approaching and called out to me.

"Smitty! I've been wonderin' when you'd get here!"

I walked up to him and took a seat in the sand beside him.

"What are you guys doin'?" I asked.

McCollum grinned at me. "We're bringin' Christmas cheer to the whole damn base! 'Jingle Bells,' 'Deck the Halls,' 'Joy to the World.' You name it, we do it!"

I chuckled. "How 'bout 'Doc Brown's Christmas Swim'? Can you do that one?"

"Absolutely!" McCollum reached back to his rear pants pocket and pulled out a folded piece of paper. He smiled at me as he opened it up. He got everyone's attention, then announced that he was going to sing a solo, but he wanted all of us to sing the song's chorus as we caught on to it.

He began to the tune of "Jingle Bells":

"Doc Brown went to bed,
too much liquor in his head,
and when he went to sleep,
his sleep was very deep.
And when the morning came,
nothing was the same,
'cause when he opened up his eyes
he got a big surprise.
Oh, on his bed
in the head,
floating on the floor.
Oh, what fun it is to ride
a mattress in the war!
On his bed
in the head
in water from the sink.
Next time he'll float a sampan,
pretending he's a dink!"

As McCollum finished the chorus, the rest of us cracked up. McCollum grinned at me and kept singing. After two more verses, we were all joining in on the chorus, singing as loudly as we could. When the song was over, we had Muck take us through the whole thing again. I was amazed at how good we sounded as we put down Doc Brown one last time. But it was all in fun. Doc had had his with his needle; now we had fun with ours.

I sang some Christmas carols with the men for another hour, drinking only one beer because I was tired of the effect alcohol had had on me lately. Then I ate lunch before going back to my cubicle to read and to write my parents. The letter was quite melancholic, as I wished I could be at home for Christmas.

At 1500 hours, I gathered with all of the SEALs on the base for religious rites for Frank Antone and the VN who had been killed. As the priest said what he gets paid to say at a funeral, I thought about Antone's parents back in the States. I knew how proud they must have been when their son had become a SEAL, just the way my parents had been proud. I knew how they'd prayed every day for their son's safety, just as my parents had prayed. I knew they were in for a terrible shock when they were told about their son's death. And I wondered how their Christmas Day was going.

By way of contrast, I realized that my Christmas was going pretty well. Even though Santa Claus hadn't made a personal appearance to deliver a gift to me, God had. He had dropped a helicopter down from the heavens in the Saint Nick of time and had given me life.

"Merry Christmas, you lucky bum," I said to myself. And the priest up front said, "Amen."

CHAPTER FOURTEEN

Mission Twenty-eight

"Human blood is heavy; the man that has shed it cannot run away."

African Proverb

DATE: 28, 29 December 1967
TIME: 281900H to 290500H
UNITS INVOLVED: PBR, Foxtrot 1
TASK: Overnight river ambush
METHOD OF INSERTION: PBR
METHOD OF EXTRACTION: PBR
TERRAIN: Nipa palm, partly defoliated
TIDE: 1900-8.5 feet, 0045-12.8 feet, 0800-2.6 feet
WEATHER: Clear
SEAL TEAM PERSONNEL:
Lt. Meston, Patrol Leader/Rifleman, M-16
RM2 Smith, Point/Rifleman, M-16/XM-148
MM2 Funkhouser, Automatic Weapons/Stoner
BT2 McCollum, Ordnance/Grenadier, M-79
HM2 Brown, Corpsman/Radioman/Rifleman,
    M-16
LDNN Ty, Rifleman, M-16
AZIMUTHS: 270 degrees-20m
ESCAPE: 090 degrees
CODE WORDS: Insert-Canada, Ambush Site-
    America, Extract-Mexico, Challenge and
    Reply—Two numbers total 10

Three days later, my squad inserted at dusk on a barren, exposed point on the Tac Ong Nghia. I didn't like that at all, as spotting us under those conditions would be easy for the enemy if he was anywhere nearby. The VC could lob in an 82mm mortar HE round while we were setting up our ambush site and wipe us off the face of the earth. Surely, Mr. Meston and my teammates must have recognized the possibility, too. It made me angry that we were being so casual about insertion so close to the end of our tour. If anything, we should have been more clandestine than ever. I'd have thought Antone's death would've strongly reinforced this.

There were only six of us on the mission: Mr. Meston, Funkhouser, McCollum, Brown, Ty, and me. I took the point and guided us a mere sixty meters to our predetermined position on the Tac Ong Nghia where the mouth of a stream entered the river. It was at this intersection of waterways that we would spend the night on ambush.

Mr. Meston had three men and himself spread out along the main riverbank, while Ty and I took places on the bank of the smaller stream. Altogether, we were stretched out over fifty meters with Ty and me on the right flank about fifty feet from Funkhouser. After giving Ty the end of my parachute suspension line for communication purposes, I moved fifteen feet to his right, stringing out the line as I went. Then I selected a little hump of dry ground for my seat and sat down.

Right away, I noticed how quiet it was. Not even the usual drone of mosquitos was evident, making for a beautiful end to the day. The sky added to my pleasure, projecting red and pink above the horizon where the sun had hidden its face.

After a minute, I abandoned my admiration for the heavens and turned my eyes upstream. I spotted three wild pigs crossing the water about seventy-five meters away. The stream was only twenty-five meters wide, and the pigs swam across quickly, climbed the opposite bank and disappeared in the brush. They reminded me of the children's story, "The Three Little Pigs," and I thought about how far I'd come since I had first heard the tale. I guess I'd turned into the Big Bad Wolf, there in the jungles of Vietnam.

Farther upstream I saw hundreds of birds, gathered in flocks, in trees along the bank. I took out my binoculars and glassed the creatures. They were large parakeets, and that was the first time I'd seen these birds in Vietnam. I assumed they were in migration. I decided to keep a close eye on them until it was too dark to see them any longer; if a human being came anywhere near those birds, whether on land or in a sampan, they would show alarm and erupt from their perches in the trees.

I continued glassing for about forty minutes as the sky gradually darkened, enjoying my bird-watching. I even located four large cranes in an old, dead tree about three hundred meters beyond the parakeets. None of the birds showed anything but placidity until it was too black to see them anymore.

During the next few hours, the stillness remained. The moon didn't show itself, but many stars did. Since I wasn't sitting in water, I found myself enjoying the serenity of the evening, although the drop in temperature was enough to chill me.

At 2300 hours, I thought I heard the sound of gunfire far away to my right. I gazed in that direction, fully aware that Foxtrot 2nd Squad was set up at the other end of the same little stream on which I was positioned, about three klicks away. I watched the skyline, and sure enough, I saw tracers arcing into the sky. Obviously, some of the fire team's bullets were ricocheting upward. As the bullets rose, the red phosphorous in the core of each bullet burned. They looked like falling stars in reverse.

I admired the show for several minutes, reminding myself a few times that I was sitting on an ambush site myself and I couldn't afford to fall into a hypnotic trance while observing the fireworks. I forced my eyes to survey my piece of the stream every few seconds, looking for any signs of movement on the water. Spotting nothing, I glanced back to where movement then reigned, which was in the night air. There I saw more tracers, and finally there was a bigger glow, which I knew was a para flare.

After a few more minutes, I heard .50s firing. This told me the PBR was arriving to extract the team. The guns continued blasting for a couple of minutes, then all was quiet. Very quiet.

I started looking around more intensely, especially upstream to my right in the direction of Second Squad's clash. I could only guess from all the shooting that they had encountered more than just one sampan or a couple of VC. In the event that they had met with a few sampans and several enemy, one or two crews may have escaped the SEAL ambush. If so, and if they stayed on the water, they'd be approaching our ambush site soon. I slowly swung Bad Girl's double barrels in half a circle to my right, as a gut feeling was speaking to me loud and clear. I just knew the enemy was coming. He will come, he will come, I repeated over and over.

An hour slowly drifted by, and the only thing that came was the tide. The water rose and crested over the bank of the stream, but only a few inches. The peak hit at 0100 hours, and I sat in half a foot of water. It was enough to wet me down, and along with a sudden strong breeze, it was enough to make my teeth chatter. I sang a couple of old country-and-western songs under my breath to the syncopated rhythm.

An hour later, the water began receding rapidly the way it always did when there was a ten-to-twelve-foot difference between high tide and low. Water rushing and gurgling everywhere made it difficult to hear any other noises in the night. I did, however, pick up the sounds of amphibious lung fish flopping in the mud and splashing into the water. Every now and then I heard the clicking noises of nearby crabs. During one short stretch, several crabs joined together in what sounded like a group of percussionists testing their castanets for speed. Thereafter, however, things began to quiet down. Even the wind backed off until an eerie silence encompassed the area.

The silence lasted almost an hour, then like all silent times, it was overcome and broken. The culprit this time was a slightly errant paddle striking against the side of a sampan to my right. I turned my eyes toward the noise. About seventy-five feet away, I vaguely saw a sampan on the starlit water with a man seated forward and another aft. My heartbeat instantly did double-time and my hands took a firmer grip on the M-16/XM-148, which was resting on my lap with its barrels pointing downstream—in the wrong direction.

Damn it all, I swore inside myself, angry that I had moved my weapon to this position only ten minutes earlier. Now I had to swing it back around with two VC right on top of me. In the starlight, there was a chance they'd see me. Maybe they'd even shoot first before they moved into our kill zone. Hell, they were going to pass by me at a distance of fifteen bloody feet or less.

I slowly pivoted Bad Girl toward the oncoming enemy, but before I got her fully turned around, the sampan turned toward the bank of the stream and the bow ran up on the beach just ten yards from my bugged-out eyeballs. The occupants remained in the grounded boat and whispered frantically to one another. Believing that they'd seen me and were plotting to shoot at me in a moment, I clicked my M-16 from semi- to full automatic. I seized the moment out from under the gooks and squeezed the M-16's trigger. Spraying the sampan from end to end, I fired the entire 30-round magazine.

In the midst of my firing, the two men tumbled out of the sampan and into the water. I moved my finger forward to the XM-148 trigger and fired a 40mm HE round to the outboard side of the sampan. It blew, visibly rocking the sampan and setting it free from the shore.

I fell to my left side on the muddy bank, keeping a low profile as I inserted another 30-round magazine in the M-16 and loaded a second 40mm canister round in the grenade launcher. Before I finished, Ty opened up with his M-16 and shot up the sampan some more as it floated past him.

As I sat up from reloading, someone down the line sent up a para flare, which brought artificial daylight to the situation. I looked downstream about forty feet and saw a human head pop up in the water. I instantly fired a 40mm round to within a foot of the head; simultaneously, McCollum shot a 40mm round into the stream on the opposite side of the head. The two grenades exploded together, and when the water settled down, there was no trace of humanity left to be seen.

A few seconds later, a package of some sort surfaced about forty meters downstream. Muck and I again fired 40mm rounds beside it and blew it sky-high. This time when the water calmed, I could see a few pieces of the bundle drifting away in the current.

Twenty seconds later, as the para flare petered out, word was passed from Mr. Meston that Ty and I were to swim out and retrieve the sampan. I hustled to slip on my fins while Ty stood over me just watching. He had no fins, which would be a big detriment in the swift stream if we had to swim some against the current.

"Let's go," I said as I climbed to my feet with my knife in my right hand. Just then, a second flare ignited high above the stream. Ty and I wasted no time in dropping down into the water and beginning our swim, Ty with his rifle in one hand.

At the start, I couldn't see the sampan ahead of us. It had drifted beyond the range of the overhead floodlight. I glanced to my left; Ty was sidestroking easily beside me, as we were going with the flow of the current.

As we progressed, McCollum placed M-79 rounds on the banks around us to keep the enemy from sticking his nose in too close. I welcomed this assistance; it made me feel secure even though I was up to my neck in an insecure position. That was what teammates were for, I thought, to lend each other the courage to attain the unattainable.

Ty and I quickly left the small stream and entered the main river, where the current was stronger. Taking advantage of the flow, we swam hard and moved along rapidly. I kept my eyes peeled for the sampan, hoping it would show up on the glittering water.

After a hundred or more yards, just when I was considering turning back, I spied a dark object floating on the water about ten yards ahead of me. I swam closer, made sure it was the sampan, then went all-out to catch it. Ty was several yards behind me as I reached out of the water and grabbed the boat. Immediately I began stroking against the current, getting nowhere until Ty laid his weapon in the sampan and helped me. We towed the boat crosscurrent toward the black shoreline, and the going was extremely tough.

Surprisingly, Ty hung in there and lasted most of the distance, finally giving out with less than thirty meters to go. I told him to hang onto the sampan until I beached it. Gathering up all my strength, I kicked furiously for the shore. I made it, but the last ten meters took a lot out of me. When the sampan struck land, I heaved it onto the muddy riverbank and uttered a sigh of relief. Then I crawled up the bank along one side of the sampan while Ty made his way along the other.

At this point I would have loved to have sat down and rested for a few minutes, but there was no way I was going to hang out a hundred yards away from my teammates with just a K-bar knife and an M-16 rifle in a totally compromised area. Instead, I jumped to my feet and grabbed the bow of the sampan. Ty took a grip beside me and we began dragging the sampan back to the ambush site through the mud.

Just before we made it back, a couple of Seawolves arrived and strafed the opposite bank for security measures. As planned, Mr. Meston and the Seawolves knew exactly where Ty and I were since I had turned on my strobe light with a blue lens cover when Ty and I had started our swim. Also, I knew Mr. Meston had been watching us through his starlight scope. As always, I was happy to see the air support, and I was now fully confident that my platoon, once again, would get back to the naval base alive and well after one more successful mission.

As Ty and I approached the others, I yelled to alert them so we wouldn't get shot accidentally. A few seconds later, I heard the PBRs coming to extract us, so Ty and I hurried our task. We pulled the sampan the last several meters and dropped it down on the riverbank where the minor stream entered the main river. Mr. Meston instructed us to gather our gear quickly so as to waste no time in departure. We retrieved our belongings as our teammates loaded the sampan onto one of the PBRs, then we joined them in boarding the boats.

Moments later, we were cruising down the Tac Ong

Nghia, and I was feeling fine. Mr. Meston didn't seem so fine as he sat down beside me in the boat.

"Smitty, you initiated the ambush prematurely," he said. "Why didn't you wait until the sampan entered the kill zone?"

I explained to the lieutenant that the VC had beached the sampan next to me and I had no choice. With that information, Meston grinned at me.

"I understand," he said, nodding his head. "When you let loose on the right flank like that, it scared the pants off the rest of us."

McCollum, sitting on my opposite side and hearing us, added, "It scared my pants off and my shit right out of me."

I chuckled. "Better your shit than my life."

Muck was grinning in the darkness. "That's a matter of opinion."

Once we got back to the base, we found out from Second Squad that they had seen four sampans at 2300 hours, which was when I'd heard and seen their gunfire. They had allowed the lead sampan, a scout boat, to move through and out of the kill zone before opening up on the trailing sampans. All of the VC had either fallen or jumped overboard during the outburst, and only one body had been found and confirmed dead. The others had sunk or gotten away. The two men I had shot must have been the occupants of the scout boat that Second Squad had let pass.

As it happened, that was the first time in which both fire teams in a platoon had gotten hits in the same area on the same night. That was good for our morale and bad for Charlie's. We'd done our job, which was to harass and destroy. Charlie had done his job, too, which from our point of view was to die. And Foxtrot Platoon lived to see another day and another mission.

CHAPTER FIFTEEN

Mission Thirty-four

"War is an unmitigated evil. But it certainly does one good thing. It drives away fear and brings bravery to the surface."

Mohandas K. Gandhi,
Non-Violence in Peace and War

DATE: 26 January 1968
TIME: 1330H TO 1630H
COORDINATES: XR698247, XR700242
UNITS INVOLVED: PBRs, MST-2, SEAL 1, SEAL 2
TASK: Recon patrol for VC hospital and prisoner-of-war camp
METHOD OF INSERTION: PBR
METHOD OF EXTRACTION: PBR
TERRAIN: Thick brush on river edge, palm groves, hootches
WEATHER: Clear
SEAL TEAM PERSONNEL: 1st Squad:
Lt. (jg) Van Heertum, Patrol Leader/Rifleman, M-16
CM3 Scott, Point/Rifleman, M-16
GMG2 Jewett, Automatic Weapons/Stoner
ENFN Hyatt, Ordnance/Grenadier, M-79
RMSN McHugh, Radioman/Rifleman, M-16
HMC Blackburn, Corpsman/Rifleman, M-16

2nd Squad:
WO1 Casey, Asst. Patrol Leader/Rifleman, M-16
EM2 DiCroce, Asst. Squad Leader/Grenadier,
  M-79
MM1 Martin, Automatic Weapons/Stoner
RM2 Smith, Point/Rifleman, M-16/XM-148
RM2 Luksik, Radioman/Rifleman, M-16
AO3 Clann, Automatic Weapons/Stoner
AZIMUTHS: Parallel stream
ESCAPE: 225 degrees
CODE WORDS: None

Foxtrot Platoon hung together for another seventeen days. On January 15, 1968, we mustered at 0800 hours, anxious to celebrate our going away on the base at the EM club later in the day. Everyone was heading back to the States in a few days, with the exception of Mr. Meston, who was leaving today, and me. I was to hook up with Bravo Platoon for another month of operations around Dung Island, which was located about eighty miles southwest of Nha Be as the crow flies.

Mr. Meston had us gather in order to say good-bye. He said a few words, commending us for a job well done, then took the time to shake each person's hand.

I approached the lieutenant with my right hand outstretched, and he looked me in the eye as he grasped my hand firmly. We shook, and I quickly tried to come out with the right words to say to him, even though words did not exist that expressed my admiration for his leadership abilities, and for the man himself.

"Thanks for everything, Mr. Meston," I blurted, doing my best. "I sure enjoyed serving under you and I learned a lot under your command." As I turned loose of his hand, I added, "If I ever have the opportunity, I'd consider it a privilege to work for you again."

With a half grin, he said, "Thank you, Smitty. You

can work point for me anytime." He looked at me, acting as if he wanted to say more, but something stopped him. Probably the wall that sort of naturally stands between an officer and his men, I thought. But he need not have said another word to me; his eyes had conveyed the rest of his message.

As I walked back to the barracks, I couldn't help but remember my first mission with Lieutenant Meston and how I had thought he was somewhat nervous and that he'd have to prove himself to me. Well, damned if he hadn't done that and a whole lot more. The man was a fine leader, in my opinion, and I hated to see him go. But as it stood, he went alone, shouldering responsibility for one terribly unfortunate accident: Katsma's death. I just knew the remembrance of that day, October 6, tormented him regularly. I knew, because I endured the same agonies 101 days later. But I was confident that Mr. Meston would go on to have a splendid naval career, and I was hoping to do the same. We then went our separate ways in life, yet we were forever unified in spirit by one comrade's passing and thirty life-and-death missions.

I entered my cubicle and slid Bolivar's cage from beneath my bunk, intent upon seeing how the snake was doing after having gotten stepped on the previous day by Flynn in the latrine. Once again, Bolivar had escaped from his box, and as Flynn had tried to catch him, he had accidentally stomped a foot on the snake. Unlike last time when Flynn had gotten bit by the snake on the finger, this time the snake had gotten mashed by the SEAL, and his chances of surviving the sustained injuries were questionable.

One look at Bolivar lying limp in his cage answered all questions: my pet was stone-cold dead. A cocky-assed beetle paraded right across Bolivar's nose. I thought for a moment about killing the arrogant one, but then I had a better idea: I'd turn him over to the guy who owned Dracula, the nine-foot python.

After snatching the aforementioned beetle from the cage and depositing it in a glass jar, I picked up my deceased snake and carried it outside. Borrowing a small folding shovel along the way, I walked to a place on the western edge of the compound. I found a nice patch of grassy ground beside a nipa palm tree and began digging a small grave.

When I ended up with a two-foot-deep hole, I laid Bolivar in it, took one last look at him, and covered him with dirt. After refilling the hole, I dropped the shovel to the side, deciding to say a few words. I glanced around to make sure no one was watching, then I addressed the grave.

"Well, Bolivar," I muttered in a quiet voice, "I guess I've gotta say good-bye to you, too." I looked around again before continuing. "Ah, you were a pretty good snake, and I'm sad that you didn't have a longer run at living. But, on the optimistic side of things, at least I don't have to try to smuggle you back through Hawaii."

I kicked a clump of ground onto the top of the grave, then tromped it down with my foot. I bent over and grabbed the shovel and whacked the turned soil with the back of the blade.

"So long, Bolivar," I said over my shoulder as I stood up, pivoted, and walked away. Again I surveyed the surrounding area, hoping no one had witnessed my snake's funeral; after all, there were some things over which you knew your teammates would torture and tease you, and presiding over a funeral for a snake was one of those things. Fortunately, I saw no living creature watching me but a brown pigeon perched on a tree branch.

I went back to the barracks for a while, then passed the day going from one errand to another. The biggest task that I completed took place in the carpenter shop, where I built two boxes. Then I filled them with some of my personal gear, nailed them shut, and loaded them in one of Foxtrot Platoon's Conex boxes. The Conex boxes, which were six feet wide, six feet high, and eight feet long, were used for storing personal and operational gear. They would be sent to the States along with the platoon.

At 1730 hours, I went to the EM club, where the going-away party was scheduled for 1800 hours, for an early beer. Funkhouser, who had just gotten back from a quick trip to Saigon, joined me at the bar.

"Give me a cold one, Al," Funky said, then he motioned toward me and added, "and another for Smitty, on me."

I looked my friend in the face and said, "Well, well, what's this? A going-away present?"

Funkhouser grinned. "That's right, and it's a helluva splurge on my behalf, if you ask me!"

I laughed. "Comin' from a tightwad like you, I'll have to agree!"

We downed our beers together, kidding one another until the rest of the platoon members started arriving. But before we were completely distracted, Funkhouser draped an arm around my shoulders and gave me a squeeze.

"You've been a good roommate," he muttered quietly. Then letting go, he said louder, "Just don't go gettin' shot up out there with Bravo Platoon!"

I patted Funky three times on the back, and standing up from my stool, I told him not to worry.

"You just have a cold six-pack ready for me when I get off the plane in San Diego," I answered him. He nodded, then I walked away and went outside the club, where a couple of the guys were grilling steaks and barbecuing chicken.

"Smitty," Doc Brown said as I approached, "I've got a damn good-lookin' steak ready for you." He stabbed a well-done T-bone with a fork and lifted it a few inches off the makeshift grill for me to admire.

I shook my head and chuckled. "Can I trust you?" I asked. "Or is that the piece you basted with manure?"

Brown grinned at me. "Come on, Smitty, let bygones be bygones. I'm not playin' any tricks anymore. We're goin' home, man!"

"That's good news," I replied as I picked up another fork and stuck it into a second well-done steak. I carried the piece of meat to a folding table on which rested paper plates, utensils, and condiments. I dropped the steak onto a paper plate, poured a small amount of steak sauce on it, grabbed a knife, and started back into the club. Before stepping inside, I turned back and called to Brown.

"If I die from eating this meat, I'll kill you!" I warned him, but I was smiling when I said it. Brown just grinned.

I entered the club and found an empty chair at a table where McCollum, Moses, and Markel were sitting and drinking beer.

"Does your last name have to begin with an M to sit with you three guys?" I inquired, hesitating before pulling the chair out from the table.

"Go ahead and sit down," McCollum said, smiling. "We can live with one misfit. After all, misfit begins with an *m*, doesn't it?"

"I'll even buy you a beer to go with that piece of meat," Moses said as he got up from his chair and headed for the bar.

"Gee," I said to the others, "everybody's buyin' me beer today. You'd think you're all goin' home and I've got to stay in Nam another month or something."

McCollum and Markel nodded their heads and

laughed. I picked up my knife and fork and cut off a piece of the steak. It tasted as good as it looked as I took it off the fork with my teeth and started chewing it.

"Well," I blurted between bites, "I guess I'll confess and say I'm gonna miss you guys."

"Ha!" exclaimed Muck, throwing his head back and guffawing. "I'll bet that was awful damn hard to get out!"

I had to laugh, too. "Yeah," I admitted, "it was, but what the hell. I knew it was what you wanted to hear, so I said it to tickle your ears."

McCollum and Markel laughed some more as Moses came back with two cans of beer.

"What's so funny?" Moses asked, sitting down and setting one beer next to my plate and keeping the other for himself.

"Smitty said he loves us," replied McCollum, eyeing me with a grin. I almost choked on a bite of meat.

"I did not!" I sputtered after a cough. Then I coughed a couple more times before saying, "I said I was gonna miss you bastards!"

Muck giggled. "That's the same thing as sayin' you love us. You only miss those you love."

The three "m brothers" heehawed some more while I took a long swig of beer, taking a moment to regain my composure. It was not that easy, though, to recover after being exposed. The fact of the matter is that I did love those nitwits. But there was no way I was going to own up to it in front of them, especially while they were splitting their sides. The worst torture the VC ever invented couldn't have forced those three little words, "I love you," out of my mouth right then.

"I'm not gonna miss you, Smitty," cracked Moses, "but I enjoyed serving time with you." He chuckled, and I shook my head and smiled.

"To Smitty!" toasted McCollum, holding up his glass of beer. "Watch your butt, protect your nuts, and may your tour with Bravo end with a 'bravo!' "

"Hoo-yah!" sang Markel and Moses as they raised their beers and drank to my future. And so the rest of the party went. Lots of drinking, eating, and joking took place. Late in the evening, many songs were sung, and the more inebriated everyone got, the more hugs were given out. The word "love" was even tossed around some, after all. I, however, left and went back to my cubicle before I got that drunk.

Eleven days later, on January 26, 1968, I was with Bravo Platoon on the USS *Jennings County*, which was an LST (Landing Ship Troop) anchored on the Bassac River about two thousand yards northwest of Dung Island. The island was Communist controlled; therefore, our ships sat a quarter of a mile outside of recoilless rifle range from the island. Also aboard the ship was a platoon from SEAL Team 2, along with a couple of Seawolf crews and five PBR crews.

As I joined the two six-man squads from SEAL Team 1 and fourteen-man SEAL Team 2 platoon on the ship's flight deck for a mission briefing at 1200 hours, led by Lt. (jg) Demo Dick Marcinko, I reflected for a minute on the past several days and our previous four missions on Dung Island. We'd blown up a VC blockade that had been built across a river to stop PBRs from passing through; we'd fired at sampans and junks on a pitch-black night and hit who-knows-what; and MM1 Martin and I had killed two VC in a sampan as it had drawn to within fifteen feet of us. I also thought about the somber fact that four SEALs had been killed in Vietnam in just the previous fifteen days; actually, all had been killed in an eleven-day period. SN Roy Keith had been killed on January 11 by small arms fire at Ba Xuyen. GMG1 Arthur Williams had been killed in the

Mekong on January 18 by small arms fire. LCDR Robert Condon of UDT-12 had been killed instantly in a Mekong River ambush when a VC B-40 rocket had hit him in the head. ADR2 Eugene Fraley had died on January 21 at My Tho when a booby trap he was setting had accidentally detonated. Death had struck down four good men in a hurry. I wondered who would be next, aware that it could easily be me.

I turned my attention to Mr. Marcinko as he ran us through the details of the day's operation. He told us we were going to patrol along a canal into an area populated by many Vietnamese families living in their hootches. Our intelligence people reported that somewhere in the locality was a POW camp where a U.S. Army sergeant had been held since 1961. We were to search for the camp and the American soldier. That information got my adrenaline flowing, as it was the kind of mission every SEAL dreamed about: rescuing a fellow warrior from the enemy. The risk involved was higher than usual due to the fact that our squads would be visible and exposed as we would investigate all of the hootches in broad daylight.

When the briefing concluded, the two squads under Mr. Van Heertum's command and the SEAL 2 platoon, led by Mr. Marcinko, boarded five PBRs and headed down the Bassac River toward Dung Island. Two Boston Whalers with 125-horsepower Mercury outboard engines and an LCPL-MK4 traveled with us. With this mission recognized as a particularly dangerous one, we were not lacking in support.

After a short ride, the boats journeyed around the western side of Dung Island on the Song Hau Giang. Six miles down the river, we turned east on the Khem Lon, which swung southeast after one thousand meters. A trip covering two klicks brought us to the mouth of a small stream called the Rach Gia, which was our insertion point. Mr. Marcinko's platoon inserted on the left bank of the waterway, while Mr. Van Heertum's twelve men were dropped on the right bank.

With the water between us, the two groups of men began advancing upstream in skirmish lines. I was positioned on the right flank with Martin and DiCroce, two teammates who had served with me at Nha Be. Bad Girl was in my hands, with her double barrels pointed ahead, ready for action.

I was instantly awestruck by the beauty of the jungle as we moved forward, as that was the first time I'd been on Dung Island in the daytime. There were coconut palm trees everywhere, and there were irrigation canals crisscrossing in front of us every ten yards. The canals were six-foot-deep ditches, about fifteen feet wide and flowing with water that was two feet deep. At each canal, we staggered our skirmish line so that only a couple of men dropped in and out of the ditch at a time. This was done for security purposes.

Between the canals I found a dozen spider traps, holes measuring four and a half feet deep and twenty inches in diameter, covered by a camouflaged, thatched lid. Enemy soldiers could hide in the spider traps, waiting for us to walk past before popping open the roofing and shooting at our backs. Those traps gave me the creeps, and my finger felt the M-16 safety to make sure it was on safe.

As I climbed out of the third canal with my eyes peeled, I saw several hootches in the trees just ahead on the opposite side of the canal. Then my ears picked up the laughter of children. When the rest of my squad came up beside me, I signaled them concerning the village.

Mr. Van Heertum moved us to the next canal, which we crossed quickly. We patrolled through a flock of domestic chickens, and as we entered the settlement, four

Vietnamese children stood and stared at us from beside the nearest hootch. They appeared to be four to seven years old and quite obviously poor, though they were relatively healthy looking. Their faces, though, expressed sheer terror, and I thought the kids were too scared to move. I didn't blame them in the least, for the twelve of us looked like a child's worst nightmare come to life.

While the others faced the hootch in the skirmish line, DiCroce and I checked around the outside perimeter of the thatched hut. Finding nothing in back but a wandering pig, we returned to the front and entered the dwelling. My eyes adjusted to the dimmer light and I saw two old women cowering in a corner.

"Toi xem choi," I said to them, assuring them that we were just looking around. DiCroce pointed at a small bunker built out of logs and mud in the opposite corner of the hootch. We checked it out, finding no one in it, then we exited the hut.

"Just two old women and a bunker for protection against machine gun and rocket attacks," DiCroce informed Mr. Casey, who was the Second Squad leader.

"Okay," said Van Heertum, "let's keep searching for the POW camp."

As our skirmish line moved toward another hootch, I glanced back at the four children who had been watching us. They saw me look, and this time they ducked into the hootch we'd searched, and they disappeared.

The growl of a dog caused me to jerk my head back to the front. I laid my eyes on a medium-size mongrel, mangy and black, which stared at me from twelve feet away. I braced myself to hit him with my rifle stock should he charge, but he chose to turn and trot away, looking back a couple times with a sneer on his ugly mug.

A few seconds later, our squads were surrounding another hootch. DiCroce and I went in and searched the dwelling, being careful not to bother anything. Having negative results, we walked back outside and reported to Bos'n Casey and Van Heertum. They had us continue ours stroll through downtown Rach Gia.

As we advanced toward another hootch, through a menagerie of ducks, dogs, and pigs, a group of women and children noticed us from the other side of the main stream. As they visibly tensed in alarm, one of them saw Mr. Marcinko's platoon approaching from downstream. That sight caused them to quickly but quietly disperse and disappear in various directions.

My attention was diverted to my right as I heard Martin and DiCroce call out simultaneously, "VC!" I swung my weapon in the direction of three men who were coming out of a huge hut about seventy meters away, but I couldn't shoot because Martin was in my field of fire. I ran up beside Martin and DiCroce.

Instinctively, the three of us spread out in a skirmish line facing the three VC, all of whom were carrying rifles. Martin opened up with his Stoner machine gun first. Instantly, the VC reacted; one dove back into the hut and the other two started running in opposite directions. I aimed Bad Girl at the man dashing to the right and squeezed the M-16 trigger. I had the weapon set on full automatic, so every round in the 20-round magazine pursued the runner like a mad hornet flying at breakneck speed. The only problem was that the magazine emptied in one and half seconds, which was so quick that if the rifleman's aim was off target in the least, every bullet would miss. As I saw the gook still sprinting for all he was worth, I knew I'd blown it.

"Dammit!" my brain screamed as my shooting finger reached for the grenade launcher trigger. I took careful aim and fired a 40mm HE round at the VC as he dropped into an irrigation ditch. The round exploded on the bank of the canal.

While I inserted a second magazine into place in the M-16, Martin sprayed the other fleeing man with his machine gun. The VC was still running when I joined my teammate in firing at him. A second later, the man, looking like he was hit, disappeared into a canal. DiCroce fired a 40mm HE round from his M-79 after the guy, which blew on the far bank.

Martin turned his machine gun on the large hootch and let loose with a barrage as I ran ahead to the next canal and jumped in. I plowed through the water in the bottom and scurried up the bank closest to the hootch. Sticking Bad Girl over the top, I fired the M-16, now on semiautomatic, at the thatched hut while Martin advanced and joined me in the canal.

When Martin rested the Stoner on the bank and started firing, I climbed out of the ditch and ran in a crouched position to the next ditch. As quick as I could, I threw my weapon over the ridge and covered Martin's advancement.

We leapfrogged in this manner until we were hiding in a canal only seventy-five feet from the entrance of the big hootch containing at least one enemy soldier. DiCroce and Clann, who was toting a Stoner machine gun, had advanced to the canal behind Martin and me.

The large hootch was at least thirty feet by twenty feet and made of intertwined palm fronds. I pointed Bad Girl at the front wall beside the door and caressed the XM-148 trigger. With a light squeeze, a 40mm round smacked into the wall and detonated. To my astonishment, the thatched roof collapsed, and the front and side walls fell completely over, revealing a large bunker made of mud, logs, and sticks. The hootch was not a hootch at all, but a huge, camouflaged hideout.

I fired another 40mm HE round at the bunker, and

DiCroce did the same from the next canal. The explosions didn't even shake the structure.

As Martin blasted the bunker with a burst of machine-gun fire, I moved a few yards to my right and looked forty-five meters down an intersecting canal. There I spotted the body of the VC whom Martin and I had shot. He was lying half in, half out of the water. I raised my weapon and shot the body twice with M-16 rounds to make sure the man was dead.

"Cover me!" I barked at Martin, then I started down the canal toward the body. Wading through the ditch water, I splashed my way to the lifeless enemy. I bent over and reached into the water beneath the man's chest. My fingers found the barrel of a rifle, and I jerked a Russian-made, bolt-action rifle out from under the body.

With DiCroce and Clann firing at the big bunker and two smaller bunkers nearby, Martin appeared on the bank of the canal. I handed the confiscated weapon up to him and got busy searching the dead man's pockets. I found nothing at first, but then I discovered a couple of ammo clips.

Meanwhile, Clann's Stoner and DiCroce's M-79 were working overtime, and with the grenades exploding to my left, the noise was earsplitting. I grabbed the dead man's right arm, intending to turn him over in order to perform a hasty search of his front pockets for any documents. I no sooner began lifting than an enemy grenade blew up fifteen to twenty yards to my left in the canal.

A burning sensation struck me in my upper left arm between my collarbone and my biceps, causing me to wince and drop the body. I looked toward the pain and found a hole the size of a dime in my shirt.

"I'm hit!" I exclaimed to Martin, who was unscathed by the blast.

"How bad?" he wanted to know, his face showing concern. I rotated my shoulder in a tight circle to check it. There was some pain, but nothing to write my congressman about.

"I'll live," I replied.

"Not if we don't get outta here!" Martin blurted. "Mr. Van Heertum is frantically motioning for us to return." We began to carefully move back toward our teammates. I saw that Martin was still carrying the Russian rifle along with his Stoner machine gun. The rifle would be one less weapon in an enemy soldier's hands, provided we made it off Dung Island alive.

DiCroce and Clann fell in behind us as we went by them in the ditch. The four of us bypassed five intersecting canals before choosing to turn and scamper down the sixth one toward Mr. Van Heertum's position.

"Smitty's hit in the shoulder," I heard Martin say to Mr. Van Heertum as they met one another.

"I'm okay," I assured them as I came to a stop next to the two worried men. "It's just a small piece of shrapnel."

"Smitty took some shrapnel," Van Heertum informed Chief Blackburn, the corpsman. I pointed at my wound and shook my head.

"No big deal," I stated strongly. "I can continue."

Mr. Van Heertum shook his head back at me. "No way! The VC are leading us into a trap! We're gonna withdraw!" His voice was excited but firm. He turned toward his squad to initiate a retreat from the village. While Van Heertum gave the orders, Chief Blackburn slapped a bandage over my wound.

"Are you ready?" the lieutenant asked in our direction. After a nod from the corpsman, he had all of us move back to the main stream. As we withdrew, there was no gunfire from either side. There was only the sound made by the walking of twelve swamp warriors in single file and the incessant barking of a dog, which grew fainter by the minute.

When a Boston Whaler came roaring up the stream, I felt like doing some bitching myself after Mr. Van Heertum told me he had radioed the boat to medevac me. The rest of the men were going to stay put and wait for Mr. Marcinko's platoon to show up on the other side of the stream, then they'd patrol out to the Khem Lon and the mouth of the Rach Gia for extraction.

Feeling guilty, I climbed aboard the Boston Whaler. The coxswain reversed the bow of the boat, and without ado we roared down the waterway. As we went, I took a final look at the coconut palm trees and the beautiful jungle I was leaving behind, realizing I might not see such a sight in broad daylight again for a long time. And again, I pondered what I'd done in this once-serene place: I'd taken part in someone's death. But better him than me. The fact was that I had almost joined the dead man in the canal where he had lain. One of his buddies had done his very best to blow my brains out after I had blown out his buddy's brains. Such was the nature of war. Some tried but died, and some somehow succeeded and survived.

The Boston Whaler crew took me to the Khem Lon River, and I transferred to the LCPL, where my bandage was changed. Since I was feeling fine and there was minimal bleeding, I told the crew chief I didn't want to go back to the LST until the mission was over and my teammates had been extracted. He granted me my wish. We sat and waited, along with the Boston Whalers and the PBRs, for about thirty minutes. Then Mr. Marcinko radioed the PBRs for extraction, and the boats responded immediately.

When everyone from SEAL Teams 1 and 2 was aboard the boats, we all headed back to the USS *Jennings County* and relative safety. I went to sick bay, where my shoulder was examined by a doctor. After considering the alternatives, they decided to leave the shrapnel in my shoulder, saying they would do more harm to my muscles than good by cutting into me. With my approval, one of them simply stitched the entry wound and released me.

I returned to the troop quarters and climbed into my upper bunk. Lying on my back, I closed my eyes and relaxed, enjoying the air conditioning. I was almost asleep when Martin called my name.

"Hey, Mr. Purple Heart," he said from below my rack. "Wake up and receive your reward."

I opened my eyes and halfway sat up. Moki reached toward me with the Russian M 1891 Mosin-Nagant rifle in his left hand.

"All the guys decided you should have this since you got wounded gettin' it," he informed me. I gripped the stock and took the rifle.

Setting the rifle on the bunk alongside me, I mumbled, "I don't know what to say."

Martin chuckled. "Try 'thank you.' That usually works."

I grinned. "Okay. Thanks, mate."

My good friend Moki Martin turned and began walking away.

"Moki!" I hollered after him. When he looked back, I said, grinning, "Try 'you're welcome.' That usually works." We chuckled together, then Martin gave me a little wave of the hand and left.

As I lay back down, my left arm brushed against the expropriated rifle. I rolled my head to the side on my pillow and gazed at the weapon. Of course, the rifle did nothing but lie there, unfeeling. Allowing my arm to rest against it, I found that it was as cold as ice. Just like war, I thought. Just like war.

I shut my eyes and dreamed of home, where love and warmth awaited me.

EPILOGUE

Eight days later, on 3 February 1968, I was back at Nha Be, where I found that my good friend Frank Toms had returned to Nam again. Frank had just arrived with Delta Platoon a couple of weeks previously while I was operating on Dung Island standing security duty at the navy's Binh Thuy base during the worst of the '68 Tet offensive. It seemed that one of the few ways I had occasion to visit with some of my teammates was at the crossroads of South Vietnam. Delta Platoon members were as follows: Lt. (jg) Tony Freedly (OIC), ENS Manuel "Manny" Isaacs (AOIC), CPO Clarence Betz, SH1 Claude Willis (LPO). PO1 "Deep Divin' " Dietz, PO3 Frank Toms, PO3 Dennis Frank. Billy McKinney, Wayne Bergeron, SM3 Jack Lee, SN Dwight "Dee" Daigle, Bob Searles, L. B. Scott, and Chuck Turner (who was later relieved by Mike Ambrose after being wounded in the T-10 area of operation).

Shortly after I departed for CONUS, Delta Platoon and a couple of SEAL-2 members went on a series of operations from one of the navy's Task Force 117, Riverine Assault Force troop barracks ships near the Dong Tam base where units of the U.S. Army's 2nd Brigade, 9th Infantry Division were located five miles west of My Tho, Dinh Tuong Province, IV Corp. It was during one of those Delta Platoon operations when they demonstrated their wisdom in devising and determination in execution.

Some time later, Frank Toms, Jack Lee, and Dee Daigle filled me in on the details. According to their story, Delta Platoon departed their troop ship by PBRs one particular night with a Vietnamese SEAL LDNN and Hoi Chanh guide (an ex-VC who had come over to the South Vietnamese way of thinking). Their mission was to locate and destroy a large VC/NVA weapons and ordnance cache. After insertion, the SEAL unit patrolled a couple klicks along a secondary stream off My Tho River to the VC weapons and ordnance cache concealed in the bottom of an old, dry water well. According to the Hoi Chanh's testimony, the cache consisted of large quantities of small arms and ammo, all forms of anti-personnel and anti-vehicle mines, recoilless rifles and rounds, mortars and rounds, RPG-2s and RPG-7s, etc. Moreover, the Hoi Chanh warned that the cache was roughly surrounded with nearby bunkers manned with depleted platoon size VC/NVA units who were still licking their wounds from their devastating defeat that took place throughout South Vietnam during the Communist Tet '68 offensive.

After the SEALs inserted, they moved slowly with their supposed ex-VC guide through the sometimes dense jungle and occasional rice paddy dikes to avoid booby-trapped trails. They eventually made it to a designated rally point near the target. From there Lieutenant Freedly (the patrol leader) sent his point man, Seaman Daigle, forward to recon the cache area for the exact location of the security guards. The Hoi Chanh wasn't allowed to accompany Dee until he had proven himself on more than one mission.

In less than an hour, Dee returned with the critical information that every patrol leader wants to know about the enemy: how many security guards were there, what

were they armed with, and where were they located.
Dee had spotted four guards with AK-47s and SKSs
within twenty to thirty meters of each other in the immediate vicinity of the covert well. So far, the Hoi
Chanh's information had been accurate.

Once the information was passed to each man, everyone knew instinctively that stealth, concealment, and
noise discipline would have to be rigidly maintained
throughout the remainder of the mission. If the VC/NVA
security forces were alerted, the SEALs would not only
be outnumbered but possibly outgunned—not to mention
that it could be a long, dark, difficult, and hazardous retreat back toward the My Tho River for extraction. There
was only one way the mission could be pulled off: the
four sentries would have to be taken out silently with
K-bar knives. Only then could the cache be quietly pil-
laged and plundered with the remainder being covered
with C-4 plastic explosives and set to detonate shortly
after the SEALs departed the bogus water well.

For maximum firepower, ten of the SEALs set up a
skirmish line facing the target. Once everyone was set,
Mr. Freedly and Daigle would take out the two right
flank sentries while Frank Toms and another mate
would eliminate the two sentries located on the left
flank.

Later, Dee Daigle explained to me what happened.
"Mr. Freedly and I moved silently forward until we
were just a few feet from our first sentry. Both of us
moved very slowly and carefully until, within range, we
leaped upon the unaware VC. While Mr. Freedly held
the VC with one hand over his mouth and the other
holding him firmly on the ground, I stuck him through
at the bottom of his sternum with my K-bar knife. The
VC's chest deflated like a punctured football. It was
quick and silent. Again, we moved on toward the second sentry where Freedly grabbed the unsuspecting fel-

low. However, all did not go well—the Communist SOB would have none of it and started struggling violently. While Mr. Freedly continued wrestling with the guy, I quickly thrust my K-bar hard into the thrashing sentry with great force. Because he was a thin and wiry fellow, my K-bar penetrated completely through his body and entered Mr. Freedly's leg just above the knee. Fortunately for us the sentry wasn't able to scream nor was Freedly's stab wound a dangerous one."

Frank Toms and his partner were also successful in eliminating their two sentries but not without a hitch. When the two of them jumped their second sentry, the terrified VC managed to scream in horror especially after he received Frank's K-bar blade in his right side just below the lower ribs.

"With little time to think," Frank Toms explained, "I cut the VC's throat to stop the noise. Within a couple minutes, we heard a VC whistle less than a hundred meters away. Shortly afterward another VC yelled an individual's name, probably one of the dead VC sentries."

Jack Lee later explained, "Knowing time was short, Mr. Freedly immediately had everyone set security around the camouflaged cache. Because I had volunteered to be the tunnel rat, I got down into the well and confirmed that it had a fairly large concave bottom as the storage area and quickly began handing up to the guys two 75mm recoilless rifles, two mortar tubes, 150mm rockets, and many other items as fast as I could remove them from the well and its tunnel."

Delta Platoon knew they had best depart from the immediate area ASAP; the day's first light would soon be slipping over the horizon. While Jack Lee worked quickly down in the well's enlarged floor area placing C-4 plastic explosives on the remaining weapons and ordnance, everyone else made last-minute preparations for their departure. Meanwhile, Mr. Freedly quietly called the senior PBR captain (usually a Chief Petty Officer) and requested Navy Seawolves to orbit over the PBRs that were located upstream near the middle of the My Tho River. Everyone, especially the SEALs, knew it was time to get out of Dodge, and quickly.

As soon as Lieutenant Freedly gave the signal for Jack to pull the fuse lighters, the SEALs silently headed back on a different route in single file toward the My Tho River for extraction. The day's first light soon reflected off their backs, which were loaded down with war trophies. Once the SEALs were out of the target area and three minutes had passed, the cache detonated, sending up a large black cloud of smoke. Immediately following the explosion, Freedly requested the Seawolves begin making their strafing and rocket runs on the VC/NVA's bunker complexes to frustrate any enemy thoughts of pursuit and reprisal.

Summarizing the operation, Dee commented, "Incredibly, there was not a shot fired. There were four VC killed in action with no rounds expended."

Interestingly, Dee Daigle recalled that the following day another Hoi Chanh from the same general area of the dry water well cache had decided to turn himself in to the Provincial Chu Hoi Center in My Tho. The navy NILO (Naval Intelligence Liaison Officer) soon learned from the army's 525 detachment that the number two Hoi Chanh eventually confessed, with physical encouragement by the Philippino adviser, that he had been assigned to assassinate Delta Platoon's now "Number One" trustworthy Hoi Chanh guide.

Not surprisingly, Delta Platoon eventually went on three to five missions a week and successfully completed their tour with several severely wounded personnel but no KIAs.

Eight days later, on 15 February 1968, I found myself

in a window seat on an airplane headed for the United States. I stared out the small window at blue sky and the heavy cloud cover below the plane, daydreaming about the missions and the things I had left behind: my teammates, the mud, the mosquitos, the man-eating man-a-cheetahs. Then there were my empty 12-gauge, 5.56mm, and 40mm cartridge cases ejected throughout the Rung Sat Special Zone and Dung Island, as well as a few dead enemy bodies scattered about, and even a bit of my own flesh and blood. On the other hand, I took with me the memories—many I was glad to retain, but there were some I wished I could send back like a 2.75-inch rocket that exploded on impact, never to be fired again.

A good-looking stewardess interrupted my train of thought, asking me if I'd like a drink.

"You bet," I replied, smiling. "I'll have one without all of the preservatives."

She smiled back. "What kind?"

I shrugged. "Surprise me."

When she returned in a minute with a Miller, I told her that she must be a mind reader, as she had brought me the brand I really had wanted.

"Then it's no surprise," she murmured with a playful sigh.

"Yes, it is, ma'am," I told her as I took the beer and glass from her hands and set them on my tray. "I'm surprised that I'm still in one piece and able to drink this beer."

She bobbed her head in an empathetic gesture. "You saw a lot of death in Vietnam, right?" she asked quietly.

"No, but I lost a very good friend," I replied reflectively. I paid her for the beer and the stewardess moved on. I was left alone with my memories.

As I gazed out the window again, a sharp pain suddenly shot through my left shoulder. I gently rubbed the spot where the piece of shrapnel was still lodged, reminding myself that it was one more souvenir I was taking back to the good ol' U.S. of A. with me.

United States of America, the country that I love. The words sounded sweet in my mind. I dwelled on them and reflected on what they meant to me for a long while. I was going home. I longed to see my mom and dad, and I could use a bit of rest, too. At home. I'd be there soon, thank God.

My tour was finished. But as this war was to go on, I'd be back with my mates soon. I'd be back.

GLOSSARY

Assistant Patrol Leader (A/PL): Second Squad's leader and A/PL of the platoon. He is to maintain command and control of the second squad, and is subordinate to the patrol leader.

AO (Area of Operation): A designated area of operation for a specific combat unit. Before a SEAL platoon could execute a mission against an enemy target, the patrol leader had to first request clearance of an AO from the U.S. or Vietnamese TOC. If the AO was under South Vietnamese control, the platoon commander would submit three to five AOs for clearance with the intention of operating in only one AO, and over a long period of time. This was necessary because Communist agents or sympathizers had penetrated all South Vietnamese TOCs. Even then, some SEAL missions were compromised before the platoon ever left base, and that was the cause of a good percentage of SEAL casualties. However, there were times when numerous friendly forces were operating in small AOs adjacent to each other. Occasionally, friendly forces would stray into another's AO and get ambushed by their buddies.

Automatic weapons man (AW man): Usually carried an M-60 or Stoner machine gun. There were usually at least two AW men per SEAL platoon, and were placed toward the middle of the patrol for tactical mobility. His main responsibility was to neutralize or suppress heavy pockets of enemy fire.

Azimuth: The azimuth of an object is its bearing from the observer, measured as an angle clockwise from true North.

Back water: Command given to oarsmen to reverse usual rowing motion.

Bitter end: The free end of a line, wire, or chain.

Boston Whaler: Eighteen feet in length and powered by assorted outboard motors. In 1967/68 the Chrysler 105-horsepower outboard engine was used. Its draft was two feet. It carried one SEAL squad of seven men and two Boat Support Unit crewmen. Using the power propeller, the Boston Whaler could speed along at about 35 knots, fully loaded. It was great for insertions and extractions, and was occasionally called upon for fire support.

Bulkhead: One of the vertical, wall-like structures enclosing a compartment.

Bunker: A protective structure made of mud, sticks, and logs. Easily made and repaired, a bunker was like a beaver dam in its ability to resist destruction. Small home bunkers were made to hold all family members, and sometimes had a tunnel leading to an escape route. The larger bunkers built in VC/NVA camps could house ten to fifteen men.

Chain of command: Succession of commanding officers through which command is exercised from superior to subordinate. Also called command channel.

Command: A term applied to a naval unit or group of units under one officer; a definite and direct form of an order.

Commanding Officer (CO): The "Old Man" of the command. In a SEAL Team, he was delegated the responsibility and authority to accomplish all tasks assigned to him and his command by NOSG (Naval Operations Support Group), which later became NSWG (Naval Special Warfare Group). During the Vietnam War, the CO was a lieutenant commander (O-4) in rank. After the war, the rank was changed to commander (O-5).

Compartment: Space enclosed by bulkheads, deck, and overhead; corresponds to a room in a building.

Compass: Instrument to indicate geographic directions.

Compass man: Usually the patrol leader, and follows the point man. The point man guides on his direction.

Coxswain: Enlisted man in charge of a boat, usually acts as helmsman.

CPO: Chief petty officer (E-7).

C rations: Individual meals for use in the field when a field mess was not available. They were balanced and sufficient. The *only* ingredient that was much needed and not furnished with the meals was Tabasco sauce. If the flavor of the meal was not quite up to snuff—just add some Tabasco sauce! One disadvantage was weight. SEAL platoons generally had to carry *all* of their food and water. "LRRP rats" (LRRPs) were light; however, because they were dehydrated they required the better part of a quart of water for each meal. Unfortunately, LRRPs required a *lot* of Tabasco sauce. Take your choice.

Crossing the line: Crossing the earth's equator.

Crossed over the bar: When a seaman had passed from this life to the next one.

Danger area: An area (i.e., river, road, hootch, base camp, mined area, etc.) that decreases the patrol's cover and concealment, security, and firepower because of terrain features, manmade obstacles, enemy forces, et cetera. SEAL patrols established SOPs for danger areas that maximized cover and concealment, security, and firepower.

Davy Jones' locker: The bottom of the sea.

Dead ahead: Directly ahead of the ship's bow; bearing 000 degrees relative.

Deck: On a ship, corresponds to the floor of a building on land.

Decontaminate: Act of removing residue of nuclear or chemical attack. Also included removing leeches and, especially, black ants that plagued the Rung Sat.

Deep: The distance in fathoms between two successive marks on a lead line, as "By the deep, four."

Deeps: In a lead line, the fathoms which are not marked on the line.

Deep six: A term meaning to dispose of by throwing over the side of a ship.

Dexamil: A stimulant in capsule form that was issued to SEALs to be used as a "stay-awake" pill while on ambush site. The platoon corpsman issued one per man per night.

Dinghy: Small, handy boat, sixteen to twenty feet in length, propelled either by oars or by sail.

Ditty bag, ditty box: Small container used by sailors for stowage of personal articles or toilet articles.

Dock: Artificial basin for ships, fitted with gates to keep in or shut out water; water area between piers.

Door: Opening between compartments; see hatch.

Dory: Small, flat-bottomed pulling boat, used chiefly by fishermen.

Douche kit: Another name for ditty bag.

Ebb tide: Tide falling or flowing out.

Eddy: A small whirlpool, especially in river streams.

Even keel: Floating level; no list.

Executive Officer (XO): Subordinate to the CO. He is responsible for carrying out the policies of the CO. During the Vietnam War, the rank of a Team XO was lieutenant (O-3). After the war, the required rank was changed to lieutenant commander (O-4).

Extra duty: Additional work assigned as mild punishment.

Fag: Frayed or untwisted end of rope.

Fair wind: A favoring wind.

Fantail: Main deck section in the after part of a flush-deck ship.

Fathom: A six-foot unit of length.

Feather: Turning the blade of an oar horizontally at the finish of a stroke to reduce resistance of air or water; changing the pitch of a variable-pitch propeller on an airplane to vary amount of bite into the air.

Field-strip: To disassemble, without further breakdown, the major groups of a piece of ordnance for routine or operating cleaning and oiling; as opposed to detailed stripping, which may be done only by authorized technicians.

Fire superiority: Gained by directing an accurate and heavy volume of fire so as to cause the enemy's return fire to cease or become ineffective.

Fire team: A subdivision of a squad. There were two fire teams per SEAL squad.

Flankers: Men of elements deployed to the sides of a moving formation to provide early warning of an enemy ambush.

Flank speed: A certain prescribed speed increase over standard speed; faster than full speed, but less than emergency full speed.

Flood tide: Tide rising or flowing toward land.

Fore and aft: Running in the direction of the keel.

Forward: Toward the bow; opposite of aft.

Founder: To sink.

Gale: A wind between a strong breeze and a storm; wind force of 28 to 55 knots.

Galley: The ship's kitchen or any area designated as such by Team personnel.

Gangplank or brow: Moveable bridge leading from a ship to a pier, wharf, or float; usually equipped with rollers on the bottom and handrails on the side. Occasionally used at Team parties as punishment/reward for one reason or another.

Gangway: Opening in the bulwarks or the rail of the ship to give entrance; also, an order to stand aside and get out of the way.

Garble: An unintentional mix-up of a message's contents.

Gear: General term for lines, ropes, blocks, fenders, et cetera; personal effects.

General alarm: Sound signals used for general quarters and other emergencies.

General quarters: Battle stations for all hands.

Go adrift: To break loose; a teammate's getting hooked on wine, women, or booze.

Granny knot: A knot similar to a square knot; does not hold under strain. Some individuals could be considered no better than a granny knot.

Grenadier: Usually carried an M-79 grenade launcher or an M-16/XM-148. There were usually at least two grenadiers per SEAL platoon, and they were placed near the center of the patrol for tactical mobility. The grenadier's main responsibility was to neutralize heavy pockets of enemy resistance as directed by the patrol leader.

Gunwale: Upper edge or rail of a ship's or boat's side. Pronounced "gunnel."

Hail: To address a nearby boat or ship. Also a ship or man is said to hail from such-and-such a home port or home town.

Hangfire: Gun charge that does not fire immediately upon pulling the trigger, but some time later. Occasionally, hangfires happened to Team ammo that had spent too much time in water.

Hatch: An opening in the ship's deck, for communication or for handling stores and cargo.

Head/john/latrine: Compartment of a ship or plane, or any designated area, having toilet facilities.

Headroom: Clearance between decks.

Headway: Forward motion of a ship, boat, rubber raft, et cetera.

Heave: To throw or toss; to pull on a line.

Hitch: General class of knots by which a line is fastened to another object, either directly to or around it. Also, a term of enlistment (slang).

Hold: Space below decks for storage of ballast, cargo, et cetera.

Holiday routine: Routine followed aboard ship on authorized holidays and Sundays. In the Teams, it was any day of the week on which to have fun. Every day was a holiday, and every meal was a feast.

Hootch: In Vietnam, a rural home made mostly of palm thatching. It usually had one or two windows with shutters. It was cool during the dry season, and warm in the rainy season. The floor was usually dirt. Sometimes, a family bunker was constructed inside the hootch. The mamma-san kept it tidy by sweeping the interior daily. The little crock charcoal stove was usually located in the corner of the floor. The simple bed may have been the only other piece of furniture in the home, and it was without a mattress; however, it did have several pillows stuffed with rice chaff.

Hug: To keep close. A vessel might hug the shore. In the Teams a hug was a form of greeting.

IBS: A seven-person boat, inflated with carbon-dioxide cartridges, referred to as an "Inflatable Boat, Small" (hence, "IBS"). It was designed and procured by the U.S. Navy as an emergency lifeboat for seagoing vessels. Since its introduction and application to the Navy's Underwater Demolition and SEAL Teams, it had been utilized for various surface uses. It could also be rigged with a parachute and dropped from an aircraft, or (with minor valve modifications) launched and recovered from the deck of a submerged submarine. The IBS could carry seven men and one thousand pounds of equipment.

Insertion/extraction: Going into and coming out of danger areas (see danger areas). Some examples of clandestine and covert insertion and extraction vehicles and methods were: boat, sampan, helicopter, truck, jeep, bus, motorcycle, parachute, patrolling, swimming, SDV (swimmer delivery vehicle), Lambretta, rappelling, and even a refrigeration truck.

Inshore: Toward land.

Irish pennant: Unseamanlike, dangling loose end of a line or piece of bunting.

Jack-o'-the-dust: Enlisted man serving as assistant to the ship's cook.

Jacob's ladder: Light ladder made of rope or chain with metal or wooden rungs; used over the side, aloft, or hanging from the bottom of a helicopter.

Jettison: Goods cast overboard to lighten a ship or boat in distress.

Jetty: Breakwater built to protect a harbor entrance or river mouth.

Jury rig: Makeshift rig of mast and sail, or of other gear, as jury anchor, jury rudder; any makeshift device.

K-bar: A knife long used by the Teams and the Marine Corps. It was not made for knife throwing. It had a nasty tendency to break just forward of the handle.

Keelhaul: To reprimand severely.

Kill zone: In a point ambush, the area where the central portion of the enemy force was caught. It was also an area where the AW and the grenadier could inflict the most casualties upon the enemy and, at the same time, maintain fire superiority. All other riflemen would concentrate their semiautomatic fire within the kill zone and maintain a sustained rate of fire.

Knot: One nautical mile (6080.2 feet) per hour. (Never say "knots per hour." This would be the same as saying "miles per hour per hour.") Also, a knob, tie, or fastening formed with rope.

Ladder: In a ship, corresponds to stairs in a building.

Landmark: Any conspicuous object on shore, used for piloting.

Lanyard: A line made fast to an article for securing it; for example, a knife lanyard, bucket lanyard.

Lash: To tie or secure by turns of line.

Lay: The direction of the twist of strands of a rope.

LCPL MK4 and LCPL MK 11: The Landing Craft, Personnel, Launch. The MK 11 had a lower free board and more stowage area than the MK 4. However the MK 11 was not adapted for lifting by whelin davits, and the hull would not fit in standard shipboard skids. The hull of the MK 11 was constructed of laminated fiberglass and plastic, and was easily maintained. The MK 11 was 36 feet in length, with a draft of 3 feet, 11 inches. It was powered by one 300-horsepower Gray marine diesel engine, with a top speed of 17 nautical miles per hour, and a maximum range of 173 nautical miles.

Leave: Authorized absence in excess of 48 hours.

Lee: Direction away from the wind.

Leeward: In a lee direction. Pronounced "lu'ard."

Liberty: Authorized absence of less than 48 hours. More accurately, a sailor's favorite time of the day.

Libsville: Same as liberty.

Line: Seagoing term for rope; also, the equator.

Lookout: Seaman assigned duties involving watching and reporting to the Officer of the Deck (OOD) any objects of interest; the lookouts are "the eyes of the ship."

Loran (**long range navigation**): A navigational system that fixes the position of a ship by measuring the difference in the time of reception of two synchronized radio signals.

LRRPs (from "Long Range Reconnaissance Patrol"): Individual combat meals designed for long-range patrols, when pack weight was a concern. They were fairly good meals if a large quantity of Tabasco sauce was applied. If there was plenty of fresh water available and we were miles from friendly lines, it sure beat having to pack a lot of heavy C rats on our backs.

Lucky bag: Locker for stowage of personal gear found adrift. The chief master-at-arms controlled the lucky bag. Depending on the gear found adrift, a mate may or may not get extra duty for his forgetfulness. This is because when at sea, if a ship catches fire or begins to founder, loose gear may well block the pumps.

Magazine: Compartment used for stowage of ammunition and explosives.

Marking panel: Generally made of satin and international orange. SEAL platoons used them to mark their positions, especially when they wished to remain tactically clandestine.

Marlinspike: Pointed iron instrument used in splicing line or wire.

Mess/mess deck/chow hall: To eat; group of men eating together. In the Teams the mess could be literally anywhere, especially while going through training or in the field.

Mighty Moe: An LCM-6 converted to a sort of gunboat, and used to insert and extract SEAL personnel. It was manned by Boat Support Unit's personnel. There was an 81mm mortar mounted for direct fire just aft of the ramp. It also had a .50-caliber machine gun adapted to mount above the mortar tube. When the ramp was lowered for the insertion of a platoon of SEALs, the 81mm mortar/.50-caliber machine gun was manned and ready. She also had a 57mm Recoilless Rifle mounted near the coxswain's area for accurate fire against distant targets. There were three .50-caliber MGs on starboard and three on port. There was also one 40mm, hand-cranked Honeywell MK-18 grenade launcher on the opposite side of the coxswain and the 57mm RR.

Most of *Mighty Moe*'s well deck was protected by a steel roof covered with sandbags. SEAL personnel felt very secure while aboard *Mighty Moe*. Sadly, she was left with the South Vietnamese Navy when the last SEAL platoon pulled out of Vietnam in December of 1971.

Mind your rudder: Warning to helmsman to watch his course carefully.

Misfire: Powder charge that fails to fire when the trigger has been pulled.

Morse code: Code in which the letters of the alphabet are represented by combinations of dots and dashes. It is used in radio and visual signaling.

Nautical mile: 6,080.2 feet, or about a sixth longer than a land mile.

Net: A group of intercommunicating radio and/or landline stations; a barrier of steel mesh used to protect harbors and anchorages from torpedoes, submarines, or floating mines.

NVA (North Vietnamese Army): The standing army of North Vietnam during the Vietnam War, frequently deployed in the South. They were generally well trained, and very well motivated. Because of the NVA's professional bearing, there were times we SEALs felt we were fighting for the wrong side. Generally, North Vietnamese military leadership was superior to the South Vietnamese.

Objective of War: Impose the will of the state, group of states, or segment of the people upon the enemy.

Officer of the deck (OOD): The officer on watch in charge of a ship or command.

Old Man: Seaman's term for the commander (captain) of a ship or other naval activity.

Order: Directive telling what to do, but leaving the method to the discretion of the person ordered.

Ordnance: Weapons of destruction (i.e., missiles, rockets, M-16s, ammunition, hand grenades, et cetera).

Out of bounds: Buildings or areas off limits to military personnel.

Overhead: On a ship, equivalent to the ceiling of a building ashore.

Pacer: Usually two men were assigned the task of recording the distance traveled by counting the paces. They generally used a knot line and were separated in the formation.

Passageway: Corridor or hallway on a ship.

Pass the word: To repeat an order or information for all hands.

Patrol Leader: Responsible for the overall conduct of the mission and the safety of his men. He had to maintain command and control at all times and make tactical decisions in a timely and decisive manner. He had to be skilled in coordinating and directing all types of fire support (i.e., helos, artillery, jets, et cetera). An effective PL would seldom have time to fire his weapon. All of his energies had to be directed toward command and control.

Pay out: To increase the length of anchor cable; to ease off, or slack a line.

PBR: Patrol Boat, River.

Peacoat: Short, heavy blue coat worn by enlisted men and CPOs.

Pelican hook: Hinged hook held in place by a ring; when the ring is knocked off, the hook swings open.

Pilot: An expert who comes aboard ships in harbors or dangerous waters to advise the captain as to how the ship should be conned (manipulated); also a man at the controls of an aircraft.

Pipe down: An order to keep silent; also used to dismiss the crew from an evolution (activity).

Pipe the side: Ceremony at the gangway, in which sideboys are drawn up and the boatswain's pipe is blown, when a high-ranking officer or distinguished visitor comes aboard.

Pitch: The heaving and plunging motion of a vessel at sea.

Plan of the day: Schedule of day's routine and events ordered by executive officer; published daily aboard ship or at a shore activity.

Plank owner: A person who has served aboard ship, or command, from its commissioning.

Platoon: Generally consisted of fourteen SEALs, with twelve enlisted men and two commissioned officers. Each platoon was made up of two squads.

PLO: The Patrol Leader's Order, given prior to the conduct of each mission, which contains detailed instructions concerning the conduct of the mission. The basic outline is: 1) situation; 2) mission; 3) execution; 4) administration and logistics; 5) command and signal.

Point man: Responsible for navigating the best and safest route for the patrol. He is to maintain an appropriate distance forward of the patrol leader, yet maintain visual contact with him, unless instructed otherwise. He must be ever watchful for booby traps and signs of enemy activity. He should be a good tracker, preferably a country boy with a lot of hunting experience.

Pollywog: Person who has never crossed the Line (the equator).

Poop deck: Partial deck at the stern over the main deck.

Port: Left side of ship facing forward; a harbor; an opening in the ship's side, such as a cargo port. The usual opening in the ship's side for light and air is also a port. The glass set in a brass frame that fits against it is called a port light.

POW: A prisoner of war.

Pricker: Small marlinspike.

Principles of War: *Mass:* The concentration of means, at the critical time and place, to the maximum degree permitted by the situation. *Objective:* The destruction of the enemy's armed forces and his will to fight is the ultimate military objective of war. *Simplicity:* Uncomplicated plans clearly expressed in orders, promoting common understanding and intelligent execution. *Surprise:* Striking the enemy when, where, or in a manner for which he is unprepared. *Unity of Command:* Obtains unity of effort by the coordinated action of all forces toward a common goal. *Offensive:* Permits the commander to exploit the initiative, and impose his will on the enemy. *Maneuver:* Positioning of forces to place the enemy at a relative disadvantage. *Economy of Force:* To conserve means. To devote means to unnecessary secondary efforts, or to employ excessive means on required secondary efforts, is to violate the principles of both mass and objective. *Security:* Those measures necessary to prevent surprise, avoid annoyance, preserve freedom of action, and deny to the enemy information of our forces.

Property pass: Signed, printed form authorizing a person to remove personal property from a ship or station.

PT: A series of physical training experiences designed to maintain maximum strength and stamina of all muscle groups. Regular PT would last approximately thirty minutes followed by a four- or six-mile run. Occasionally there would be a "burn-out" PT which lasted forty-five minutes to one hour. These usually occurred on Friday mornings, which gave the old timers Saturday and Sunday to recover.

Punt: Rectangular, flat-bottomed boat usually used for painting and other work around the waterline of a ship.

Pyrotechnics: Chemicals, ammunition, or fireworks that produce smoke or lights of various colors and types.

Quarterdeck: That part of the main (or other) deck reserved for honors and ceremonies, and as the station of the OOD in port.

Quarters: Living space; assembly of the crew (all hands assembled at established stations for muster, drills, or inspection).

Radar (radio detection and ranging): Principle and method whereby objects are located by radio waves. A radio wave is transmitted, reflected by an object, received, and the results displayed on an oscilloscope or cathode ray screen.

Radioman: Located directly behind the patrol leader. He is responsible for maintaining communications with support elements, as directed by the PL.

Radio direction finder: Apparatus for taking bearings on the source of radio transmissions.

Rake: Angle of a vessel's masts and stacks from the vertical.

Rakish: Having a rake to the masts; smart, speedy appearance.

Rally point: Usually designated, on the spot, by the patrol leader by pointing his index finger toward the sky and moving his hand in a circular motion. In the event individuals within the squad or platoon later become separated, they will regroup and reorganize at that rally point.

Rank: Grade of official standing of commissioned and warrant officers.

Rate: Grade of official standing of enlisted men. A rate identifies a man by pay grade or level of advancement; within a rating, a rate reflects levels of aptitude, training, experience, knowledge, skill, and responsibility.

Rat guard: A sheet metal disc formed into a conical form, with a hole in the center, and slit from the center to the edge. It is installed over the mooring lines to prevent rats from boarding ship from the shore over the mooring lines.

Rating: Name given to an occupation that requires basically related aptitudes, training experience, knowledge, and skills. Thus, the rating of yeoman comprises clerical and verbal aptitudes, filing, typing, and stenographic skills, and knowledge of correspondence, reporting forms, et cetera. Men in pay grades E-1, E-2, and E-3 are not considered as possessing ratings.

Ready room: Compartment on aircraft carriers in which pilots assemble for flight orders.

Rear security or rear point: Usually a rifleman who provides rear security, and is the last man in the patrol. He and the point man will generally alternate. He is responsible for insuring that no enemy forces are tracking the patrol, and he covers the patrol's tracks when necessary.

Recon by fire: A technique of firing to draw fire, in order to locate an enemy's position.

Reef: Chain or ridge of rocks, coral, or sand in shallow water.

Reefer: Refrigerator vessel for carrying chilled or frozen foodstuffs.

Relative bearing: Bearing or direction of an object, in degrees, in relation to the bow of the ship. The bow of the ship is taken as 000 degrees, and an imaginary circle is drawn clockwise around the ship; objects are then reported as being along a line of bearing through any degree division of this circle.

Relieving (the watch, the duty, et cetera): To take over the duty and responsibilities, as when one sentry relieves another. Those who relieve are "reliefs."

Request mast: Mast held by captain or executive officer to hear special requests for leave, liberty, et cetera

R&R (Rest and Relaxation): A welcome policy established and used by U.S. Armed Forces in Vietnam. Individuals generally became eligible for a five-day R & R after six months in country. They could choose such places as Bangkok, Thailand; Manila, Philippines; Sydney, Australia; Taipei, Taiwan; and Vung Tau or Nha Trang, Vietnam. Honolulu, Hawaii was especially popular with the married men, who would arrange to meet their spouses there.

Rig: General description of a ship's upper works; to set up, fit out, or put together.

Rigging: General term for all ropes, chains, and gear used for supporting and operating masts, yards, booms, gaffs, and sails. Rigging is of two kinds: standing rigging, or lines that support but ordinarily do not move; and running rigging, or lines that move to operate equipment.

Ropeyarn Sunday: A time for repairing clothing and other personal gear. (Usually Wednesday afternoon at sea.)

Sampan: A small Vietnamese boat propelled by paddle or motor.

Scow: Large, open, flat-bottomed boat for transporting sand, gravel, mud, et cetera.

Scullery: Compartment for washing and sterilizing eating utensils.

Scuttlebutt: Container of drinking water, or a drinking fountain. Also, a rumor, usually of local importance.

Sea lawyer: Enlisted man who likes to argue, usually one who thinks he can twist the regulations and standing orders around to favor his personal inclinations.

SEAL Teams: SEAL Teams 1 and 2 were commissioned on 1 January 1962, and were located at Coronado, California, and Little Creek, Virginia, respectively. All of the original SEALs were formerly UDTs. However, as the Vietnam War escalated, some individuals were assigned directly to a SEAL Team from the training unit. Shortly thereafter, UDT training was renamed BUDS (Basic Underwater Demolition SEAL). SEAL is an acronym formed from sea, air, and land. SEALs can attack from the sea, the air, and the land. SEAL Teams are organized, trained, and equipped to conduct unconventional warfare, counterguerrilla, and clandestine operations in maritime areas and riverine environments. This includes, but is not limited to, the following: demolitions, intelligence collection, and training and advising friendly military and paramilitary forces in the conduct of Naval Special Warfare.

Seaworthy: Capable of putting to sea and meeting usual sea conditions.

Secure: To make fast; to tie; an order given on completion of a drill or exercise, meaning to withdraw from drill stations and duties.

Semaphore: Code indicated by the position of the arms; hand flags are used to increase readability.

Service stripes: Diagonal stripes on the lower left sleeve of an enlisted man's uniform denoting periods of enlistments. Usually referred to as "hash-marks."

Set: Direction of the leeway of a ship or of a tide or current.

Shellback: Man who has crossed the equator and been initiated.

Shipshape: Neat, orderly.

Shore patrol: Naval personnel detailed to maintain discipline, to aid local police in handling naval personnel on liberty or leave, and to assist naval personnel in difficulties ashore.

Sick bay: Ship's or command's hospital or dispensary. On Monday the dispensary is filled; on Friday the dispensary is empty.

Skivvy: Slang for underwear.

Slick: Common, cross-service slang for a UH-1 "Huey" helicopter armed only with two M-60 machine guns, located on each side and aft of the passenger/cargo area. Each slick can carry one squad, or seven men, with full combat gear.

Smoking lamp: A lamp aboard old-time ships used by men to light their pipes; now used in the phrase, "The smoking lamp is lit (or out)," to indicate when men are allowed (or forbidden) to smoke.

Snipes: Slang for members of the engineering department.

Sonar (sound navigation and ranging): Device for locating objects under water by emitting vibrations similar to sound, and measuring the time taken for these vibrations to bounce back from anything in their path.

SOP: Standing operating procedure based upon lessons learned and military wisdom.

Sound: To measure depth of water by means of a lead line. Also, to measure the depth of liquids in oil tanks, voids, blisters, and other compartments or tanks.

Squad: A subdivision of a platoon. The squad was made up of seven men. There were two squads in each SEAL platoon.

Squall: Sudden gust of wind.

Square away: To get things settled down or in order.

STAB (SEAL Team Assault Boat): Twenty-six feet in length, powered by two 325-horsepower motors, and drew four feet of water. Its maximum range was 450 nautical miles. It was manned by Boat Support Unit personnel and used to insert and extract one squad of SEAL personnel. It was also used for fire support.

Staff officer: Officer of staff corps, (medical, dental, supply, et cetera), whose duty was primarily within his specialty, and not of a military character. Also, a line officer when assigned to the staff, or group of assistants, of a high-ranking officer.

Stage: Platform rigged over ship's side for painting or repair work.

Stand by: Preparatory order meaning "Get ready," or "Prepare to."

Starboard: Right side of a ship looking forward.

Stateroom: Officer's shipboard bedroom.

Stern: After part of a ship.

Stow: To put gear in its proper place.

Striker: Enlisted man in training for a particular rating.

Swab: A rope or yarn mop.

Sweepers: Men who use brooms in cleaning ship when "clean sweep down" is ordered.

T-10: An operational area within the northeastern portion of the RSSZ (Rung Sat Special Zone). It was composed of very dense vegetation and double-canopy forest. It was generally surrounded by swampy terrain and numerous streams that were very difficult for any foot soldier to penetrate. For these reasons, the United States and its allies rarely penetrated its interior. Even then, it was done carefully and by warriors who were specially trained to deal with the riverine environment. The NVA/VC used the T-10 extensively for an R & R and troop-staging area to include several field hospitals, training camps, et cetera. SEALs preferred operating in the T-10 area because they encountered the enemy on every mission. Success was always good for morale. And last, but not least, a good portion of the T-10 had good, solid, dry land—a luxury in the RSSZ!

Tide: The vertical rise and fall of the sea, caused by gravitational effect of sun and moon.

TOC: The tactical operations center. In Vietnam, the Vietnamese TOCs were located in all provincial cities and district villages. These were *always* considered to be compromised. There were also TOCs located in all U.S. military locations, which were considered secure and not penetrated by Vietnamese Communists.

Topside or topsides: Above decks.

Trades: Generally, steady winds of the tropics that blow toward the equator. NE in the northern hemisphere, and SE in the southern.

Trice up: To hitch up or hook up, such as trice up a shipboard bunk/bed.

Turn to: An order to begin work.

UDT (Underwater Demolition Teams): Initially formed as the Navy Combat Demolition Unit, after the lessons learned from the amphibious invasion of Tarawa in November of 1942. Later, they were reorganized into UDTs until a much later reorganization in 1983. At that time, the UDTs were decommissioned. On the west coast, UDT-11 became SEAL Team 5, and UDT-12 became SDV Team 1. On the east coast, UDT-21 became SEAL Team 4, and UDT-22 became SDV Team 2. All UDT/SEALs were graduates of UDT Training until 1968, when it was renamed BUDS (Basic Underwater Demolition/SEAL). Today, all Team personnel are graduates of BUDS training at the Naval Amphibious Base located near Coronado, California.

Uncover: To remove headgear/hat.

Underway: A ship is underway when not at anchor, made fast to the shore, or aground. She need not be actually moving; she is underway as long as she lies free in the water.

Unit: An entity in itself, made up of one or more parts. The unit itself is a member part. Thus, two destroyers (units) form a section; two sections form a division; two divisions form a squadron.

VC (Viet Cong): The South Vietnamese Communist NLF's (National Liberation Front) regular/guerrilla forces. These poor fellows got much of their training in actual combat. And to add insult to injury, they were generally led by North Vietnamese officers. During the 1968 Tet offensive, the VC military units assigned to attack IV Corps districts and provincial capitals were slaughtered by the U.S. and allied forces. Many of them were forced to serve the Communist cause, and defected to the American and South Vietnamese forces under the *Chieu Hoi* (open arms) program.

Very well: Reply of a senior (or officer) to a junior (or enlisted man) to indicate that information given is understood, or that permission is granted.

War: A bitch, except for those professionals who seem to enjoy it. Use of force or violence, by a state or group of states, against another state (or group of states), or by a segment of a people against the established government.

Wardroom: Officers' mess and lounge aboard a ship.

Warning Order: Always precedes a standard patrol order. Its purpose is to provide the men with sufficient information to prepare adequately for the problem in advance. The basic outline is: 1) a brief statement of the situation; 2) mission of the patrol; 3) general instructions; 4) specific instructions.

Watch: A period of duty, usually for four hours' duration. Watches call for a variety of Navy skills, and are of many types: quarterdeck watch, messenger watch, damage-control watch, evaporator watch, signal watch, radio watch, et cetera.

Watchcap: Knitted wool cap worn by enlisted men below CPO in cool or cold weather; also, a canvas cover placed over a stack when not in use.

Watch officer: An officer regularly assigned to duty in charge of a watch or of a portion thereof; for example, the OOD, or the engineering officer of the watch.

Webb belt: A heavy-duty belt made of cotton or nylon. Pistols, magazine pouches, canteens, first aid kits, et cetera, may be attached to it.

Wheelhouse: Pilothouse; the topside compartment where, on most ships, the OOD, helmsman, quartermaster of the watch, et cetera, stand their watches.

Yard: Spar attached at the middle to a mast, and running athwartships; used as a support for signal halyards or signal lights; also a place used for shipbuilding and as a repair depot, as Boston Naval Shipyard.

Yardarm: Either side of a yard.

Yarn: Twisted fibers used for rough seizings, which may be twisted into strands; also, a story, as to "spin a yarn," meaning to tell a story not necessarily true.